Is Art Good for Us?

Is Art Good for Us?

Beliefs about High Culture in American Life

Joli Jensen

ROWMAN & LITTLEFIELD PUBLISHERS, INC.
Lanham • Boulder • New York • Oxford

ROWMAN & LITTLEFIELD PUBLISHERS, INC.

Published in the United States of America
by Rowman & Littlefield Publishers, Inc.
A wholly owned subsidiary of The Rowman & Littlefield Publishing Group, Inc.
4501 Forbes Boulevard, Suite 200, Lanham, Maryland 20706
www.rowmanlittlefield.com

PO Box 317
Oxford
OX2 9RU, UK

British Library Cataloguing-in-Publication Information Available

Library of Congress Cataloging-in-Publication Data

Jensen, Joli.
  Is art good for us? : beliefs about high culture in American life /
Joli Jensen.
      p. cm.
Includes bibliographical references and index.
  ISBN 0-7425-1740-3 (cloth : alk. paper)—ISBN 0-7425-1741-1 (paper :
alk. paper)
  1. Arts, American—Psychological aspects. I. Title.
  NX503 .J46 2002
  306.4'7—dc21

                                                      2002001194

Printed in the United States of America

∞™ The paper used in this publication meets the minimum requirements of
American National Standard for Information Sciences—Permanence of Paper for
Printed Library Materials, ANSI/NISO Z39.48-1992.

Contents

Acknowledgments

I feel some chagrin at having received public funding to write a scholarly book that questions our rationale for public funding of the arts. Nonetheless, I am deeply grateful to the National Endowment for the Humanities for their 1994–95 Fellowship for College Teachers and Independent Scholars, and for their summer stipend in 1999. I can only hope that my analysis of how we think about the arts will contribute to the public good—in expressive if not instrumental ways.

Several colleagues have been particularly helpful at crucial junctures in this project. John Pauly helped me figure out how to begin; Steve Jones encouraged me as I continued; and Gwenyth Jackaway gave me much-needed support during its final phases. I am also grateful to the University of Tulsa for a sabbatical and a summer stipend; I am especially indebted to Dean Tom Horne; my department chair, John Coward; and other colleagues at TU who understood my need to focus on writing and teaching, rather than on administration.

I have had the opportunity to work out some of these ideas at conferences, as a guest lecturer and in print. I appreciate discussions at several Politics, Social Theory and the Arts meetings, as well as during guest lectures at St. Louis University and University of Wisconsin–Stevens Point. Earlier versions of chapters 1 and 2 appeared as "Questioning the Social Powers of Art: Toward a Pragmatic Aesthetics" in *Critical Studies in Mass Communication* 12, no. 4, December 1995, and other portions as "Arts, Intellectuals and the Public: The Legacies and Limits of American Cultural Criticism 1910–1950" in *American Cultural Studies*, ed. Catherine Warren and Mary Douglas Vavrus, University of Illinois Press, 2000. Earlier versions of parts of chapter 5 and the conclusion appeared as "Art, The Public and Deweyan Cultural Criticism," in *American Pragmatism and Communication Research,* ed. David K. Perry, Longmans, 2000.

This project has had a number of incarnations, and I have benefited from the editorial guidance of Sheldon Meyer, Ann Miller, Bill Regier, and especially Patricia Reynolds Smith, as well as from the suggestions of several anonymous reviewers. I have also received welcome advice about publication options from Daniel Horowitz, Michael Schudson, Horace Newcomb, and, especially, James W. Carey.

Additional thanks go to Brenda Hadenfeldt, Jehanne Schweitzer, and others at Rowman & Littlefield.

And finally, my thanks to my parents, brothers, and friends for their advice, encouragement, and support throughout this period. And to my husband Craig Walter, and sons Charlie and Tom, my continuing gratitude for accepting the ways in which writing takes me away but brings me back, too.

Introduction:
Is Art Good for Us?

THE LIMITS OF INSTRUMENTAL LOGIC

Of course the arts are good for us. Exactly how and why they are good for us isn't clear, but we firmly believe that the arts are good, and that the media are bad. Social critics, especially those in the media, frequently argue that the media should be more like the arts—more uplifting, more enriching, more challenging, more worthwhile.

If only the media would "do" what the arts supposedly "do." But mass culture, we believe, is up to something very different from high culture. We assume that we need the arts to offer an alternative, more valuable cultural experience to each of us, now that we are "drowning" in the "media onslaught." The presumption is that we need the good influence of the arts to offset the bad influence of the media.

These arguments—that the arts are good for us, the media bad for us, and the arts can counteract the effects of the media—depend on an instrumental view of culture. An instrumental view of culture assumes that cultural forms do something to us. This view presumes that good culture does us good, and bad culture does us harm. If we are exposed to good stuff, we become better people; if we are exposed to bad stuff, we become worse. This treats high culture like a tonic, and mass culture as a toxin: in either case, culture is imagined as something we ingest that has direct effects. The instrumental view of the arts relies on a medicinal metaphor: the arts are good medicine, especially in today's "sick" society. The mass media, in contrast, are bad medicine, poisoning a healthy society.

1

But is any of this true?

In this book I explore our widely held faith in the arts as social medicine. I challenge assumptions that the arts can and should counterbalance the bad effects of the mass media. I want all of us to give up faith in the arts as *doing* good, and commit instead to a faith in the arts as *being* good.

American social thought has long depended on an instrumental view of culture. My first analytical claim is that *American social criticism is built on an unquestioned faith in the power of certain forms of culture to transform individuals, and thereby improve society.* I demonstrate how this instrumental view of culture has shaped the assumptions and conclusions of a variety of American intellectuals throughout the twentieth century. Then I compare this dominant instrumental view with an alternative expressive view, found in Alexis de Tocqueville and John Dewey.

In the end, I want to convince you that Tocqueville and Dewey have it right, and everybody else has it wrong. The instrumental view of the arts has untoward consequences. It misidentifies the causes and cures of social ills, which means it is a story that misdirects our energies—diverting us both from direct social engagement, and from more effective arguments for the arts.

We cannot build sustained social support for the arts in schools and communities if we base our arguments on nonexistent "art effects." These claims are too flimsy to be sustained—there is no convincing empirical evidence for the good effects of good culture, just as there is surprisingly little evidence for the bad effects of the mass media. If we want to improve our children, our schools, our inner cities, and the lives of the marginal, the elderly, the impoverished, then we should do so directly, rather than argue for an injection of "more arts." We must stop making arguments for arts funding using sweeping claims and spurious evidence.

Another reason we should give up instrumental arguments is that they are insulting—and therefore rhetorically ineffective. The medicinal metaphor tells people that they need high culture to be good people. The backlash against this elitist notion (from both the right and left) about what is "good for" others has made for understandably contentious debates about arts funding. Arts supporters cannot convince people to support the arts by defining them as "cultural spinach."[1]

There are better ways to make a case for the social value of the arts, tied directly to what is socially valuable about varieties of experience. The expressive perspective is evident in Tocqueville as he evaluated the costs and benefits of democratic taste in 1830s America. It was developed philosophically by Dewey in the 1920s as he explored the nature and value of democratic aesthetic experience. Because the expressive view believes that culture *is* something, rather than that it *does* something, it offers a more respectful, more effective, and (I believe) more accurate view of what the arts and the media are up to.

From an expressive perspective, culture—high, low, popular, commercial—is an aspect of experience, in its creation, circulation, and consumption. It can and should be evaluated, like any experience, for what it offers us. We cannot assume that it does something "to" us: good or bad. From an expressive perspective, the stuff we find distasteful and upsetting will not necessarily harm us or harm anyone else, and (alas) the stuff we find delightful and uplifting will not necessarily improve us or improve anyone else. All we can say is that we find some cultural forms more meaningful and worthy of our time and energies, and presume that others can and will make their own, often very different, assessments of aesthetic meaning and worth.

In contrast, the instrumental perspective assumes bad and good culture a priori. We already "know" what is good and bad, if we assume that the arts are generally good, and the media are generally bad. We take for granted that there are big differences between good and bad stuff. The instrumental view of the arts assumes that good culture is canonical culture—institutionally sanctioned, requiring a certain kind of training to appreciate, commercially unsuccessful, and rarely disseminated by the mass media. So classical music is automatically "good culture," and so—it is assumed—it will have good effects on us.[2]

The instrumental view, with its a priori categories of good and bad, and implicit assumptions of automatic effects, is the reason that the unproven "Mozart effect" gained such wide popular currency, and remains a robust commercial phenomenon. Because it was Mozart, it seemed somehow more believable that brain structure and math scores could be positively affected by brief exposure to a Mozart sonata. How wonderful—Mozart, undeniably good culture, helped rewire the brain to do better in math.

Unfortunately, the preliminary study that began the hoopla was soon disproved, and the many studies done since have only confirmed that there is no clear-cut Mozart effect. This has done little to stem the tide of commercial spin-offs and curricular deployments: "Best-sellers were written, lecture tours mounted, infomercials clogged the airwaves, Mozart-effect tapes and CDs flooded the market. A device to deliver Amadeus in utero became standard equipment for parents-to-be. Mozart cured everything from backache to writer's block."[3]

There is also widespread belief in what could be called the Muzak effect. Many of our public commercial spaces pipe pre-set music into them, because store owners believe, as Muzak claims, that music affects behavior. Faith in the Mozart effect can be contrasted with faith in the Muzak effect. Muzak—the syrupy essence of commercialized, mass-mediated culture—has various programs that are alleged to affect mood, and thereby (apparently) behavior.[4] Muzak's promotional literature argues that different tempos and styles of music can encourage and discourage behaviors such as shopping, lingering, and eating—that music can affect mood and mood can affect behavior.

The Muzak effect and the Mozart effect give us parallel versions of an instrumental view of culture. If we spend our lives in shopping malls and fast-food joints, listening to Muzak, we are being manipulated by mass, commercial culture. If we instead spend our lives in classrooms and concert halls, listening to Mozart, we will be increasing our brainpower while uplifting our souls.[5] For many social and cultural critics, the passive, unproven effects of Muzak are a form of social control, while the passive, unproven effects of a single Mozart sonata are examples of social benefit.

Under the combined logic of the Mozart/Muzak effects, we believe that music is medicine: different forms of culture can do different things to us. With an instrumental view, we make automatic assumptions about what happens to us when we spend time with high culture rather than with mass culture. We assume, ludicrously, that the effect is embedded in the cultural form itself, released when it is "consumed." If this were true, then it would be relatively easy to give each of us doses of good culture, making us into model citizens. Few carry faith in cultural effect that far. Yet the popular accounts of the Mozart effect implied just that—a dose of a sonata would improve brain wiring and math ability.

Why did the Mozart effect become so widely believed? Because it fit a dominant discourse about the good effects of good culture. It also resonated with previous (also disproved) claims about the ways that classical music helps plants grow better, and with other (far more reliable) studies about correlations between mathematical and musical abilities.

The issue here is *not* whether there is a connection between music and mood, or with musical exposure and other abilities. It is likely, and unsurprising, that familiarity and practice connect with abilities of various kinds, and that people's moods are shaped by listening to music they find pleasant or unpleasant. It is unsurprising that exposure and experience with various kinds of music—low, high, mass, commercial, ethnic—can affect mood, musical ability, and other cognitive functions. What is typical, and questionable, is the assumed connection between canonical "good" culture and social categories of "good" outcomes—like increased brain power, or docility, or—as claims about the social value of the arts often have it—lowered crime rates, or increased property values.

I want us to question the widespread assumption that there is universal good culture that can have automatic good effects, and that there is universal bad culture that has automatic bad effects. Clearly, many of us yearn to find an easy way to make our cities better, our lives safer, our children smarter. It would make classroom life so much easier if a half-hour of Mozart helped make students productive, tractable, and focused, no matter what. But this is a dangerous illusion—we must stop imagining that we can inject children, classrooms, or communities with "good culture" and make them better.

WHY BELIEVE IN ART EFFECTS?

Why do we maintain faith in the instrumental power of culture, in art as tonic and media as toxin? My second analytical claim is that *believing in the instrumental power of the arts gives us a simple and palatable explanation for why things are bad in society, and a simple and palatable way to make them better*. If good culture can make things better, then all we have to do is support more of what "we" (the so-called cultured) know to be good—the arts. And if bad culture makes us bad, then "we" know what to blame—not "the people" of course, but "the media." In the following chapters I show the varieties of forms this instrumental cultural logic can take.

Among communication scholars, there has been much criticism of the media effects model. Communications research has been dominated by a statistically oriented model, measuring the variables involved in "who said what to whom with what effects." This research model generates lots of publishable data relatively easily, while fitting well with the instrumental perspective. But it has become clear to many inside and outside the field that communication doesn't operate like a hypodermic needle, directly injecting meaning into us. It is increasingly taken for granted that culture isn't a message being transmitted, via a sender to a receiver. Communication is not linear, and the sender-message-receiver transmission model of communication has largely been abandoned, in favor of a more interpretive, cultural, ritual view.[6]

And yet, in public commentary, the transmission view continues to reign. It does so partly because both advertisers and journalists want to believe that what they say and do has direct, measurable effects. As Schudson has argued, this does not appear to be true of advertising,[7] and studies of news coverage and public opinion show how vexed and complicated the relationship is between what journalists say and what people believe.

It is also handy for all of us to be able to scapegoat the media for causing things that are frightening and mysterious, like eating disorders, gang violence, and school-yard shootings. Blaming communication technologies like video games, movies, music, and television shows is an easy way to locate causes for social pathologies outside of ourselves. When scapegoating the media, we find ways to place blame on something we think of as "other"; to do so strengthens the implicit claim that bad culture has bad effects.[8]

The instrumental view of the arts, based in a transmission view of communication, is dominant because it allows commentators and social critics to have hope (the arts can make us better) and place blame (the media make us bad). But the instrumental and transmission views also make it possible to tell stories about social improvement that rely on the very activities that social critics themselves are most fond of and adept in—critical thought, nuanced writing, sophisticated dramas, elaborate argumentation, and debate. It also allows stories that denigrate the taste, abilities, and worth of those who do *not* participate in those kinds of activities.

Social critics from across the political spectrum agree on the "badness" of contemporary popular culture, as evidenced in the badness of most media fare. That lots of people actually like the cultural forms that the critic knows to be bad only "proves" the transmission view—

those people have been deformed by their exposure to bad culture, brainwashed into liking it. If they were instead to be exposed to "good" culture, in the schools and by the media, they would have better taste and become better people.

And they would then, the argument goes, be less susceptible to the "bad" influence of the media. The counterbalancing argument imagines the arts as an inoculation against the media. If we make sure that people are made good by art, they will be less likely to choose to spend time with bad influences like television. It certainly seems to hold for most social critics, who rarely seem to watch television, read best-selling novels, go to blockbuster movies, or spend time in shopping malls.

Popular opinion is dominated by this instrumental view of culture, but it is a view that has a much longer, more complex history than I ever imagined. I began this project with the certainty that there were many perspectives on the social role of the arts among American intellectuals; my goal was to excavate a "usable past" of differing arts beliefs. To my surprise, and growing dismay, I found relentless similarity. It became increasingly clear that the differing perspectives on the social role of the arts I'd hoped to find were based in a single story, told over and over, across generations and political perspectives.

That people of such different times, with differing politics, loyalties, and social goals, share a faith in the instrumental effects of culture could mean that culture really is "good medicine"—good art makes good people, bad art makes bad people. But because there is so little empirical evidence for this, and because the consequences of this belief are so unpleasant, I have written a very different book—a critique rather than a comparative analysis. Because the stories we tell have consequences—and I do not like the consequences of the stories we tell about the social effects of the arts—I want us to examine, question, and ultimately abandon, our instrumental faith.

The story being told serves mostly the people doing the telling. It leads to social policies that don't really help anyone, arts policies based on effects that can't be proven, and endless essays on how bad contemporary culture is and how much better the world would be if only the "right" kinds of culture were dominant. If we tell the story of culture, democracy, and commerce differently, we might be able to come up with more effective social policies, more inclusive arts support, and better accounts of what is wrong, why it is wrong, and what needs to be done about it.

AMBIVALENCE AND DESIRE

My third analytical claim is that *beliefs about the arts are connected to deeper ambivalences about modern life, particularly about democracy, technology, and commerce.* When we talk about "today's society" we are almost always talking about some aspect of egalitarianism, industrialization, and consumerism. What does it mean to let go of an inherited social hierarchy? What does it mean to live in the machine age, or the electronic age, or the digital age? And what does it mean to sell our time and energy for money to buy products?

Commercial culture references the products, habits, and symbols of contemporary life, and it is too broad a category. But "commercial culture" offers a shadow alternative to the arts, imagined to be non-commercial culture. Noncommercial culture is not mainstream or egalitarian or about making money—therefore it supposedly does not share the traits of modernity about which we are so ambivalent. Noncommercial art, whether it is classical, progressive, avant-garde, revolutionary, or alternative, is presumed to be more "authentic" and therefore better culture. It is better because it does not "contain" or "spread" the contamination of modernity. Our mistrust of commercial culture is a cover for deeper, more difficult, more interesting mistrusts of our social, technical, and economic order.

Our desire—an admirable one—is to find ways to make ourselves, and our society, better. Our faith in the power of arts to do this is misplaced, however. My final analytical claim is a conclusion: *The arts are not an intervening variable that can change the world.* When we imagine the arts as a way to make things better, we are assuming that the arts do something that we cannot. An imagined category of "good culture" becomes the way to challenge, subvert, uplift, refine, ennoble, enliven, and do other good things. We look to certain forms of culture to make the world a place we want to live in, with people we might actually want to live with, rather than looking to ourselves and taking responsibility for our own actions.

HERITAGE OF PRECONCEPTIONS

In the following chapters I explore—and deplore—the two dominant rhetorical claims I find in the discussions of social role of the arts. Discussions among American intellectuals and social critics rely on either a rhetoric of redemption (the arts can save us) or a rhetoric of counter-balance (the arts can counteract modernity and the mass media), or some combination of the two. I argue that both the redemptive and counterbalancing perspectives take us somewhere we don't want to go—to claims in support of the arts that are wrongheaded, self-serving, and unconvincing.

If we are to support the arts effectively, we need to understand how they might actually be important and valuable *in themselves*. To do so is to be respectful of varieties of aesthetic experience. This requires that we adopt an expressive view of the arts, defined by Dewey, and prefigured in Tocqueville. I want us to understand all culture, and all communication, as forms of experience. If we do this, we can evaluate these experiences for ourselves, in moral, ethical, and aesthetic terms, and let others evaluate them for themselves, in whatever terms they want to use.

Using an expressive perspective, we are more likely to support cos-mopolitan, pluralistic, and egalitarian notions of artistic creativity, and engage in more diverse, "from-the-ground-up" aesthetic expression. We will focus more on giving all people access to varieties of creative encounters, rather than on defending "our" cultural forms for what we think they can do to make other people better.

The rest of the book considers the nature and consequences of various versions of redemptive and counterbalancing perspectives in American social thought. I end by arguing for an expressive approach to the social role of the arts, so that we can begin to think more clearly, and act more wisely, about culture in contemporary life.

NOTES

1. This phrase draws on the term *theatrical spinach,* used by Gerald Nachman, "Break a Leg, Willy," *San Francisco Chronicle,* 30 November 1979, quoted in Lawrence W. Levine, *Highbrow/Lowbrow: The Emergence of Cultural Hierarchy in America* (Harvard University Press, 1988), 31.

2. For an analysis of how this belief is used in the marketing of classical CDs, see Gwenyth Jackaway, "Selling Mozart to the Masses: Crossover Marketing as Cultural Diplomacy," *Journal of Popular Music Studies* 11–12, 1999/2000, 125–50.

3. *Bangor Daily News,* 31 August 1999.

4. See Stephen H. Barnes, *Muzak, the Hidden Messages in Music: A Social Psychology of Culture* (Lewiston, N.Y.: Edwin Mellow Press, 1988), for a direct critique of Muzak as a form of social control; for a history and analysis of this form of popular

culture, see Joseph Lanza, *Elevator Music: A Surreal History of Muzak, Easy-Listening and Other Moodsong* (New York: St. Martin's Press, 1994).

5. An example of how this perspective is played out in popular discourse is Betty Casey, "Is Your Child's School Flunking Art?" *Tulsa Kids*, August 1998, which begins, "What if you were told that certain parts of your child's brain just didn't develop for lack of proper stimulation? Or that because certain neural circuits in the brain weren't stimulated before kindergarten, your child will never reach her potential? On the other hand, what if someone came to you and promised to boost your child's SAT scores? And pump up his grasp of math? Would you enroll your child in a school that had the curriculum to increase self-esteem, improve problem solving skills, enhance creative and expressive abilities, prepare her for life, give her cultural understanding, improve communication skills, enhance math and language skills, and add joy to her life? Research shows that making the arts an integral part of a child's environment will do all these things and more" (11).

6. For critiques of the transmission view, in relation to a developed cultural approach to communication, see James W. Carey, *Communication as Culture: Essays on Media and Society* (Boston: Unwin Hyman 1989). For accounts of several decades of definitional controversy in media studies and communication research, see *Ferment in the Field*, [special issue] *Journal of Communication* 33, no. 3 (1983); and Mark R. Levy and Michael Gurevitch, eds., *Defining Media Studies: Reflections on the Future of the Field* (New York: Oxford University Press, 1994).

7. Michael Schudson, *Advertising, the Uneasy Persuasion: Its Dubious Impact on American Society* (New York: Basic Books, 1984).

8. For a discussion of how this operates in media criticism, see Joli Jensen, *Redeeming Modernity: Contradictions in Media Criticism* (Berkeley, Calif.: Sage, 1990).

Chapter One

Exemplary Voices:
Tocqueville, Whitman, and Mumford

It is always difficult to examine the ideas, values, and beliefs we live by, because they seem natural. Our taken-for-granted assumptions have an "of course" quality to them that makes them so obvious that they are almost invisible. But we must learn how to denaturalize our constructs if we are to examine their consequences. If we live by stories, and seek the best stories by which to live, then we must first figure out what stories we are already telling ourselves, so that we can decide if we like where they are taking us.

What stories are we telling ourselves about the arts? I have found two basic stories—that the arts can redeem us, or that they can counteract what is harming us. I don't like where either of these stories takes us. Instead, I want us to question those stories, so that we can adopt a better one: that all forms of culture—including what are called the arts—express us.

One way to demonstrate the nature, and consequences, of these three kinds of stories—redemptive, counterbalancing, and expressive—is to connect them with particular thinkers. By tracing the contours of these perspectives in particular individuals, I can show how each of them operates, and consider (and compare) their consequences. In this chapter, I use Tocqueville as an example of expressive logic, Whitman as an example of redemptive logic, and Mumford as an example of counterbalancing logic.

I first describe the basic claims Tocqueville makes about the role of art in 1830s American democracy. Then I contrast Tocqueville's analysis with the assumptions used by Whitman in his 1860s essay "Democratic Vistas." Finally, I explore the assumptions used by Mumford in the 1940s to the 1960s—how does Mumford's instrumental perspective compare with Whitman's, in contrast with Tocqueville's expressive approach? These three sketches are designed to highlight characteristics of the expressive, redemptive, and counterbalancing perspectives. Having demonstrated these perspectives in particular, we can then, in later chapters, explore how they operate in various twentieth-century debates about the arts in American life, up to the present time.

My ultimate goal is to denaturalize our discourse on the arts, in ways that allow us to recognize and dislodge our dominant assumptions. Ideally, reading this book will make you more and more aware of the varieties of ways the arts are imagined as "doing" something, rather than as "being" something, in contemporary discussions. In the end, I want you to realize how the logics of redemption and counterbalance do not serve us well, and how different, and preferable, the expressive perspective can be.

CHOOSING TOCQUEVILLE

I had long assumed that Tocqueville was an early critic of mass or commercial culture, because he is so frequently quoted in collections addressing the mass culture debates. When I returned to his two-volume *Democracy in America,* however, I was startled to discover a very different terrain of assumptions, not just about the arts, but about democracy, commerce, religion, and public life. I then assumed that Tocqueville would offer me one of a series of different takes on the arts; I would use him as one example of a variety of perspectives I would locate, describe, and trace throughout twentieth-century discussions.

The more I read, the more I realized how unusual Tocqueville's approach really is, and I struggled to sort out why. What made his thought seem so alien, especially in comparison with that of Whitman and Mumford? Tocqueville is still widely quoted by contemporary social and cultural critics, so his thought is obviously not hopelessly anachronistic. Eventually, I worked out why Tocqueville—unlike Whitman and Mumford—sounds so unlike other commentators on the social role of the arts. In doing so, I recognized the difference between what I am now calling instrumental and expressive perspectives on the arts: what makes Tocqueville seem so "odd" is that he presumes that the arts are expressions of, rather than causal agents in, social life.

Congruent with an expressive perspective (although not required by it) is that Tocqueville also does not assume that democratic culture is intrinsically less worthy than aristocratic culture. He acknowledges democratic culture as different from aristocratic forms, because of its necessarily different relationship to the social order. Both these assumptions—that art is not causal, that arts can differ in sophistication and style but not in social value—are addressed only in relation to his larger argument about the risks and possibilities of American democracy.

Tocqueville's analysis of early American social, cultural, and political life offers us a powerful way to explore how an expressive perspective on the arts addresses concerns about democracy, commerce, and new cultural forms. When Tocqueville considers the arts, he is doing so in relation to his own more pressing concerns about the future of democracy in general—what can the American instance tell him, and his French readers, about what is yet to come?

Tocqueville's Logbook

Democracy in America was published in 1835 and 1840, after Tocqueville spent nine months touring America. During his travels he sought, he says in the introduction to volume 1, "the image of democracy itself, with its inclinations, its character, its prejudices and its passions, in order to learn what we have to fear or to hope from its progress" (14).[1]

Tocqueville's goal was also to explore, concretely, what both threatens and protects democracy. For Tocqueville, democracy is equality where liberty is not guaranteed. Democratization will inevitably spread, but the multiple consequences of democracy were still, in the 1830s and 1840s, largely unknown. How does American democracy manifest the qualities that Tocqueville, and his contemporaries, most fear and most value? How can the American experience be used to illuminate what the future holds?

Tocqueville's analysis of the influence of democracy on civic life is an extended argument about how to "endeavor to make the best of that which is allotted to us." We do this, he argues, by "finding out both [democracy's] good and its evil tendencies," thus learning how to "foster the former and repress the latter to the utmost" (vol. 1, 253).

So Tocqueville is not making a simple causal argument about "democracy" as a modernizing force, one that transforms all that it touches.

He is not merely describing the consequences of social leveling, or the effects of capitalism, or the costs of the loss of aristocratic leadership. These are twentieth-century—and no doubt twenty-first-century—appropriations of Tocqueville's philosophy, ones that turn him into a social critic whose observations give historical weight to the critics' own presumptions about modernity's effects on culture and society.

Rather, Tocqueville is describing how he believes various American social forms *mitigate against* the worst aspects of, or threats to, democracy. And, when the mitigation seems insufficient, he suggests that these aspects of democracy are necessary, and bearable, losses. When neither mitigation nor trade-offs seem enough, he invokes religion as a final guarantor. For Tocqueville, it is not art but commerce that directs and channels the passions; and it is not art but religion that can turn men's hearts and minds to higher things.

Tocqueville addresses two fundamental and recurring fears of democratization: that democracy leads to social fragmentation, and that people may not be trustworthy as "their own masters." These two fears—of fragmentation and of the masses—still worry social and cultural critics. Unlike Tocqueville, Whitman and later social critics exalt the arts to assuage their own fears of egalitarianism. They can rest easy, all is well, if the arts have the power to unify the nation and transform the masses into citizens.

Tocqueville's need, instead, is to imagine a force that will enhance cohesiveness and deflect anarchy and revolution, without curtailing liberty. The ultimate force that Tocqueville invokes to ensure a liberal and stable democracy is religion. Religion is endowed with the power to strengthen moral ties (defending against anarchy) while offering necessary checks to imagination and desire (defending against endless revolution). In this way, religion serves Tocqueville in the ways that "the arts" serve later social critics—as an instrumental force that can ensure a good social outcome.

In volume 2, Tocqueville develops his analysis of religion as countering the worst potential influences of egalitarianism on individuals. He argues that one of the principal advantages of religion is "to furnish to . . . fundamental questions a solution that is at once clear, precise, intelligible, and lasting, to the mass of mankind." Religions impose, as he argued in volume 1, a "salutary restraint on the intellect," because they counter paralytic doubt, and the "confused and changing notions" that can assail members of a society of equals.

Tyranny is the threat that concerns him here. Doubt, change, uncertain opinions "cannot but enervate the soul, relax the springs of the will, and prepare a people for servitude" (21). Frightened of unbounded independence, in constant agitation, alarmed, and exhausted, the people, without religion, are at risk of surrendering their freedom to some firm, fixed master.

Religion, Tocqueville argues, inspires principles that are diametrically contrary to the "dangerous propensities" of equality. "Equality, which it must be acknowledged brings great benefits into the world, nevertheless suggests to men . . . some very dangerous propensities. It tends to isolate them from one another, to concentrate every man's attention upon himself; and it lays open the soul to an inordinate love of material gratification" (22). Religion places objects of desire above and beyond the earth, imposes duties on man toward others, and draws his attention outside himself, thus countering the individualistic and material propensities of equality.

Equality unleashes many human passions, for Tocqueville, but the dominant one is the taste for well-being. Tocqueville argues that religion cannot destroy such a deep-seated passion; men cannot be weaned entirely from the contemplation of the good things of this world. "Men cannot be cured of the love of riches, but they may be persuaded to enrich themselves by none but honest means." The chief concern of religion, argues Tocqueville, is to "purify, to regulate, and to restrain the excessive and exclusive taste for well-being that men feel in periods of equality" (26).

This is the last in an extraordinary series of claims Tocqueville makes for the power of religion. In his analysis, religion functions individually and socially to deflect threats to democracy's stability, and to mitigate against democracy's worst propensities. Its power ranges from the mundane, increasing material success through spiritual energizing, to the exalted, social glue, a requirement for freedom, and a bulwark against despotism. It precludes rash or unjust acts. It mitigates against atomism and individualism. By offering certainties it prevents tyranny, without itself becoming tyrannical.

The channeling of passions and intellect that religion offers is invariably salutary, purifying, regulating, restraining—never stifling or smothering. For Tocqueville, religion takes what is natural in man and shapes it toward the purposes he most values. With religion, stable, liberal, and beneficent democracy can triumph.

Religion becomes, in Tocqueville, a form of spiritualized commerce. The same salutary effects he attributes to commerce are attributed, in greater degree, to religion—it prepares men for freedom, and preserves them from revolution, tyranny, and anarchy. The key difference is that religion simultaneously counters the deleterious effects of commerce. It contains the same seeds of salvation, while curtailing commerce's seeds of destruction. Through religion, the selfishness and anxieties of materialism are counterbalanced. Religion is therefore the sole single-edged concept in Tocqueville's thought—it does only good things.

The Value of Intervening Variables

The characteristics of religion in Tocqueville's account directly parallel the many powers ascribed to the arts by later thinkers. Religion functions in Tocqueville's analysis as an intervening variable—a fudge factor—that guarantees desired outcomes. Religion is a multifaceted, pervasive, beneficent force whose influence is, happily, just what is required to foster a stable, free, equal society. The best of democracy can flourish, thanks to the powers religion is presumed to have.

Religion is not the only factor Tocqueville invokes as enhancing the best aspects of democracy and protecting against the worst. Virtually every trait or characteristic of 1830s American life that Tocqueville discusses is evaluated in terms of enhancing democracy or mitigating threats against it. Tocqueville finds abundant evidence for the enhancing capabilities of (potentially dangerous) traits like self-interest, individualism, the taste for well-being, and for the stabilizing powers of commerce, as well as laws, the press, and free associations. But religion trumps them all—it functions as the crucial, most powerful, and least-defined element in his analysis. Religion is, for Tocqueville, the ultimate antidote, emollient, and tonic for democracy.

The arts play no such exalted role in Tocqueville's analysis. They do not protect against dangers to democracy. He does not analyze the arts in terms of their power to channel or purify, to temper or deflect individual traits. He does not invoke them as crucial democratic forms, like the press, or the legal system, or free associations. For Tocqueville, the arts are expressions of deeper, more fundamental characteristics of political and social life. They do not activate, energize, corrupt, or destroy elements of democracy. In his analysis, painting and sculpture, literature, poetry, and drama are dependent on the social and political context of democracy; they are neither central to its development nor factors in its potential demise. For Tocqueville, democracy depends on other forces.

Yet later commentators, especially in the 1950s and early 1960s, have claimed Tocqueville as an early critic of mass culture, as someone who sensed the dangerous consequences of commercial cultural forms designed for mass consumption. They quote from his sections, in volume 2, on the nature of the arts, without locating his ideas in his larger argument. This means that Tocqueville is being misappropriated as a precursor to twentieth-century critics, as an early observer of the American arts being contaminated by commerce.

But Tocqueville's perspective on the arts is fundamentally different from that of most contemporary critics. Tocqueville is *not* arguing that commerce ruins art's ability to serve social ends, because he does not argue that art has the power to transform people or societies. Instead, for Tocqueville, different social arrangements result in different kinds of artistic expressions. Democratic arts have characteristics particular to democratic societies. He believes that there is sometimes less great work in democratic societies, but there is, overall, greater involvement with new and different forms. There may be fewer examples of perfect art, but, in democratic life, the arts are more widespread and abundant.

Tocqueville marshals an array of forces that can deflect threats to democracy's potentials. Yet he *never* suggests the arts as a crucial or necessary way to redeem democracy or counterbalance mechanization. Instead, he analyzes the nature of the arts he finds in American life and considers the possible consequences of egalitarian, commercial society for its nature and characteristics. Unlike later critics, he thinks in terms of middle grounds, of finding ways to make the best of necessary changes. He seeks the benefits in what appear to be losses. His expressive notions of the arts are developed in this spirit.

Illumination and Leveling

The conceptual dichotomy Tocqueville foregrounds in his discussion of democracy and the arts is civilization vs. barbarism. This dichotomy is implicit in much of the rest of his analysis, and responds to widespread concerns among his contemporaries. They wanted to know if democracy would lead to an increase in civilization, or instead foster a stagnant culture that would decline into barbarism. Analyzing the state of the arts in American democracy helps Tocqueville address widespread fears that democratization leads inevitably to civilization's stagnation or decay.

But what, exactly, is civilization, and what would constitute its stagnation or decay? For Tocqueville, civilization represents advancements in knowledge (*lumiere*), as manifested in the sciences, and in the imagination, as manifested in the arts. Civilization is a condition where "the higher faculties" are widely deployed. Barbarism is a condition where emotions and passions reign, where the higher faculties are neither valued nor cultivated. Societies have moved from the darkness of barbarism to the light of civilization, from a low, animalistic state to a higher, more spiritual, state. Societies can sink into darkness or rise into light, in Tocqueville's perspective.

This imagery is crucial to understanding how leveling works in Tocqueville's analysis. He conflates the high/low and light/dark images, suggesting, ultimately, that society is not rising, but is perhaps spreading more, or a different kind of, light. Tocqueville speaks to his times by asking questions about the "level" of civilization possible in a democracy in relation to a larger sense of the advance of civilization—he addresses nineteenth-century concerns about where democracies stand on a hypothetical barbarism–civilization scale. Tocqueville usually *answers* such questions in relation to an inclusive standard—how many in the population have achieved a certain level of knowledge and imagination, or are engaged in new, comparable forms of mental activity?

Civilization, defined in Tocqueville's refraction of Enlightenment vocabulary, is not a unitary standard that offers a simple way to evaluate a society. Crucial to understanding Tocqueville's perspective on the arts is recognizing that *he offers a different scale against which to evaluate the progress of democracy*. What Tocqueville does is give us a different yardstick to evaluate democratization.

Tocqueville moves the discussion from "Is democracy good or bad for civilization?" to a different question—"What do we want from society and government?" Once that question is asked, different answers can be offered. Those answers do not endlessly celebrate or critique the consequences of equality for civilization, but address, instead, different visions of a good society. They also reveal the role Tocqueville ascribes to the arts—dependent on conditions that cannot, and perhaps should not, prevail. He asks:

> Is it your object to refine the habits, embellish the manners, and cultivate the arts, to promote the love of poetry, beauty and glory? Would you constitute

a people fitted to act powerfully upon all other nations, and prepared for those high enterprises which, whatever their results, will leave a name forever famous in history? If you believe such to be the principal object of society, avoid the government of democracy, for it would not lead you with certainty to the goal.

But if you hold it expedient to divert the moral and intellectual activity of man to the production of comfort and the promotion of living in the midst of a brilliant society, you are contented to have prosperity around you; if, in short, you are of the opinion that the principal object of government . . . is to ensure the greatest enjoyment and to avoid the most misery to each of the individuals who compose it—if such be your desire, then equalize the conditions of men and establish democratic institutions. (vol. 1, 252–53)

In this passage, "the arts" are linked to refined habits, embellished manners, and the love of beauty and glory, as well as the potential for heroic, enduring action. All these result, he implies, from nondemocratic conditions. They are opposed, in the following paragraph, with the production of comfort and the promotion of general well-being, which result from a "diversion" of moral and intellectual activities. An aristocratic world of dramatic and grandiose action for some is contrasted with a democratic world of comfort and prosperity for many. The fine arts are a product of, not a causal mechanism in, that former world.

Human Nature and the Arts

Tocqueville's implicit theory of the arts involves a set of assumptions about individual human nature. We have, with Tocqueville, a tripartite scheme, soul-mind-body. "The interests" are rational and mental, a middle state, neither exaltedly spiritual nor debasingly material. Man's interests, rationally based, are neither spirit nor passion, but can be harnessed by either. Thus the passions can anchor men's thoughts to finite, earthly, utilitarian things, but the mind, motivated by interest, can still be drawn upward, toward infinite, spiritual, beautiful things.

These become assumptions from which Tocqueville analyzes the arts in a democracy. Individuals are mixtures of passion, intellect, and spirit; given the opportunity of leisure, they naturally turn toward higher, more intellectual and spiritual matters. People not "strictly confined to the cares of the practical life" will be able to "indulge in the pursuits and pleasures of the intellect . . . for if it is true that the human mind leans on one side to the limited, the material and the useful, it

naturally rises on the other to the infinite, the spiritual, and the beautiful. Physical wants confine it to earth, but as soon as the tie is loosened,
it will rise of itself" (vol. 2, 38–39).

The pursuits and pleasures of the intellect are scientific, literary, and
artistic, and will emerge naturally among those freed from the necessity of material activities. Further, it will become obvious, in an egalitarian society, that excelling in "the labors of the mind" is a powerful
means of acquiring fame, power, or wealth." This will lead to a general increase in those who cultivate science, letters, and the arts (vol. 2,
40). This is Tocqueville's prediction for American society, and the final
statement in his chapter "The Example of the American People Does
Not Prove That a Democratic People Can Have No Aptitude and No
Taste for Science, Literature or Art."

Tocqueville claims that American society, for a number of reasons,
has not yet offered a context for a natural turning toward the pleasures
and pursuits of the mind. The Puritan heritage, "austere and almost
harsh in its principles, and hostile to external symbols and to ceremonial pomp, is naturally unfavorable to the fine arts and yields only re-
luctantly to the pleasures of literature." Furthermore, "in America
everyone finds facilities unknown elsewhere for making or increasing
his fortune. The spirit of gain is always eager, and the human mind,
constantly diverted from the pleasures of imagination and the labors of
the intellect, is there swayed by no impulse but the pursuit of wealth."

Finally, Americans have had access to "learned and literary Europe"
and can thus afford to neglect the pursuit of science, literature, and the
arts "without relapsing into barbarism."

But in an egalitarian society focused on procuring comfort, the taste
for the useful always predominates over the taste for the beautiful, in
science as well as the arts. "Democratic nations," Tocqueville argues,
"will therefore cultivate the arts that served to render life easy in pref-
erence to those whose object is to adorn it. They will habitually prefer
the useful to the beautiful, and they will require that the beautiful be
useful."

Further, democratic societies lack the segmentation that trained specialized artisans and offered them a livelihood of selling their perfect
work to fastidious customers. Democratic societies instead "offer large
numbers of people whose desire for acquiring objects can often exceed
their purse, or their desires for perfection." The artisan finds ways to
work more quickly and cheaply, sacrificing quality. "When none but

the wealthy had watches, they were almost all very good ones; few are now made that are worth much, but everybody has one in his pocket. Thus the democratic principle not only tends to direct the human mind to the useful arts, but it induces the artisan to produce with great rapidity many imperfect commodities, and the consumer to content himself with these commodities" (vol. 2, 50).

For the fine arts, particularly painting, sculpture, and architecture, this tendency means that artists "cultivate what is pretty and elegant, and appearance is more attended to than reality." Vast numbers of insignificant pictures are made, versus a few great ones; statues are plaster, not bronze; buildings are painted wood, not marble.

Tocqueville develops his spiritual and material split to suggest that artists in democratic life tend to "follow nature with fidelity. This is not true of great artists in the past, who "sought for something better than nature." Raphael, for example, "discloses in his works a glimpse of the Deity." The fine visual arts of the past offered fleeting access to the divine, unlike the utilitarian, imitative arts that predominate in democratic society.

> The social condition and institutions of democracy impart certain peculiar tendencies to all the imitative arts, which it is easy to point out. They frequently withdraw them from the delineation of the soul to fix them exclusively on that of the body, and they substitute the representation of motion and sensation for that of sentiment and thought; in a word, they put the real in the place of the ideal. (vol. 2, 52)

So in addressing the arts in general, and the visual arts in particular, Tocqueville develops a set of critical distinctions: soul/body; sentiment/sensation; ideal/real; beautiful/useful; spiritual/material. These distinctions are used, when convenient, to evaluate the quality of particular art forms in American life.

Evaluating American Arts

Architecture is discussed as "monuments of the arts" in a chapter considering "Why Americans Raise Some Insignificant Monuments and Others That Are Very Grand." Tocqueville's answer is that democracy, by making men feel individually insignificant but nationally grandiose, "leads men to a vast number of inconsiderable productions; it also leads them to raise some monuments on the largest scales; but between these two extremes there is a blank."

In "Literary Characteristics of Democratic Times," Tocqueville suggests that a large number of Americans "take an interest in the productions of the mind and make them, if not the study of their lives, at least the charm of their leisure hours" (55). But these "productions" are not by and for Americans. In an often-quoted line, Tocqueville says, "The inhabitants of the United States have, then, at present, properly speaking, no literature."

Tocqueville notes that England provides both actual books for American readers, and literary models for American authors. Thus, he argues, Americans "transport into the midst of democracy the ideas and literary fashions that are current among the aristocratic nation they have taken for their model. They paint with colors borrowed from foreign manners."

But he believes that Americans will develop a literature, with a "character peculiarly its own." He goes on to trace that character, by first considering the literature that appeals to "aristocratic people, among whom letters are cultivated." These men have strict and traditional codes of behavior, and "have learned to understand literature as an art, to love it in the end for its own sake, and to feel a scholarlike satisfaction in seeing men conform to its rules." They have a taste for "carefully chosen gratifications and a love of refined and delicate pleasures. . . . They would rather be amused than intensely excited; they wish to be interested, but not to be carried away."

Writing designed for this audience follows particular rules, is carefully wrought, and values style and form as much as content. It has a "dignified, seldom very animated, tone." But Tocqueville also notes the perils of such writing—authors disconnect from the rest of the world, are infected with a false and labored style, and "write in a remote, affected language." This taste for a distanced, artificial world is dangerous; Tocqueville warns that "an aristocracy that keeps itself entirely aloof from the people becomes impotent."

He then turns to democracy, where we find a "motley multitude" who "live in a state of incessant change of place, feelings and fortunes . . . it is from the bosom of this heterogeneous and agitated mass, however, that authors spring; and from the same source their profits and their fame are distributed."

For such a people, literary rules and traditions seem ludicrous, since "each new generation is a new people." Further, few have the leisure to engage fully with literature; instead, they can only "taste occasionally and by stealth the pleasures of the mind." These pleasures become "transient and necessary recreation amid the serious labor of life." Since they have little time, they "prefer books which may be easily procured, quickly read, and which require no learned researches to be understood. They ask for beauties self-proffered and easily enjoyed; above all , they must have what is unexpected and new. Accustomed to the struggle, the crosses, and the monotony of practical life, they require strong and rapid emotions, startling passages, truths or errors brilliant enough to rouse them up and to plunge them at once, as if by violence into the midst of the subject."

The democratic literature Tocqueville expects to emerge, then, will have "more wit than erudition, more imagination than profundity; and literary performances will bear marks of an untutored and rude vigor of thought, frequently of great variety and singular fecundity. The object of authors will be to astonish rather than to please, and to stir the passions more than to charm the taste."

Notice how this contrast between an imported, refined, aloof aristocratic literature and a native, crude, but lively democratic literature is not an attack on "barbaric" mass culture. Instead it describes the costs and benefits of two very different literary styles, displacing caricatured differences between Europe and America onto literary forms. The imagined new literature becomes an embodiment of perceived differences in individual types: the aristocrat versus the democrat. Both authors and audience are presumed to have literary tastes congruent with more general stereotypes about manners and temperament.

The linking of commerce and art that characterizes twentieth-century cultural critics seems to appear in Tocqueville in chapter 14, "The Trade of Literature." This half-page chapter is an astringent indictment of writers who seek to obtain, without great effort, a moderate reputation and a large fortune with readers who are far too easy to please. In a democracy, "the ever increasing crowd of readers and their continual craving for something new ensure the sale of books nobody much esteems." Tocqueville notes that democratic literature is always "infested" with writers who look upon letters as a mere trade—"for some few great authors who adorn it, you may reckon thousands of idea-mongers."

What later critics miss, when they quote his half-page chapter, is that Tocqueville's critique is of writers, not democratic literature, or art in a capitalist era, or the inevitable corruption of art by commercial interests. Tocqueville is angry at writers who approach literature "in the trading spirit" rather than as an arduous exertion. His hostility is for those who "infest" democratic literature, not for the literature itself, or the commercial basis of its production. What he dislikes is authors pandering to the market, not the existence of the literary marketplace itself.

The market exists in both aristocracies and democracies, but it is, in Tocqueville's analysis, a significantly different market. Aristocratic and democratic audiences influence the style and substance of the literature circulated in it by influencing the author—it is the size and kind of audience that determines what authors produce. Tocqueville is criticizing those authors who see literature as mere money-making, who "sell out" by producing, with minimal exertion, literature that a crowd of readers will like, but not respect.

Another section that it is easy for critics to misuse in current debates is the following chapter, "The Study of Greek and Latin Literature is Peculiarly Useful in Democratic Communities." Here, apparently, is the first salvo in contemporary debates about canon and curriculum. And Tocqueville indeed says, "All who aspire to literary excellence in democratic nations ought to frequently refresh themselves at the springs of ancient literature; there is no more wholesome medicine for the mind."

But the argument that precedes this statement is equivocal, and limits the utility of classical literature to those who seek to be true scholars or extraordinary writers. Ancient literature, he argues, displays aristocratic society's special merits *and defects.* A brief survey of classic authors shows they used exquisite care and skill in details, with each line written for the connoisseur, and the whole shaped toward a conception of ideal beauty. But, extending his previous aristocratic/democratic stereotypes, Tocqueville says those writers were sometimes "deficient in variety and fertility of subject, or boldness, vivacity and power of generalization in their thoughts."

Further, their social and political conditions were not truly democratic, and so the study of their literature may not be appropriate to true democratic wants. In a passage conveniently absent from Tocquevillian appropriation by conservative voices in today's culture wars, Tocqueville offers an extraordinary warning *against* teaching only Greek and Latin literature to a community where everyone seeks to augment his fortune. He says, "the result would be a very dangerous set of citizens" who would have an education that would not teach them to meet the wants of their social and political condition, so they would "perturb the state, in the name of Greeks and Romans, instead of enriching it by their productive industry."

Tocqueville argues that it is better, in democracies, that the majority be educated in ways that are scientific, commercial, and industrial, rather than literary. Classical literature is best taught to those who are "destined to cultivate letters." Literature is set off from science, commerce, and industry, as a separate sphere for particular people of particular predisposition and ability.

But literature has two subsets: drama and poetry. Tocqueville calls drama "the literature of the stage," and argues it is the most democratic literary form in an aristocratic age. Poetry, in contrast, is an aristocratic form that must transform itself in a democratic age. In Tocqueville's analysis, drama excites the emotions and poetry delights the imagination. Each is treated in a separate chapter, and they are never explicitly compared.

Tocqueville's analysis of "the literature of the stage" is fresh and lively. He argues that drama will be where literary changes will first be manifested, because in the theater, authors quickly discover public tastes and respond to them. This means that drama can both indicate an approaching literary revolution and complete it.

Drama takes the spectator by surprise; the spectator has no time to "refer to his memory or to consult those more able to judge than himself." Theatrical presentations do not require preparation or study, "they lay hold on you in the midst of your prejudices and your ignorance." This accessibility means that at the theater, and the theater alone, the classes mix. And often the tastes of the people prevail over the tastes of "men of cultivation and literary attainment . . . the pit has frequently made laws for the boxes."

This means that drama quickly shows the influence of democracy on literature: "In written productions the literary canons of aristocracy will be gently, gradually and so to speak, legally modified; at the theater they will be riotously overthrown."

Tocqueville claims that the theater brings out most of the good qualities and almost all of the defects inherent in a democratic literature. He makes direct comparisons: "On the stage, as elsewhere, an aristocratic audience wishes to meet only persons of quality and to be moved only by the misfortunes of kings," while in democratic communities, spectators "prefer to see on the stage that medley of conditions, feelings, and opinions that occurs before their eyes." This means that, in a democracy, drama becomes "more striking, more vulgar, and more true."

Canons and rules cannot control theatrical representations—"If the effect of democracy is generally to question the authority of all literary rules and conventions, on the stage it abolishes them altogether, and puts in their place nothing but the caprice of each author and each public." Those who go to the theater "do not go there to seek the pleasures of mind, but the keen emotions of the heart." Logical plots and stylistic niceties are not required, "if you succeed in bringing your audience into the presence of something that affects them, they will not care by what means you brought them there, and they will never reproach you for having excited their emotions in spite of dramatic rules."

Tocqueville suggests that Puritan animosity toward amusements, especially the stage, has "left deep traces on the minds of their descendents." Regular habits, strict morals, and a country "which has witnessed no great political catastrophes and in which love invariably leads by a straight and easy road to matrimony" does not yield an audience receptive to theater. Tocqueville notes that, in many cities, theatrical presentations are censored by municipal authority, and dryly adds that "this may serve to show how much communities are like individuals; they surrender themselves unscrupulously to their ruling passions and afterward take the greatest care not to yield too much. . . ."

Democratic drama, with its intense, direct appeal to the emotions, can be contrasted with aristocratic poetry, with its subtle, indirect appeal to the imagination. Tocqueville defines *poetry* as "the search after, and the delineation of, the Ideal." The Poet "completes and extends the work of nature." The goal of poetry is not "to represent what is true, but to adorn it and present to the minds some loftier image."

Democratic poets, Tocqueville argues, "lose sight of gods and heroes," and "set themselves to describe streams and mountains," but this descriptive poetry is only a transitional phase. In the end, democratic poetry will be about man, because "democratic nations may amuse themselves for a while with considering the productions of nature, but they are excited in reality only by a survey of themselves." And such a survey will be oriented not to the past, or the present, but to the unfolding future.

These, then, are the new, democratic springs for poetry. Democratic poets will write about passions and ideas, not persons and achievements, because democratic life, by bringing diverse lives into close proximity, destroys the mystery. Everyday people and events become "too familiar for the poet to speak of them." The poet must seek below the surface, to the inner soul, and "nothing lends itself more to the delineation of the ideal than the scrutiny of the hidden depths in the immaterial nature of man."

In his own burst of poetry, Tocqueville describes the new wellspring from which he presumes democratic poems will develop:

> I need not traverse earth and sky to discover a wondrous object woven of contrasts, of infinite greatness and littleness, of intense gloom and amazing brightness, capable at once of exciting pity, admiration, terror, contempt. I have only to look at myself. Man springs out of nothing, crosses time, and disappears forever in the bosom of God; he is seen but for a moment, wandering on the verge of the two abysses, and there he is lost.

For Tocqueville, democratic poetry will not be "fed with legends or the memorials of old traditions" but by man himself, with "his passions, his doubts, his rare prosperities and inconceivable wretchedness." The new springs of poetry will replace the old. Equality does not destroy all subjects of poetry, Tocqueville concludes, but rather transforms them. Equality renders poetic subjects "less numerous, but more vast."

Tocqueville's Expressive Logic

The Tocquevillian perspective is one that deeply values, and seeks to protect, the freedoms that democracy can bring. Tocqueville's work is a chronicle of transformations, as he finds them in America, and as they can be imagined, and worked toward, in France.

Equality is inevitable; what is at stake for Tocqueville is liberty in its largest sense.

Liberty, from a Tocquevillian perspective, is always at risk—vulnerable to the cruelties of revolution, the chaos of anarchy, the confines of harsh and of gentle tyranny. Liberty can be lost because it is loved too little, ignored in favor of the daily pleasures of material acquisition.

Like all social theorists, Tocqueville sought ways to ensure the development of better worlds. For social critics, descriptions of current social conditions always serve as foundations for prescriptions for achieving better ones. But Tocqueville embeds his prescriptions in his analysis. Unlike Whitman and Mumford, and most contemporary social critics, Tocqueville does *not* exhort us to change. He makes no calls for personal or cultural transformations that must occur if democracy is to survive. His work is a form of convincing himself, and his readers, that in spite of many fears, American democracy offers many good things.

The main value of a Tocquevillian perspective is that it offers us an analysis of democratic life that relies on factors *other* than the arts for its worth and survival. This is in direct contrast to Whitman, who along with most twentieth-century critics, considers the arts to be crucial to social improvement, and Mumford, who believes that the arts must offset the dangers of rampant mechanization. Tocqueville does *not* claim, for art, the power to channel, or uplift, or unify, or subdue. He ascribes such powers to other forces—most notably commerce and religion.

There is much in Tocqueville that need not be deployed in an expressive perspective. Tocqueville's tripartite view of human nature as body-mind-spirit means he presumes that bodily passions can be tempered and channeled by the mind, through reason, and that the mind can be "lifted" or made more sublime, through spirit. For Tocqueville, rationality is a tempering force, a middle ground that can seek both immediate pleasures (under the influence of commerce) and exalted, universal ones (under the influence of religion). The exigencies of everyday activities keep men "bound" to immediate gratification of self-interest, but leisure time can free men to pursue "higher" pleasures of the intellect and imagination.

These are assumptions that reappear in the New Humanists of the early twentieth century, in conservatives of mid-century, and in neo-conservatives in the culture wars. This mind-body-spirit division is not a necessary component, however, in an expressive perspective—Dewey operates instead (and I believe much better) with beliefs about what he calls social intelligence. In fact, as I discuss in the final chapter, faith in the powers of social intelligence serves Dewey much as faith in religion and commerce serves Tocqueville. All social criticism needs "fudge factors"; the question is, which ones make the most sense?

Tocqueville answers those who attack democracy as barbarism with his view of the arts as *diverse forms of imaginative practice*. Yes, he says, the arts in America tend to be less embellished and refined, and more lively and crude. Yes, there is less exquisite art, but there is also lots of artistic activity, widely available to a variety of peoples. What is lost, he argues, is not nearly as important as what is being gained—new forms of artistic expression for new forms of social order.

Tocquevillian aesthetic theory defines the arts as symbolic expression dependent on the social order. This is the key claim of expressivist logic—the arts are elements of, rather than causal mechanisms in, society. Tocqueville does not ascribe transformative powers to something called "the arts," but he *does* ascribe such powers to commerce and religion. These factors, in combination, channel human passions, while purifying human motives. Commerce and religion are the intervening variables in Tocqueville's analysis, allowing him to believe in democracy, in spite of his view of human nature.

I have come to believe that democratically inclined social critics need intervening variables, so that they can muster enough faith in people to sustain faith in democracy. For many critics, that intervening variable has been, and continues to be, art. For Tocqueville, it is a combination of religion and commerce. Some force or thing allows the critic to keep faith with an idealized populace—"the people"—while having grave doubts about current people's habits and tastes. I hope to convince you that social critics imagine the arts as powerful so that they will have a way to guarantee that the people are worthy of the power that democracy bestows upon them.

In Tocqueville's analysis, people are self-interested, and so they are vulnerable to revolution, anarchy, tyranny. But self-interest, he then argues, also draws men into relationships with each other, in voluntary associations and business relationships, and draws them toward God, through desires for material success. Virtuous behavior, including regularity, temperance, moderation, are supported by both commerce and religion. These two forces offer ways to subdue and channel the isolating and destructive aspects of human nature; in combination they ensure that men act in worthy ways.

This is how Tocqueville guarantees his vision of a democratic middle ground, where more are included in a world that has less extraordinary virtue, but also less depravity. His view of democratic art is congruent with this—there is less exquisite beauty, but more useful and lively art available to the many. The arts are various, interesting expressions of more basic and fundamental characteristics of society.

They are not crucial to a good life, nor are they threatened by the domination of commercial habits and beliefs.

They are not powerful forces for good or ill, they cannot change people or societies. They are, instead, pleasurable activities dependent on time, energy, leisure, and temperament. This expressivist perspective may seem a prosaic view of the arts, but it has, I firmly believe, many advantages.

CHOOSING WHITMAN

Just as with *Democracy in America*, I came to my rereading of Walt Whitman's "Democratic Vistas" with faulty preconceptions. I assumed it was an overwrought call for more democratic art. My memory of Whitman's essay was as an incoherent prose poem that was mercilessly critical of "high" forms of literature, and energetically supportive of emerging American forms of writing. As with Tocqueville, Whitman is often quoted out of context, and I had come to imagine him, as do many others, as deeply populist.

He is not. He is instead deeply supportive of his own notions of what democracy is and should be, against an actuality that he finds repugnant. This faith in an imaginary people, in combination with a disdain for an actual populace, came as a complete surprise to me. But I now believe it is a defining characteristic, not just of Whitman, but of most redemptive perspectives on the arts. We imagine that the arts have the power to transform individuals (and thereby society) only if we want and need individuals to become something very different from what they already are. Whitman needed the American populace to be transformed before he could believe in them.

In "Democratic Vistas," Whitman called for a new class of poets who could bring into existence a new, democratic American literature, and thereby bring into existence new and better people, and a new and better society. Whitman believed that a new literature could allow America to fulfill its destiny. This is why Whitman offers us—in his poetry and in his cultural criticism—the consummate example of faith in the power of the arts to redeem democracy.

Where Tocqueville uses logic and analysis, Whitman uses metaphor and exhortation. Where Tocqueville sees potential good in apparent bad, Whitman sees only the contrast between what is and what should be. Whitman exhorts us, always, to create the possibilities he sees, inchoate. Tocqueville asks much less of us—in fact, he mostly reassures us that what we fear will not come to pass.

Tocqueville describes; Whitman criticizes, blusters, and thunders. Where Tocqueville imagines possible outcomes, Whitman prophesies doom or destiny. Where Tocqueville suggests development, Whitman demands action. Tocqueville is the outsider who describes and analyzes American experience to reveal underlying patterns, dangers, and possibilities of equality. Whitman is the insider, exhorting America to fulfill its promise, seeking to call into being his ideal democracy.

Whitman's Quest

Whitman's goal was to create himself as a new American poet who could write poetry that could transform the reader, and thereby transform American life. To accomplish this transformation he had to directly connect with the reader. Whitman's intense desire to merge with the reader precipitated his use of innovative literary techniques. His desire to connect—to draw the reader into a personal relationship—led him to a direct, emotional, visual, lyric style. This is what made his poems so startling, and keeps them seeming modern and fresh.

Whitman sought an adhesive connection between himself and the reader, and this justified and validated his belief in the power of the arts to transform. In Erkilla's insightful terms, Whitman had "designs" on the reader: "He wants them to be not spectators but actors in the work of democracy. His design is not merely to 'record' but—with the cooperation of the reader—to 'make' democratic history."[2] To transform readers from spectators to actors requires a kindling, an energizing, an enlivening force—himself incarnated in literature.

By incarnating himself in his poems, Whitman must become what he wants his poems to be. Whitman must embody the qualities he believes poetry must have, to work the changes he hopes to accomplish. He demands of himself a naturalness, a robustness, a perfect healthiness—a mode of being required for the race of people that will create and sustain his ideal democracy.

"Democratic Vistas"

"Democratic Vistas" is a remarkable assemblage—contradictory, sweeping, and grandiose in its social and political analysis; cosmic, passionate, and shading into incoherence in its vision of an ideal future. It is Whitman at his most Whitmanesque.

Literary critics read "Democratic Vistas" mostly for its call for a new native form of literature, but expend their critical energies on the poems. Social critics read it, occasionally, for its indictment of (nineteenth-century) contemporary life; as with Tocqueville, brief excerpts appear in anthologies of social and cultural history. Political critics see the essay, understandably, as exhortation masquerading as political analysis, and have mostly ignored it.

We can read the essay in all three of these ways—it is indeed a call for a native American literature, as well as a fervent critique of nineteenth-century life, and an exhortation addressing democracy, suffrage, and party politics. But "Democratic Vistas" is best read, I believe, as Whitman asks us to read it: "a collection of memoranda, perhaps for future designers, comprehenders" about "New World politics and progress."

Whitman writes, he says, "to admit and face the dangers" of universal suffrage. He writes this essay for an audience "within whose thought rages the battle, advancing, retreating, between democracy's convictions, aspirations, and the people's crudeness, vice, caprices."[3] This "battle" between faith in democracy and fears of the people's "crudeness" is at the heart of *all* American social criticism. American intellectuals, if they value democratic life, write from Whitman's embattled juncture between the possibilities of democracy and the inadequacies of the people. What is refreshing about Whitman's essay is that he explicitly faces the struggle, and presumes that the reader shares it.

"Democratic Vistas" has been seen as a "dark night of the soul," for Whitman,[4] an expression of his own doubts, in the Civil War era, about the future of America. But it is also a response to all those who are skeptical of democracy's promise. "Democratic Vistas" is framed as a series of thoughts and claims, a beginning and an imagining, a collection of related convictions, hopes, and fears, oriented to the future of America.

Whitman begins by saying that the terms *America* and *democracy* are "convertible," and each must triumph to guarantee the other. The stakes are high: "the United States are destined either to surmount the gorgeous history of feudalism, or else prove the most tremendous failure of all time" (363). He writes to preclude such failure, to describe what can and should be, to suggest what is needed to counteract current tendencies.

Whitman constructed "Democratic Vistas" by combining two previously published works—"Democracy" and "Personalism"—with notes for an unpublished third essay to be titled "Orbic Literature." The seams are still evident, and the lack of headings or sections makes the whole seem even more disheveled. For our analysis, I address in serial order Whitman's claims about democracy, personalism, and literature. I pay special attention to three recurring threads in his overall argument: the power of literature, the nature of the masses, and the failed promise of American life.

During the period in which "Democratic Vistas" was written, Whitman returned to revisions of *Leaves of Grass*, after discarding the notion of becoming a "wanderer-teacher." His hopes of being "affectionately absorbed" by the nation have dimmed. His beliefs about America's promise and destiny have been challenged. His poetry was becoming both more intensely personal (the Calamus series) and more grandiose and public. He has been deeply affected by the Civil War, and by his months ministering to wounded soldiers in Washington.

The essays struggle with a central contradiction between promise and actuality. Whitman writes, elliptically and luxuriously, about the gap between what democracy can be and what it actually is; between what the people can be and what they actually are; and between what the American arts can be and what they actually are.

Whitman offers various formulae to collapse the gap, to usher in the future vistas he imagines. These formulae vary across the three sections, but combine and narrow near the end of the essay into a paragraph that summarizes where he finally ends up—calling for "a class or institution—a new and greater literatus order" that can offer a "subtle and tremendous force-infusion" to confront the "artificial and materialistic bases of modern civilization" (424).

Democracy

Whitman begins with the claim that variety and freedom are the greatest lessons in New World politics and progress. By variety he means, he says, a large variety of character; by freedom, he means offering full play to human nature to "expand itself in numberless and even conflicting directions." Whitman opens by locating what he (later in the essay) calls "personalism" as the defining possibility of democracy.

Democracy is not, for Whitman, simply enfranchisement, or a more Tocquevillian focus on equality, or freedom from tyranny. It is primarily the opportunity to develop a self, and a society of selves, unlike any that have gone before. America "cheerfully" accepts the past, including feudalism, but "counts . . . for her justification and success . . . almost entirely on the future." It is for the results to come that the New World is important, the putting into practice of "moral political speculations of the ages, long, long deferr'd, the democratic republican principle, and the theory of development and perfection by voluntary standards, and self-reliance" (362).

He then defines his subject—a call for "vigorous, yet unsuspected Literatures, perfect personalities and sociologies, original, transcendental and expressing (what, in a highest sense, are not yet express'd at all,) democracy and the modern" (364). He defines his audience as people who, like him, sense the battle between democracy's possibilities and the people's characteristics. Whitman always writes from the disjuncture between democracy's ideals and actualities. Tocqueville, as we saw, writes instead to allay fears by locating aspects of democracy's ideals *in* its actualities.

Whitman argues that democracy will prove itself when it "founds and luxuriantly grows its own forms of art, poets, school, theology," displacing the feudalism that still lurks in the "very subsoil" of American education, social standards, and literature. A new class of native authors will "permeat[e] the whole mass of American mentality, taste, belief, breathing into it a new breath of life, giving it decision, affecting politics far more than the popular superficial suffrage . . . radiating, begetting appropriate teachers, schools, manners, and, as its grandest result, accomplishing . . . a religious and moral character beneath the political and productive and intellectual bases of the States" (365).

Literature has, according to Whitman, significant, even therapeutic power. The problem of the civilized world, Whitman claims, is "social and religious, and is to be finally met and treated with literature" (365). Few realize, Whitman claims, the ways that "great literature penetrates all, gives hue to all, shapes aggregates and individuals, and after subtle ways, with irresistible power, constructs, sustains, demolishes at will" (366).

Whitman concludes, "A single new thought, imagination, abstract principle, even literary style, fit for the time, put in shape by some great literatus, and projected among mankind, may duly cause changes, growths, removals greater than the longest and bloodiest war, or the most stupendous merely political, dynastic, or commercial overturn" (366). This is as clear (and grandiose) a claim for the power of literature as we are likely to find. Whitman's belief in literature's ability to penetrate, shape, cause, vivify allows him to posit a new, as yet unimagined form of it as a way to ensure that democracy will fulfill its potential.

The key to understanding the rest of Whitman's essay is to remember his logic: by endowing an as yet nonexistent cultural form (orbic literature) with the power to transform people and society, *Whitman can rely on it to bring into existence his ideal democracy.* The essay is simultaneously an account of the power of literature, an argument for the necessity of its (and America's) transformation, and an attempt to demonstrate that power and accomplish that transformation.

Diseased Actuality

In a section that in an early draft was titled "The Gravest Question of All," Whitman begins his impassioned critique of contemporary society. Whitman has become popularly known as a champion of the common man, the Poet of Democracy, but this essay shows that he is repulsed by what he finds when he looks around him. To Whitman, the actualities of American society are never what they can or should be, and neither are the American people.

Whitman is not alone in this tendency to idealize The People in the abstract and deplore them in the concrete. As we shall see, American social critics are extraordinarily uncomfortable with the habits and values of everyday people; they seek to change society partly to change most of the people in it. It is usually the middle classes who are most deplored, the people who have succumbed to whatever is presumed to be the toxin of contemporary life. Both the redemptive and the counterbalancing perspectives call for an instrumental use of the arts to make these necessary improvements.

In this way, social critics avoid seeming snobbish or cruel—they aren't elitists, they are simply writing, in the name of the people, to change the social conditions that are turning them into such inadequate specimens. Ironically, Whitman, the Poet of Democracy, offers us a particularly clear example of how this logic works.

Whitman describes his contemporary society as "canker'd, crude, superstitious, and rotten," in spite of its unprecedented material advancement (369). He suggests we "look at our times and our lands . . .

like a physician diagnosing some deep disease"; the disease he finds
is "a hollowness of heart. . . . Genuine belief seems to have left us. The
underlying principles of the States are not honestly believ'd in, (for all
this hectic glow, and these melodramatic screamings,) nor is humanity
itself believ'd in. What penetrating eye does not everywhere see
through the mask? The spectacle is appalling. We live in an atmosphere of hypocrisy throughout" (369–70).

Whitman (as he so often does) offers a long list—this time of what
is so wrong with mid-nineteenth-century "modern" life. His list
should sound familiar—it resonates well with more recent accounts,
from the right and from the left, about what's wrong with modern life:
men do not believe in women nor women in men; a scornful supercil-
iousness rules in literature; churches usurp the name of religion; conversation is mere badinage; the business class is depraved; the official
branches of government are saturated in corruption, bribery, and
falsehood.

Whitman continues:

> The great cities reek with respectable as much as nonrespectable robbery
> and scoundrelism. In fashionable life, flippancy, tepid amours, weak infi-
> delism, small aims, or no aims at all, only to kill time. In business, (this all-
> devouring modern word, business,) the one sole object is, by any means, pe-
> cuniary gain. . . . The best class we show, is but a mob of fashionably dress'd
> speculators and vulgarians. (370)

Whitman catches his breath to say that yes, behind this "fantastic
farce" there are "solid things and stupendous labors to be discover'd"
but they exist crudely, in the background. He summarizes: "I say that
our New World democracy, however great a success in uplifting the
masses out of their sloughs, in materialistic development, products,
and in a certain highly deceptive superficial popular intellectuality, is,
so far, an almost complete failure in its social aspects, and in really
grand religious, moral, literary and esthetic results" (370).

Here is a critique that will become increasingly prevalent—hollow,
superficial, hypocritical modern American society, having lost track of,
or access to earlier beliefs. Notice how very different it is from Tocqueville's sense that material development and commercial relations *themselves* offer salutary results, and even some interesting aesthetic forms.
Not for Whitman. His is a much more Manichaean rhetoric, with the
good being smothered under the evil. The business class is greedy and
corrupt. The fashionable are supercilious and flip. There may be some

"solid" things, but they are crude, inchoate, hidden behind the facade of modern life.

Whitman's critique does not yet depend on a full opposition between moral and material development. A full counterbalance model (evident in Mumford, and in the mass culture debate of the 1950s) assumes that material development *automatically* taints or corrupts religious, moral, literary, and aesthetic development. Whitman's analysis presumes mostly that material prosperity has not been matched, or paralleled, or succeeded by (he varies his claim) the necessary moral development. At the end of his essay he resorts to a simpler and more powerful metaphor of counterinfusion. This foreshadows later critics, like Mumford, who make the material and the moral into opposing tendencies—material development causes moral corruption, moral development prevents material corruption.

Whitman later makes a case for social development that presumes a series of necessary stages, where the political and material developments are "matched" or "crowned" by spiritual ones. Here he corporealizes material and moral, making material development the social body, and moral development the social soul. Whitman diagnoses a "disease," a loss of connection to founding principles. He sees around him the development of a prosperous, expanding but hollow empire—as if, he says, "we were somehow being endow'd with a vast and more and more thoroughly appointed body, and then left with little or no soul" (370).

But that "thoroughly appointed body" truly fascinates Whitman. Every extended critique of the ills of American life is followed by either an idealized portrait of an alternative or, in this case, a paean to the beauty of material progress, as actualized in urban life. Whitman diagnoses the disease of hollowness, then launches into a description of the

> splendor, picturesqueness, and oceanic amplitude and rush of these great cities, the unsurpass'd situation, rivers and bay, sparkling sea-tides, costly and lofty new buildings, facades of marble and iron, of original grandeur and elegance of design, with the masses of gay color, the preponderance of white and blue, the flags flying, the endless ships, the tumultuous streets, Broadway, the heavy musical roar. (371)

All this, he says, gives his aesthetic conscience "a continued exaltation and absolute fulfillment."

But then he reins himself in, saying we must sternly discard, and shut our eyes to "the glow and grandeur of the general superficial effect."

Why? This paragraph reads like his poems, and were we to know only Whitman's poetry, we might imagine him as arguing *for* the aesthetic power of the industrial and mechanical, *for* the dissolution of boundaries between the material and the spiritual, the artistic and the commercial.

But Whitman urges us to "shut our eyes" to this "superficial" (yet exalting and fulfilling) aesthetic effect. Why? Because for Whitman there is only "one real question: Are there, in these cities, worthy people? Are there men, athletes, perfect women? Are there crops of fine youths and majestic old people? Are there arts worthy of freedom and a rich people?" In short, "Is there a great moral and religious civilization—the only justification of a great material one?" (371)

Here, the problem of The People, which bedevils Whitman (and American social criticism), takes over the argument. The answer to this "gravest question of all—do we have a moral and religious civilization?"—is, of course, no.

The Problem of The People

The beautiful material city he loves is full of people he characterizes as "petty grotesques, malformations, phantoms, playing meaningless antics," men who are "puny, impudent, foppish," women who are "painted, padded, dyed, chignon'd, with muddy complexions and bad blood" (372). *Whitman, the poet who celebrates the people, has first to call into existence people worth celebrating.*

A new form of Divine Literature is Whitman's way to create The People from these "petty grotesques." A new literature can transform these people, because it can breathe into "all this" a breath "recuperative of sane and heroic life" (372). Whitman describes his tonic literature: it doesn't copy or reflect surfaces, or pander to taste, or amuse, or pass away time, or celebrate the beautiful, the refined, the past. It is, therefore, neither the commercial nor imported culture of his time. Instead, it is a literature that underlies life, is religious, consistent with science, teaches men, and, "perhaps most precious of its results" redeems women from "webs of silliness, millinery, and every kind of dyspeptic depletion" (372).

Whitman describes, in the first sections of "Democratic Vistas," what has gone wrong with American life, and how to put it right. There is a lack of moral and artistic identity, which, if present, would give unity ("compaction") to the States. There is a loss of belief in founding principles. There is institutional corruption. There are superficial chat and muddied complexions. And even though material prosperity, as actualized in the city, gives Whitman extraordinary pleasure, he exhorts himself, and us, to shut our eyes to its "superficial" effect, and look hard at the people who live there—malformed phantoms.

The new literature he proposes can create and sustain national unity; can restore faith in founding principles, can (apparently) address the corruption in government and business, and can make people and cities sane and heroic. It can even redeem women from silliness, millinery, and dyspepsia. Strong stuff, indeed!

"Democratic Vistas" is shadowed by Thomas Carlyle's "Shooting Niagara: and After," a wry, devastating commentary on the consequences of enfranchisement in England.[5] Carlyle's article was published in the *New York Tribune,* and Whitman says he wrote the essay "Democracy" as a "counterblast or rejoinder."[6] But it was, I believe, only a partial "counterblast." Whitman addresses the question of the people's worthiness and their value, once properly trained, but avoids the center of Carlyle's attack—the poignant faith of social reformers in millennial transformation.

Carlyle wrote in response to the Reform Measure of 1867, where Disraeli proposed to extend voting privileges to the working class. Such an extension, Carlyle writes, will call in "new supplies of blockheadism, gullibility, bribability, amenability to beer and balderdash." Unconditional liberty, he points out, can be disastrous—it is fine to allow a good man to be free, permitted to unfold himself in works of nobleness, but what about a bad man—is he to be free to unfold himself in his particular way? Those who call for universal suffrage are buzzing and swarming in an absurd manner, expecting a millennium when "there is nothing but vulgarity in our People's expectations, resolutions or desires, in this Epoch."

Whitman says he was originally roused "to much anger and abuse" by the essay, but had come to read it with respect, as coming from an earnest soul, and contributing certain "sharp-cutting metallic grains." Those grains are, I believe, the problem of the people's worthiness, and the possibility of millennial transformation.

Carlyle's essay is a sardonic description of the foolishness of believing in dramatic social change. Obviously Whitman's whole project depends on his being able to maintain his own faith in personal and social transformation. His essays and poems, even his own biography, are about the possibility of, and necessity for, dramatic change. "Democratic Vistas" is written in the belief that America *must* change. While Whitman offers literature (not suffrage) as the vehicle of millennium, the fact remains that Whitman's faith is what Carlyle ridicules. Whitman must continue to believe in the possibility that Carlyle disdains. That "sharp-cutting metallic grain" of faith, central to Carlyle's attack, cannot be questioned by Whitman. To suggest that dramatic change cannot and will not occur would undermine Whitman's life's work.

The second "grain" in Carlyle's essay, the worthiness of the people, haunts Whitman. *Are* the people worthy? Can (should) they be presumed to be "properly trained" by freedom? Carlyle says, in his cynical way, no. Whitman disparages the kinds of people he already finds in the cities, but *still* cannot bring himself to critique The People he seeks in America. Instead, as we have seen, he posits a Literature that can redeem them.

Whitman addresses the paradox between everyday people and The People elliptically. He compares how the artist-mind appreciates in the populace what is not evident to the merely educated, or the cultured. "Man, viewed in the lump, displeases, and is a constant puzzle and affront to the merely educated classes. The rare, cosmical, artist-mind, lit with the Infinite, alone confronts his manifold and oceanic qualities— but taste, intelligence, and culture, (so-called,) have been against the masses, and remain so" (376).

He goes on to say that literature never recognizes The People, that there is some natural repugnance between a literary and professional life, and "the rude rank spirit of the democracies." He continues:

> I know nothing more rare, even in this country, than a fit scientific estimate and reverent appreciation of the People—of their measureless wealth of latent power and capacity, their vast, artistic contrasts of lights and shade— with, in America, their entire reliability in emergencies, and a certain breadth of historic grandeur, of peace or war, far surpassing all the vaunted samples of book-heroes, or any *haut ton* coteries, in all the records of the world. (376–77)

Whitman contrasts himself, his "rare, cosmical, artist-mind," with those (like his shadow antagonist Carlyle) who are affronted by the masses. He, unlike the others, confronts man's oceanic qualities, latent power and capacities, vast artistic contrasts, reliability, and historic grandeur. But notice—these are characteristics of The People, but not, yet, qualities found in actual people (puny, shallow, malformed, and painted), members of a society he just finished describing as canker'd, supercilious, diseased, and hollow.

Whitman did find some actual people who are, to him, evidence of The People's worthiness. During the Civil War, wounded soldiers supplied, for Whitman, "the last-needed proof of democracy, in its personalities":

> Grand common stock! to me the accomplish'd and convincing growth, prophetic of the future; proof undeniable to sharpest sense, of perfect beauty, tenderness, and pluck, that never feudal lord, nor Greek, nor Roman breed, yet rival'd. Let no tongue ever speak in disparagement of the American races, north or south, to one who has been through the war in the great army hospitals. (379)

This is the evidence Whitman needs to counter Carlyle's "sneering question" about popular sovereignty. Yes, Whitman continues, there are "crude, defective streaks in all the strata of the common people," indeed we can find specimens and collections that are ignorant, credulous, unfit and uncouth, incapable, very low, and poor. But:

> We believe the ulterior object of political and all other government . . . is . . . not merely to rule, to repress disorder, etc., but to develop, to open up to cultivation, to encourage the possibilities of all beneficent and manly outcroppage, and of that aspiration for independence, and the pride and self-respect latent in all characters. (Or, if there be exceptions, we cannot, fixing our eyes on them alone, make theirs the rule for all.) (379)

The resolution to Whitman's paradox of unworthy people and a worthy People is to focus on the majority, not the minority, and to trust in "latent powers and capacities," evidenced in the character of Civil War soldiers. These latent capacities, hidden in the painted, foppish, and supercilious, as well as in the crude and defective, can be recognized by the true artist-mind, and brought out, under the right conditions.

Democracy and Commerce

Commerce figures, in Tocqueville's analysis, as a salutary democratic influence—its workings enact and cultivate many of the best characteristics of the citizenry. In Whitman, social stability is guaranteed by "the vast, intertwining reticulation of wealth" (383). Commerce appears as a topic after adhesiveness, religion, love, and full personal development have previously been offered as guarantors of democratic felicity.

Whitman's original essay, published in *Galaxy*, included a direct refutation of Carlyle: "No community furnished throughout with homes and substantial, however moderate, incomes, commits suicide, or 'shoots Niagara.'"[7] Whitman left out this reference in "Democratic Vistas," but then goes on to suggest that "a great and varied nationality, occupying millions of square miles, were firmest held and knit by the principle of the safety and the endurance of the aggregate of its middling property owners" (383).

The role commerce plays in Whitman's analysis varies. Unlike many contemporary social commentators, Whitman does not simply oppose material interests with moral, aesthetic, or spiritual interests. Instead, he says in a footnote, "My theory includes riches, and the getting of riches, and the amplest products, power, activity, inventions, movements, &c. Upon them, as upon substrata, I raise the edifice design'd in these Vistas" (385).

Yet Whitman ended the essay with a different substratum, Literature, that all the other parts were "founded on." Although Whitman recognized and embraced his own contradictions, passages like this one, where he directly opposes earlier statements, are places we should linger—how can both "riches" and "literature" be a necessary substrate for democracy?

The answer has, once again, to do with the shaping of the people into an appropriate People. Whitman argues that "democracy looks with suspicious, ill-satisfied eyes upon the very poor, the ignorant, and on those out of business. She asks for men and women with occupations, well-off, owners of houses and acres, and with cash in the bank—and with some cravings for literature, too; and must have them, and hastens to make them" (384).

In a footnote, he adds, "I perceive clearly the extreme business energy, and this almost maniacal appetite for wealth present in the United States, are parts of amelioration and progress, indispensably needed to prepare the very results I demand" (384–85).

In short, democracy of the kind Whitman imagines requires as a beginning shared participation in the getting of houses, acres, property; commercial engagement is a prerequisite for democratic engagement. Through interests in "farms, stores, offices, dry-good, coal and groceries, enginery, cash accounts, trades, earning, markets, &c" (384), the people become and remain unified, active, available to new literatures, and ready for the kind of spiritual, moral, and aesthetic democracy Whitman believes and hopes will follow.

Already involved, then, with commercial democracy, The People find, in political democracy, "a training-school for making first-class men." "Freedom's athletes" are training in "life's gymnasium." The body/body politic metaphor continues—"I know of nothing grander, better exercise, better digestion, more positive proof of the past, the triumphant result of faith in humankind, than a well-contested American national election" (385).

Whitman offers a variety of ways that dyspeptic, hollow-hearted people can become a robust People, fit for democracy. Unity, national and international, achieved through adhesiveness, or religion; or participation in commerce; or participation in party politics—at this juncture in the essay, literature is barely mentioned while other potentially ameliorative forces are lavishly described.

Whitman then returns to his earlier argument—that of a hidden worthiness, latent, beneath the surface. To make the argument this time, he develops a contrast between the real and the artificial.

Whitman says: "Shams, &c. will always be the show, like ocean's scum; enough, if waters deep and clear make up the rest. Enough, that while the piled embroider'd shoddy gaud and fraud spreads to the superficial eye, the hidden warp and weft are genuine, and will last forever" (387).

Evidence of this genuine "hidden warp and weft" is in crowds in major cities, when Whitman mixes with "these interminable swarms of alert, turbulent, good natured, independent citizens, mechanics, clerks, young persons." And then Whitman reinvokes literature, in connection with his own "singular awe" in the presence of "this mass of men, so fresh and free, so loving and so proud" (388).

"Few or none have yet really spoken to this people, created a single image-making work for them, or absorb'd the central spirit and the idiosyncrasies which are theirs." Whitman claims that "I have not seen a single writer, artist, lecturer, or what not, that has confronted the voiceless but ever erect and active, pervading, underlying will and typic aspiration of the land, in a spirit kindred to itself" (388). In this portion of Whitman's argument, The People are already worthy, loving, proud, fresh, and free, and are being deprived of a literature that celebrates their manifest characteristics.

Instead, the public mind is filled with foreign works, "poisonous to
the idea of the pride and dignity of the common people, the life-blood
of democracy. The models of our literature, as we get it from other
lands, ultramarine, have had their birth in courts, and bask'd and
grown in castle sunshine; all smells of princes' favors." Works mod-
eled on foreign lines will "wither to ashes" if "touch'd by the national
test, or tried by the standards of democratic personality" (388).

Whitman concludes by admitting the fruition of his vision "resides
altogether in the future." It is there we will find the "source and test of
all the moral, esthetic, social, political and religious expressions and
institutes of the civilized world." The future will show us, "with unparallel'd success, a new earth and a new man" (390).

The seams between the original essays show. Whitman, for his longer
combined essay, must move from this triumphant vision of a new future, to a consideration of the characteristics of the people in his future
democracy. He must connect the more abstract and political arguments
of "Democracy" with the more social and psychological arguments of
"Personalism."

He does this by noting that he is presuming to "travel by maps yet
unmade, and a blank" and claiming that what he calls (tellingly) his
speech, is "without polish'd coherence, and a failure by the standard
called criticism." Nonetheless, it is "hot from surrounding war and
revolution" and thus "real at least as the lightnings" (391). He assures
us that his is a prophetic vision, and writes of "the joy of being toss'd
in the brave turmoil of the times." He makes himself a multiple "we"
who lives with the "proud consciousness that amid whatever clouds,
seductions, or heart-wearying postponements, we have never deserted, never despair'd, never abandon'd the faith" (391).

Personalism

And yet, the faith in democracy's future that Whitman proclaims he
never deserted, despair'd of or abandons is a faith that requires much
bolstering. "Personalism" is a more direct attempt to address the problem of democracy's reliance on an unreliable people. It is an essay on
how democratization is not simply leveling, the reduction of all to
some level of shared mediocrity. Rather, "the unyielding principle of
the average" is shadowed, joined, confronted, modified by another
principle—what Whitman calls personalism—the "pride and cen-
tripetal isolation of a human being in himself" (391).

The quality of personalism is "shooting Aurora-like" about the world, and forms, Whitman argues, "the compensating balance-wheel of the successful working machinery of aggregate America" (392). In fact, personalism offers Whitman yet another substrate, this time for civilization:

> What does civilization itself rest upon—and what object has it, with its religions, arts, schools, &c. but rich, luxuriant, varied personalism? . . . The literature, songs, esthetics, &c. of a country are of importance principally because they furnish the materials and suggestions of personality for the women and men of that country, and enforce them in a thousand effective ways. (392)

Here literature becomes a vehicle (furnishing materials and suggestions) for the varied personalism which is the object and substrate of civilization. In a footnote, Whitman argues that great poets and "literasuses" have been "creators, fashioning, making types of men and women," and gives examples in ancient world literatures of heroic "models, combined, adjusted to other standards than America's, but of priceless value to her and hers" (392).

Whitman is now making his argument for literature's ability to bring into existence a certain kind of person, in this case a more "perfect" version of the person that he has claimed could come into existence through participation in commerce, or politics, or religion. In this section he seeks to more fully characterize "the democratic personality," but with only intermittent reference to the role literature can play in the creation of "a copious race of superb American men and women, cheerful, religious, ahead of any yet known" (395).

Whitman is concerned with his perceived dichotomy between natural and artificial personalities, in relation to natural rather than artificial literatures. Earlier he had talked of the honest "warp and weft" hidden under the "gaud and fraud" of society. This is a metaphor of the genuine and reliable being underneath, latent, the true inside the false.

This section changes, and modernizes, the metaphor—the true personality is that which has been allowed to fully develop by its own lights; the false is that which constricts and confines such development. A genuine or true personality is both "natural" and "democratic." A fake or false personality is artificially created, unnatural, and (therefore) undemocratic. The inner/outer metaphor is here combined with a new freeflowing/confined metaphor. Authenticity resides, latent and inchoate, in each person. It can be allowed to fully flourish and develop, or it can become deformed or deflected by inappropriate cultivation.

This individual deformation—gentility—breeds social corrosion. "In our times," Whitman writes, "refinement and delicatesse are not only attended to sufficiently, but threaten to eat us up, like a cancer. Already, the democratic genius watches, ill-pleased, these tendencies. Provision for a little healthy rudeness, savage virtue, justification of what one has in one's self, whatever it is, is demanded" (394).

Whitman can now combine his characterization of a hollow, superficial society with his developing claims about the role of genteel, Old World–inspired literature in sustaining such a society. He argues that "to prune, gather, trim, conform, and ever cram and stuff, and be genteel and proper, is the pressure of our days"(394). The issue that the United States has to face is not how to educate or uplift a barbarous nation, but what is most applicable and pertinent to "conventional, overcorpulent societies, already becoming stifled and rotten with flatulent, infidelistic literature, and polite conformity and art" (395).

So Whitman argues for a new kind of democratic literature that is *neither* the genteel literature of the upper classes, *nor* the increasingly popular commercial literature of the middle classes. This new democratic literature calls on the "high average" of all men, and is accessible to all the masses. Genteel and commercial forms of culture are detrimental to the development of a true "democratic personality"; only a New World literature can foster personalism.

Whitman begins this portion of his argument with the often-quoted statement, "America has yet morally and artistically originated nothing" (395). Instead, she has adopted "models of persons, books, manners &c., appropriate for former conditions and for Europeans lands," appropriate only for "exotics and exiles." Such models are "thoroughly upholster'd exterior appearance and show . . . built entirely on the idea of caste, and on the sufficiency of mere outside acquisitions," elevating "glibness [and] verbal intellect. Such upholstered glibness goes under the name Culture" (395).

When the word *Culture* is invoked, Whitman says, "we find ourselves in close quarters with the enemy."

As now taught, accepted and carried out, are not the processes of culture rapidly creating a class of supercilious infidels, who believe in nothing? Shall a man lose himself in countless masses of adjustments, and be so shaped with reference to this, that, and the other, that the simply good and healthy and brave parts of him are reduced and clipp'd away, like the bordering of box in a garden? (395)

Whitman imagines "cultivation" by high culture as stifling. He wants, instead, a culture that will

> always be that of the manly and courageous instincts, and loving percep-
> tions, and of self-respect—aiming to form, over this continent, an idiocracy
> of universalism, which, true child of America, will bring joy to its mother, re-
> turning to her in her own spirit, recruiting myriads of offspring, able, natu-
> ral, perceptive, tolerant, devout believers in her, America, and with some
> definite instinct why and for what she has arisen, most vast, most formida-
> ble of historic births, and is, now and here, with wonderful step, journeying
> through Time. (396)

In short, Whitman is calling for a form of literature that can make people manly, courageous, loving, self-respecting, adhesive, able, natural,
perceptive, tolerant, devoutly patriotic, and committed to America's
destiny. Whitman blames genteel culture for the existence of "supercilious infidels." As with later critics, the "wrong" kind of culture is responsible for making repugnant people.

Whitman's essay on "Personalism" is a way to detail his vision of an
ideal democratic citizen, and democratic literature is offhandedly
brought in as the route to achieve such a "native personality." The energy of this portion of the essay is spent in detailed description of
what the ideal, should be, for individual people, rather than on what
has prevented the ideal, or on how to achieve it.

What Whitman argues, in passing, is that native personalities are
not yet in full flower because of the presence of upholster'd Old World
literature, which offers perfumed, false models. The route to a full-
flourishing self is through New World literature, native, robust. What
this New World literature is, actually, is the focus of the final section of
the essay. The ideas in it originated in the proposed but never published essay on "Orbic Literature." The section functions in the overall essay of "Democratic Vistas" as a grounding of Whitman's vision
of democracy and personality in the potential of ideal literature to
work the necessary transformations.

Orbic Literature

In "Democratic Vistas" Whitman moves from a discussion of democracy's possibilities to a discussion of the people's possibilities to, finally,

a discussion of literature's possibilities. In each section, the key tension is between what is, and what could and should be. The essay combines and recombines its key elements: the potential of all three—democracy, the people, literature—to create each other in ideal form.

Democracy can and should result in an ideal people and literature. The people deserve and should create an ideal democracy and literature. Literature should cultivate democracy and an ideal people. When attempting to locate a final cause or source for social development, Whitman offers various substrates: democracy, commerce, literature, or religion.

But literature remains, for Whitman, the most frequently invoked shaping force of character and social life—it is the cause/cure he returns to in most detail. In this final section of the essay, he describes what he imagines as an ideal democratic literature, and contrasts it not only with genteel literature, but with the new popular, commercial literature of the 19th century.

Whitman begins by suggesting that New World literature should be "fit to rise upon, cohere, and signalize in time, these States" (405). Thus it is not, in this portion of the essay, a substrate, cause, or cure. It is instead a development, a cohesive force, and a historic emblem. "Politics, materials, heroic personalities, military eclat" will remain crude until "vitalized by national, original archetypes in literature" (405).

These are tamer claims than previous ones, with literature serving an energizing and refining, rather than a causal, function. But Whitman quickly returns to a more dramatic call: for Old World literature to breed a spirit that will ultimately destroy the aristocratic tradition itself. The genuises of the ages have offered us "beacons that burn through all the nights," but they were designed for America's foes "the feudal and the old" while "our genius is democratic and modern" (406).

"Yet could ye, indeed, but breathe your breath of life into our New World's nostrils—not to enslave us, as now, but, for our needs, to breed a spirit like your own—perhaps (dare we say it?) to dominate, even destroy, what you yourselves have left!" (407). He concludes with his famous call: "I demand races of orbic bards, with unconditional uncompromising sway. Come forth, sweet democratic despots of the west!" (407). The rest of the essay is a discussion of how the commercial, popular literature and drama of the time is absolutely *not* the genuine democratic art Whitman calls for.

The heading Whitman proposed for his first section was "Is Literature Really Advancing?" Does democracy bring cultural advance? Whitman surveys "our current so-called literature" which he compares to "an endless supply of small coin." He find that it "performs a certain service"—that of preparation, as children learn to spell. He admits to being impressed with the "mountain stacks of white paper piled in the press-vaults, and the proud, crashing, ten-cylinder presses." But, in all this productivity, he does not find "a single first-class work" (407).

In earlier sections Whitman has defined the effects he ascribes to "genuine" literature—creation of perfect people, unity, patriotism. What he finds in the copious literary productions of the time is writing designed to "amuse, to titillate, to pass away time, to circulate the news, and rumors of news, to rhyme and read rhyme." Such stuff is successful, Whitman notes, because it "strikes the mean flat average, the sensational appetite for stimulus, incident, persiflage, &c., and depicts, to the common calibre, sensual, exterior life." The audiences for such works are "limitless and profitable; but they cease presently" (408).

This popular literature ("prolific brood of the contemporary novel, magazine-tale, theatre play &c.") is still influenced by "over there in Europe" and is "just as sensational, just as strain'd." Thus there has been no real advance, Whitman concludes. Instead, we are beset by "a parcel of . . . dapper little gentlemen from abroad, who flood us with their thin sentiment of parlors, parasols, piano-songs, tinkling rhymes, the five-hundredth importation—or whimpering and crying about something, chasing one aborted conceit after another, and forever occupied in dyspeptic amours with dyspeptic women" (408).

Whitman combines a critique of popular literature with his critique of imported and genteel literature—his desired "genuine literature" has nothing in common with them. Its subject matter is the revolutionary changes of the time, its object the transformation of its readers and the nation. Whitman claims that "the grandest events and revolutions, and stormiest passions of history, are crossing to-day with unparallel'd rapidity and magnificence over the stages of our own and all the continents, offering new materials, opening new vistas, with largest needs, inviting the daring launching forth of conceptions in literature. . ." (408).

These events, revolutions and passions can be inspired by these new conceptions in literature, "soaring in highest regions, serving art in its highest, (which is only the other name for serving God, and serving humanity)" (408). For Whitman, here, history calls for a new kind of literature, and literature makes a new kind of exalted, spiritual history.

In the historical trajectory that Whitman describes, America is entering a new phase, one that builds on and makes "illustrious" political and material progress. It is a phase defined by a "native expression-spirit," which will be evidenced in literature, and in a new kind of religious democracy that can reconstruct society.

True revolutions, Whitman continues, are of the interior life, and the arts. Enfranchisement, elective government, orderly and prosperous citizens are "mediums of deeper, higher progress," spiritual progress. The "spirit" must be changed, otherwise change of appearance is to no avail. This "spirit" is metaphorically compared to "the inherent soul, nativity, idiocrasy, free, highest-poised, soaring its own flight, following out itself," Whitman returns to a notion of genuine spirit as unfettered and free-flowing. The spirit of America is not free, he implies, as long as it is fettered to "the distant, the partial, and the dead," the Old World (411).

He finds "swarms of poems,[8] literary magazines, dramatic plays" to be "useless, a mockery" because they "strengthen and nourish no one, express nothing characteristic, give decision and purpose to no one, and suffice only the lowest level of vacant minds" (412). Dramatic presentations deserves to be treated on par with "ornamental confectionery at public dinners." Poetry is but "copious dribble" (412).

America demands, instead, "a poetry that is bold, modern, and all-surrounding and kosmical, as she is herself." It must "bend its vision toward the future," and "extricate itself from even the greatest models of the past, and, while courteous to them, must have entire faith in itself, and the products of its own democratic spirit" (412).

Such poetry will come from unexpected places, Whitman believes, "in some western idiom" in slang or local song or allusion, by men living in huts or mountains or alongside railroads, by farmers or boatmen. "Rude and coarse nursing-beds, these; but only from such beginnings and stocks, indigenous here, may happily arrive, be grafted, and sprout, in time, flowers of genuine American aroma, and fruits truly and fully our own" (413).

He then makes a nationalistic plea. It is a disgrace, Whitman continues, that a nation "distinguish'd above others by the variety and vastness of its territories, its materials, its inventive activity, and the splendid practicality of its people" does not "rise and soar above the others also in its literature and art" (413). Whitman predicts that the States, made more vast by the addition of Canada and Cuba, will lead the world.

But the United States can assume this position of eminence only if it has "the mightiest original non-subordinated SOUL" which Whitman now claims "This Soul—its other name, in these Vistas, is LITERA-TURE" (413). World leadership is now added to the list of beneficent results of a genuine democratic literature.

The "orbic literature" Whitman calls for is to be written, as he has claimed, by a new race of orbic bards. Such a race will have "character, not merely erudition or elegance." They will have a "strong-fibred joyousness and faith, and a sense of health *al fresco*," they will not contain any idea of "the covert, the lurid, the maleficent, the devil, the grim estimates inherited from the Puritans, hell, natural depravity and the like." Instead, the "great literatus" will be known by "his cheerful simplicity, his adherence to natural standards, his limitless faith in God, his reverence, and by the absence in him of doubt, ennui, burlesque, persiflage, or any strain'd and temporary fashion" (414).

And he will believe in "adhesiveness," which Whitman again addresses in a footnote, as the "counterbalance and offset of our materialistic and vulgar American democracy" (414). Whitman claims that democracy implies loving comradeship "as its most inevitable twin or counterpart."

So Whitman also relies on what he calls "intense and loving comradeship, the personal and passionate attachment of man to man" to enter into the third phase he proposes. Notice—it seems as if adhesiveness, not literature, is what matters at this stage of the historical process he describes. This is not a contradiction if we assume that adhesiveness is the unspoken intent of democratic literature—the binding of writer/reader and reader/America. In other words, democratic literature embodies adhesiveness.

It is the author, the literatus, who can embody all the ideal qualities of democratic literature. By experiencing and manifesting adhesiveness, as well as joyousness, health, faith, and cheerful simplicity, the literatus contributes to what Whitman now calls "moral civilization." The author can be great only if he has the necessary absences and presences described by Whitman; only great authors can contribute to democracy.

There is an even more important role for genuine authors. In times of danger, native philosophers and orators can "fend off ruin, and defection."

> The problem of the future of America is in some ways as dark as it is vast. Pride, competition, segregation, vicious willfulness and licence beyond example brood already upon us. Unwieldy and immense, who shall hold in behemoth? who bridle leviathan? Flaunt it as we choose, athwart and over the roads of our progress loom huge uncertainty, and dreadful, threatening gloom. It is useless to deny it: Democracy grows rankly up the thickest, noxious, deadliest plants and fruits of all—brings worse and worse invaders— needs, newer, larger, stronger, keener compensations and compellers. (422)

Whitman depicts modernity as a noxious, deadly jungle, requiring the services of new, large, strong, keen "compellers." This dark view of modern life, linked to a heroic view of artists and intellectuals, continues into the present. Unlike Tocqueville, who presumes that intellectuals, artists, and aristocrats have a relatively tangential role in the new democracy, Whitman (and almost all who follow him) imagines them as engaged in a mighty struggle to redeem the promise of America.

"What prospect have we?" Whitman asks, as we "sail a dangerous sea of seething currents, cross- and under-currents, vortices—all so dark, untried?" It is as if the Almighty had spread out before us a chart of "imperial destinies, dazzling as the sun, yet with many a deep intestine difficulty, and human aggregate of cankerous imperfections" (422). To have greatness, a price must be paid:

> For you too, as for all lands, the struggle, the traitor, the wily person in office, scrofulous wealth, the surfeit of prosperity, the demonism of greed, the hell of passion, the decay of faith, the long postponement, the fossil-like lethargy, the ceaseless need of revolutions, prophets, thunderstorms, deaths, births, new projections and invigorations of ideas and men." (423)

To accomplish the revolutions, projections, and invigorations, Whitman posits his "new and greater literatus order," as the "counter-infusion" to all that weakens, corrupts, and poisons contemporary life. He ends his central argument by offering a cautionary prophecy:

> I say of all this tremendous and dominant play of solely materialistic bearings upon current life in the United States, with the results as already seen, accumulating, and reaching far into the future, that they must either be confronted and met by at least an equally subtle and tremendous force-infusion for purposes of spiritualization, for the pure conscience, for genuine esthet-

ics, and for absolute and primal manliness and womanliness—or else our modern civilization, with all its improvements, is in vain, and we are on the road to a destiny, a status, equivalent, in its real world, to that of the fabled damned." (424)

WHITMAN AND TOCQUEVILLE: COMPARING VIEWS

It is tempting to dismiss Whitman's analysis—overheated, often incoherent, awash in idiosyncratic metaphors and absurd claims. But Whitman offers an unmistakable, and poignant, example of the consequences of believing in the arts as a multiply powerful force. The strengths and weaknesses of his argument are—writ very large—the key characteristics of the redemptive perspective.

Whitman's purposes are very different from Tocqueville's. Tocqueville writes to suggest that democracy can survive, while Whitman writes to redeem what he perceives as America's failed promise. Tocqueville writes to locate and encourage the tendencies that will ensure democracy's felicity. Whitman writes to bring into existence a new, extraordinary democracy, to unleash the latent capacities in people, and to catalyze a new phase in civilization, through the powers of (among other things) literature.

Whitman marshals potential vehicles for America's hoped-for transformation, just as Tocqueville marshals various vehicles for democracy's hoped-for protection. For Whitman, Literature is the most powerful vehicle of change—it can cause transformations more lasting and stupendous than wars, or "political, dynastic or commercial overturn," and foster a "sane and heroic life," creating a race of "superb men and women."

Unlike Tocqueville, who sees the arts as dependent on, and expressive of, the social order, Whitman sees the arts as fundamental, powerful processes that shape selves and societies. Literature is the way to guarantee that the people become The People, worthy of the powers that democracy offers them. As simplistic as this sounds, it is the essence of the instrumental view, the perspective that still dominates discussion of the social role of the arts.

Whitman barely addresses the dangers of revolution, anarchy, and tyranny that so concern Tocqueville, and that only intermittently trouble today's social critics. What Whitman worries about is the inadequacy of contemporary life. Like today's critics, he worries about the ways in which the society he lives in falls short of the society he believes is possible. Whitman's concern is with an unfulfilled destiny, evidenced in the "grotesque" peoples and literatures that surround him.

Amid the sea of claims in "Democratic Vistas" are simple metaphors that combine into an argument about the need to change a weak, false, cramped people/nation into a strong, honest, free people/nation. The oppositions Whitman uses (sickly versus robust, the sham versus the authentic, the feudal versus the democratic) are applied to people, literature, and society as a whole. To change one is to shape all. Literature is the Archimedean point he chooses—the right literature, written by the right race of orbic bards, can and will release the latent capacities of individuals, and of American society.

This may seem ridiculous, even after a prolonged steeping in Whitmanian rhetoric. But the same logic continues, in less fervent language, today. While Whitman picks up many of the threads we find in Tocqueville, including the opposition of material and spiritual, the potentials of democracy, and the necessity of community, he weaves them into a much more familiar, and therefore contemporary-sounding, argument. Whitman sounds more modern partly because he is making familiar arguments about modern life—the loss of authenticity, the need for communal bonds, the threats to social "health."

Commerce, in Tocqueville, can channel men's passions in ways that support the stability and decency of common life. Whitman adopts this claim, but then goes on to imagine a world that has moved into a third, religious/spiritual/literary phase, building on but superseding material interests. In particular passages, the material is almost, but not quite, seen as the antithesis of the spiritual/literary. This opposition is what characterizes the counterbalancing perspective, exemplified by Mumford.

Democracy for Tocqueville is equality and liberty. For Whitman, democracy is a condition that liberates, and thereby perfects people. Tocqueville and Whitman both tend to see freedom as freedom from constraints, but Tocqueville's constraints are political and social, and some of them are necessary for the social good. Whitman's constraints are psychological and personal—petulance, fraud, greed, lethargy—and they must *always* be transcended. The redemptive perspective begins with the individual—he or she must be transformed, so that society can be saved.

The new, free, robust self "naturally" forms community; Whitman's concept of adhesiveness is a bonding that allows unity and self-development. Where Tocqueville soberly discusses voluntary and commercial associations, Whitman rhapsodizes about adhesiveness—community is mystical and spiritual for Whitman. Social cohesion, a key problematic for all social theorists, finds characteristically different solutions in each view.

The most striking conceptual difference between Tocqueville and Whitman is in the issue of authenticity. Whitman's democracy, ultimately, offers everyone a life of "genuineness." It is therefore a more familiar utopia to contemporary readers—authenticity has become a dominant theme in critiques of twentieth-century life.[9]

Whitman is obsessed with the problem of modern "gaud and fraud." Tocqueville simply does not see America in these terms. The democratic world Tocqueville finds is different from, but not more or less "authentic" than, the hierarchical world being left behind. For Tocqueville, the aristocratic world may be overly refined, out of touch, insubstantial, but it is not "foppish" or "fake." The existence, and fears, of "simulacra" that haunt modern and postmodern social criticism make little sense in a Tocquevillian view.

But Whitman's characterization of the European or feudal world adds the notion of the false, hollow, sham. These traits also characterize, for him, the commercial, popular literature of his time. That which is imported or successful in the marketplace is confining as well as fake. For Whitman, the imported and the popular are also the confining and the false; the new and the democratic are the liberating and the true. This critique of popular, commercial, mediated culture continues, virtually unquestioned, into the twentieth century; it is a central element in the mass culture debates, and in Mumford's counterbalancing perspective.

For Whitman, the feudally inspired literature which causes "spasms" in literary coteries is not the healthy brew that creates robust men and women. The fops and phonies currently being sustained by such literatures will become, under the influence of truly democratic literature, a "copious race of superb men and women." In marked contrast to Tocqueville, who seeks mostly to channel self-interest, Whitman seeks dramatic, permanent change in individuals. Surprisingly, the French aristocrat is far more accepting of "the people" as they already are than is the Poet of the Common Man.

Whitman believes that the arts are therapeutic. He sees literature as counteracting sickness and restoring latent health. That there is implicit soundness in The People is crucial to Whitman's argument. That art—his art—can somehow call it forth is the claim upon which his whole essay (and life's work) depends. His is the redemptive perspective at its most egocentric—Whitman dispensing the artistic elixir America needs.

Tocqueville never imagines that his work is world-changing. Whitman does. Tocqueville sees America as having multiple processes that protect and sustain liberty and equality; he takes interest and delight in the ways that everyday people express their interests and desires. Whitman sees America as already infected, as not achieving the democratic potential it has, and is distressed and even repulsed by the choices that people make. Whitman sees American society as needing just what he happens to be, an Orbic Bard, who creates just the kind of art it needs, Orbic Literature.

In that way, too, a Whitmanian perspective continues. American cultural and social critics continue to believe not only in the social power of the arts, but in the social power of their own work—criticism. I think it is because faith in the redemptive power of the arts gives them, like Whitman, a way both to call for an ideal democracy, and to believe they have a special responsibility to bring it into being. The Whitmanian view is self-serving in the extreme: it describes a powerful role for the arts in ways that *simultaneously* imagines a powerful role for artists, critics, and intellectuals.

Tocqueville makes no such claims about the potential transformative power of his work. His is a more humble view of the world; democracies bustle along quite well without aristocrats (and critics) like him. Tocqueville is able to appreciate the possibility that tastes and habits that are foreign, perhaps even repugnant to him, might still have value. Tocqueville's respect for the propensities and choices of everyday people is admirable and rare.

Faith in the instrumental power of the arts fosters a social criticism that is Whitmanian—and as we will see, Mumfordian—rather than Tocquevillian. The consequence is a philosophy that reifies art and criticism, while denigrating the practices of ordinary life. If we question Whitman's faith in the redemptive power of the arts, perhaps we can develop a more Tocquevillian appreciation of the nature, and possibilities, of our democratic experiment.

CHOOSING MUMFORD

Interpretations and Forecasts is a collection of Lewis Mumford's essays that span fifty years.[10] It is through this collection that I realized that the Mumford of the 1960s was not the Mumford of the 1920s, and that I liked his early work far more than his later essays. Why? In rereading his work, in order, for this project, I realized that Mumford had undergone an intellectual evolution, moving from a brief encounter with an expressive perspective to a redemptive and finally to a counterbalancing perspective on the arts. By sketching Mumford's intellectual trajectory, we can explore the characteristics and consequences of these differing perspectives

In a prolific and influential writing life that spanned sixty years, Mumford sought first to merge, then to balance, then to restore a dual vision of art and technology in modern society. Mumford's dualistic vision—where the arts must counterbalance the mechanistic imperatives of technology—continues in contemporary criticism.

We have long taken for granted Mumford's insistence on distinguishing the arts from technology and from commerce—art is to remain separate and distinct, free from the "taints" of mechanization and the marketplace. That there is contemporary consternation about the blurring of lines between art and commerce (with blockbuster museum exhibitions) and with art and technology (in new forms of techno-art) shows how much these distinctions still matter. In Mumford we see what those divisions make possible, and preclude.

Mumford's Intellectual Trajectory

When Mumford died in 1990, the *New York Times* described him as "a visionary social critic, philosopher, literary critic, historian, city planner, cultural and political commentator, essayist and perspicacious writer on the subject of architecture."[11] Another commentator offered a more vivid description—Mumford was "one part historian, one part critic, and a more prodigious part preacher, goading us on toward the utopia that he has always understood would never be attained but that he could not restrain himself from striving for."[12]

Mumford's body of work is unified by his insistence that the world we have made is not the world that we need if we are to live rich, rewarding, fulfilling lives. Like most utopians, including Whitman,

Mumford critiqued this world through imagining a better one. In tracing his claims and dreams throughout this period, we find a consistent refiguring of his perceived dichotomy between art and technics. This dichotomy remained central to his thought from the 1920s to the 1980s while he, the world he critiqued, and the world he imagined, changed. Mumford used his art/technics divide to anchor his chronological discussions of utopias, literature and politics, the social role of the arts, and the limits of mechanization

Mumford's first book, written in 1922, *The Story of Utopias*, evaluated historical ideals of "the good life." Its insistence on imagined, then enacted, social change was the conceptual foundation for all his subsequent work. Unlike his fellow Young American critics, Mumford went on to connect aesthetic analysis to the history and implications of technology, in conjunction with urban life, architecture, international politics and everyday experience. The wedding of art to technics is evident in his earliest works and continues throughout his writing career.

Mumford had published five books by the 1930s, when his focus became less literary and more technological. In the 1930s he began his four-book series, *The Renewal of Life*, which addressed the consequences of science and technology in the history of Western Civilization, a series added to by two major books in the 1960s: *The Myth of the Machine I: Technics and Human Development* and *The Myth of the Machine II: The Pentagon of Power*. By the end of his active writing career, he had published more than a thousand essays and reviews, as well as thirty books.

Mumford's first book analyzed the utopian project in general; his next four addressed nineteenth-century architecture and literature (*Sticks and Stones*, 1924; *The Golden Day*, 1926; *Herman Melville*, 1929; and *The Brown Decades*, 1931) as they offered a foundation for twentieth-century critique and action.

Mumford offers himself as an example of someone who has made choices against the grain of contemporary life, toward a more humane and organic vision.[13] His autobiographical writings are voluminous, and in his role as moral philosopher (see in particular *Faith for Living*, 1940; *The Conduct of Life*, 1951) he directs the reader toward the habits and practices he himself has chosen. These are values of simplification, balance, and reflection, in order to be more fully present, focused, and engaged in everyday life.

These goals were ones that did not come easily to him, it seems. The Mumford evidenced in his memoirs *Green Memories* (a wrenching memoir of his son, Geddes, killed in combat in Italy in 1944); *My Work and Days; Findings and Keepings,* and in his biography[14] is a self-scrutinized and self-controlled creation, someone whose thoughts and feelings are scrupulously directed toward productivity, growth, and self-improvement.

Mumford has been dismissed by some as a Luddite and technophobe, a Cassandra who wrote endless diatribes about the evils of mechanization. This an unfair reading.[15] His work does, at times, have an exhortative tone that becomes shrill, and a strenuousness that can seem priggish. But these characteristics are due to his unyielding (and enacted) faith in the possibility of personal and therefore social transformation. He arranged his life to heal and overcome the art/technics split, but he could only exhort others to restore or heal it in the social body.

Mumford was not a technophobic agrarian utopian, but a social critic increasingly frustrated by the refusal of transformational possibilities in the people he addressed. It is his faith in transformation, based in his conceptualization of an art/technics divide, that explains his intensifying frustrations. It also connects him to the Whitmanian tradition of insisting that the reader embody transformation. The instrumental perspective supports, and is supported by, the need to make the world into what the critic needs it to be.

As the century wore on, the mechanistic forces that Mumford critiqued so forcefully were flourishing, seemingly unopposed, in spite of his best efforts. The solutions he called for—the concerted efforts of a new generation—did not materialize. For a reader in the 1990s, his trajectory of essays[16] addressed, years in advance, the issues that have come to matter most in American social and cultural criticism. To write so accurately and presciently, and to so little social effect, can only have increased the polemical tendencies in his work.

On Art, Technics, and Utopias

The young Lewis Mumford was actively engaged in an exhilarating intellectual movement that used literary magazines and essay collections to define and foster an aesthetic-and-thus-social renewal. He was also a new husband and young father who delighted in aspects of New York, and who moved with his wife and son to the experimental community of Sunnyside. The Mumford of the 1920s was living out his vision of an organic, aesthetic intellectual, alive to the possibilities of the postwar world.

Two books demonstrate his early hopes for an integration, even a synthesis, of art and science: *The Story of Utopias* and *The Golden Day.* The key aspects of his thought are here in their earliest forms: the necessity of renewal; the nature of the "idola"; the balance between art and technics; the nature of the good life.

The Story of Utopias[17] gives Mumford a way to critique the premises by which others have imagined better worlds. It clears the ground, and serves as the foundation, for his later work. It offers selective descriptions of Utopian thinkers, including Plato, Sir Thomas More, Francis Bacon, Charles Fourier, Edward Bellamy, William Morris, and H. G. Wells. After comparing their visions of a better world,[18] Mumford offers his own description and critique of three peculiarly modern utopian visions: the Country House, Coketown, and Megalopolis.

These three mythic sites have been both imagined and enacted in recent times, Mumford writes. The Country House is an aristocratic institution based on power and wealth; Coketown an industrial conglomeration built by engineers and centered on the factory; Megalopolis a paper-based world of impersonal systems of goods and services. Each myth defines and connects with the other, so that the Country House is offered (for some) as a weekend retreat from the exigencies of Coketown, and Megalopolis imagined as the sanitized, systematized "paper purgatory which serves as a medium through which the fallen sons of Coketown, the producer's hell, may finally attain the high bliss of the Country House, the consumer's Heaven."[19] Each myth has its attendant view of the role of art and of technology.

The key to Mumford's critique here, and in all his later work, is that these social myths are not merely literary imaginings, but social visions that shape our everyday lives. These myths make the reality in which we live. They form the beliefs and values from which social practices and institutions spring. Our unexamined faith in dominant social myths keeps them dangerous. The myths of Country House, Coketown, and Megalopolis, Mumford says, are "the source of a great many evils that threaten, like stinking weeds, to choke the good life in our communities" (*SoU,* 233).

Why are these three myths dangerous? Because, says Mumford, they do not address the problem of living a full, balanced, humane life in community. Instead, they offer fake utopias, partial solutions that deepen our dissipation. The Country House works only for the rich and powerful, and is separated from the life of the community as a whole. Coketown offers a life of endless production-for-consumption, and defines a good life as a "goods" life. Megalopolis offers a uniform, desiccated world of loyal, passive citizens.

Mumford's assessment of the contemporary (1920s) situation is blunt: "In so far as we have accepted the modern social order we are in ruin . . . and in so far as we have pinned our hopes to current movements for reconstruction or revolution, our plans are sickly and debilitated" (*SoU*, 263). If what Mumford calls here "the dissipation of Western Civilization" is to cease, we must form a new foundation for knowledge and projects. Instead of accepting available social myths, or available progressive or radical options, we must join together to imagine and then enact a new utopian vision. We must recognize the role that our beliefs play in maintaining our institutions, and develop a new, modern understanding.

This means, in *The Story of Utopias*, a call for a new kind of inquiry, what he calls social science. We must, Mumford argues, "return to the real world, and face it, and survey it in its complicated totality. Our castles-in-the-air must have their foundations in solid ground" (*SoU*, 281). He describes (drawing on Patrick Geddes's ideas of the regional civic survey) a social science that consists of "definite, verifiable, localized knowledge." This kind of knowledge has been absent in previous utopias, and so they have been abstract, simplistic, and partial.

This is the key moment in Mumford's early conceptualization of the art/technics dichotomy—an imagined integration, a truly social science, that studies local life in its complexity and offers empirical evidence that infuses knowledge back into social choices, fostering a concrete, complex, complete social vision toward which to aspire.

But such social science–based knowledge is only a necessary start. This is where Mumford's brief beginnings as an expressivist give way to his redemptive, and then counterbalancing, perspective. Mumford adopts an instrumental perspective on the social role of the arts because he believes that we need to make ourselves over. The need to remake the human personality is central to all of Mumford's calls for renewal.

In *The Story of Utopias*, Mumford cites the need for us to become "fully energized human beings." This is possible when science and art are combined and allowed to contribute to the "exuberance of intellectual life" (*SoU*, 283–84). The works of artists, in conjunction with the social science described above, offer clues to the establishing of a "concrete eutopia which shall rise out of the real facts of the everyday environment, and, at the same time, turn upon them and mold them creatively a little nearer the heart's desire" (294). Art must connect with science to reveal the human world, and then it can and must mold the world and us into more natural and humane patterns.

It is, Mumford argues, the absence of a vision of a new world "informed by science and ennobled by the arts" that has weakened and made ineffective both classical and more recent partisan utopias. Previous versions have been abstract, have not taken into account the actual complexity of human beings and their environment, and have not created a moving, vivid pattern toward and through which men can work. This becomes Mumford's lifelong project: to define an alternative toward which we can aim.

Mumford uses history, both literary and technological, to make his case for renewal. It is through his histories that he can demonstrate what has been lost, what needs to be reconstituted, what can be newly created. Mumford's subsequent work flows from this initial utopian project. His combination of historical, aesthetic, technological, and social analysis is designed to locate previous patterns of change, and then demonstrate the possibilities of current and future transformation. Much like Whitman, Mumford exhorts us to become who we need to become in order to enact his vision of an ideal future.

This location of past patterns (to argue for future ones) structures his next book, *The Golden Day*.[20] Later critics remember it for its definition of, and analysis of, an American literary renaissance that helped to define the study of American literature and the development of American Studies. But they rarely note that the book is about Emerson, Whitman, and Thoreau only in relation to what they can reveal about what has been lost in American thought. It begins Mumford's turn away from notions of social science–based utopias and toward an argument for the restoration of lost balance.

Mumford begins his analysis of nineteenth-century American literary values by describing the breakdown of the medieval order. He ends it with a lengthy critique of pragmatism.[21] Along the way he makes extended claims about the power of art to enrich, transform, and vivify. The "golden day" of Emerson, Whitman, and Thoreau offers a lost moment of balance, one that serves as a foil for Mumford's developing critique of the American mind as increasingly influenced by Protestantism, technological development, the Puritan, pioneer, and business ethos, and what he terms pragmatic acquiescence.

The transcendentalists offer Mumford the vision and life he seeks to revive:

> In their work, we can see in pristine state the essential characteristics that still lie under the surface; and from their example we can more readily find our own foundations, and make our own particular point of departure. In their imaginations, a new world began to form out of the distracting chaos; wealth was in its place, and science was in its place, and the deeper life of man began again to emerge, no longer stunted or frustrated by the instrumentalities it had conceived and set to work. For us who share their vision, a revival of the moribund, or a relapse into the pragmatic acquiescence is equally impossible; and we begin again to dream Thoreau's dream—of what it means to live a whole human life. (*Golden Day*, 142)

In *The Story of Utopias*, Mumford talks about wedding science and art into a newly imagined social science. By *The Golden Day*, he is using a metaphor of restoration, completion, balance, wholeness. We must "rectify the abstract framework of ideas which we have used, in lieu of a full culture, these last few centuries" (*GD*, 144). This incomplete culture has created a "sinister world," the power to escape it can be found "only by the double process of encountering more complete modes of life, and of reformulating a more vital tissue of ideas and symbols to supplant those which have led us into the stereotyped interests and actions which we endeavor in vain to identify with a full human existence" (*GD*, 144).

On Technics and Civilization

A decisive turn in Mumford's work is in *Technics and Civilization*, written and revised in the early 1930s. It is an extraordinary work, full of details about technical developments like clocks, mining, hunting, warfare, engineering, and weaving. It argues, overall, that advances in mechanical, technical understanding have not been brought into proper relation to human purposes, and it calls for a revitalization of humane purposes so that mechanization can serve our needs.

Mumford's hope is that a recognition of the dangerous consequences of mechanization, when combined with intensified attention to what he calls "living processes," can work to change the historical relationship between mechanization and life. "With a change in ideals from material conquest, wealth, and power to life, culture, and expression, the machine, like the menial with a new and more confident master, will fall back into its proper place: our servant, not our tyrant" (*TC*, 427).

This model is based on a set of assumptions that he develops earlier—assumptions about how mechanization dehumanizes, depersonalizes, is antithetical to "life" and "culture" and "expression." Notice, in the following quote, how science is equated with "lifelessness" and ultimately a wasteland:

> Science . . . singled out the most negotiable set of relations, mass, weight, number, motion. Unfortunately, isolation and abstraction, while important to orderly research and refined symbolic representation, are likewise conditions under which real organisms die, or at least cease to function effectively. . . . In their desire to achieve exact result, the physical sciences scorned true objectivity: individually, one side of the personality was paralyzed; collectively, one side of experience was ignored. To substitute mechanical or two-way time for history, the dissected corpse for the living body, dismantled units called individuals for men-in-groups, or in general the mechanically measurable for the organically whole, is to achieve a limited practical mastery at the expense of truth and the larger efficiency that depends on truth. . . . The physical scientist denuded the world of natural and organic objects and turned his back upon real experience: he substituted for the body and blood of reality a skeleton of effective abstractions which he could manipulate with appropriate wires and pulleys. What was left was the bare, depopulated world of matter and motion: a wasteland. (*TC*, 51)

Here we have the theme that becomes, in the 1960s and 1970s, *The Myth of the Machine I* and *II*—descriptions of technical knowledge combined with a critique of them as "abstract" and "bloodless," a form of dismemberment, the antithesis of that which is concrete, organic, alive, human. In *Technics and Civilization*, he focuses on history and the critique, with only passing reference to ways to rehumanize the "wasteland." In fact, he can sound quite cavalier about solutions—"we merely have to use imagination and intelligence and social discipline in our traffic with the machine itself" (*TC*, 427).

Twenty years later, this dichotomy continues, and emphasis on restored balance structures *Art and Technics*.[22] But Mumford's plea for balance is now more simple, and more desperate:

The great problem of our time is to restore modern man's balance and whole-ness: to give him the capacity to command the machines he has created in-stead of becoming their helpless accomplice and passive victim; to bring back, into the heart of our culture, that respect for the essential attributes of personality, its creativity and autonomy, which Western man lost at the mo-ment he displaced his own life in order to concentrate on the improvement of the machine. In short, the problem of our time is how to prevent ourselves from committing suicide, precisely at the height and climax of our one-sided mechanical triumphs. (*AT*, 11)

Now the stakes are higher, our prescribed role a more difficult one, and the world that we must save ourselves from even more sinister.

Synthesis, Equilibrium, and the Good Life

Mumford's earliest work imagines art and technics in a synthesis that can inform our social choices and direct our conjoint actions. Like Dewey, he imagines a social science that is lively and humane as well as empirical and rational. This synthetic perspective gives way, in the 1930s, to a darker vision of the consequences of mechanization as ab-straction and dismemberment. Mumford still maintains a relatively cheerful view of social possibility—if we find ways to support hu-mane processes and purposes, we can achieve a social equilibrium. By the 1950s this cheer has disappeared. Mechanization is rampant, hu-mane purposes are eclipsed, the human race is on the verge of suicide.

Mumford's calls for "balance" make it easy to misread him—he is not simply calling for "more art" to counteract "more technics." He calls, in-stead, for *a view of life that includes the processes he ascribes to art as a coun-teractant to a view of life that is created by the processes he calls technics.* By the 1950s, Mumford calls for a world that is structured and defined by the values, powers, possibilities he finds in the arts, as they are in har-mony with those of technological development. This makes the arts into bearers of humane values—and comes perilously close to assuming that they can inject those values into those who partake of them.

Mumford's view of art and technics in his middle period usually depended on dynamic equilibrium. When artistic and technical processes are brought into balance, then the "higher functions—those that promote art, morality, freedom—can flourish" (*AT*, 145). There have been times, Mumford argues, when the balance has skewed the other way, when "it is the overdevelopment of the inner life, the over-proliferation of symbols, the excessive claims of subjectivity that are responsible for the mischief" (*AT*, 145). But in our times, "we suffer chiefly because of the result of the unlimited license we give to the machine" (*AT*, 145).

The purpose of life, for Mumford, was always growth, abundance, passion, intensity, fullness. His critiques are of things that are stagnant, sparse, dead, dull, empty. His opposition between full/empty; alive/dead; abundant/sparse, can conflate, all too easily, into his distinction between art and technics. Art draws from, enhances, vivifies life; mechanization (run rampant) weakens, corrodes, numbs life. His later work became increasingly simplistic in these ways.

Remember, Mumford's version of the good life began, in the 1920s, with a contrast between a scrabbling for money, power, glory and a concrete delight in life's basic elements. In *The Story of Utopias* he argues that:

> Our attempts to live the good life are constantly perverted by our efforts to gain a living; . . . by juggling gains and advantages, by striving after power and riches and distinction, we miss the opportunity to live as whole men. People become the nursemaids of their furniture, their property, their titles, their position; and so they lose the direct satisfaction that furniture or property could give. (78)

To this picture of distractions and squandered possibilities he offers a countervision: "To cultivate the soil rather than to simply get away with a job; to take food and drink rather than to earn money; to think and dream and invent, rather than to increase one's reputation; in short, to grasp the living reality and spurn the shadow—this is the substance of the Utopian way of life" (*SoU*, 78).

The Dangers of Dichotomies

Why does Mumford give up his faith in the combination of art and technics? In *The Story of Utopias*, Mumford calls for a new synthesis, one that recombines artistic and scientific imaginations *and* restores connections between the artist and the community. He believes that the intellectual exuberance of the Renaissance was largely because "both literature and science were regarded as coeval phases of man's intellectual activity" (*SoU*, 283).

Mumford concluded: "There is no genuine logical basis, as far as I can see, in the dissociation of science and art, of knowing and dreaming, of intellectual activities and emotional activities. The division between these two is simply one of convenience; for both these activities are simply different modes in which human beings create order out of the chaos in which they find themselves" (*SoU*, 284).

If there is, as Mumford says in his first book "no genuine logical basis for the dissociation of science and art," why, then, does all his subsequent work rely upon it? How does the separation of art and technics "work" for Mumford? What does it make possible? What does it prevent? If we understand what this counterbalancing perspective achieves for Mumford, we can recognize how and why the art/technology dualism continues to shape contemporary discourse.

In Mumford, and in current discussion, the dichotomy allows mechanization to be blamed for the ills of modernity, and the arts to be posited as a form of restoration and, thereby, salvation. Through this dichotomy, we can deplore what Mumford finds wounding and troublesome about contemporary experiences—technics. And we can imagine an alternative and a solution—art.

To do this, he and we must posit art as a transformative force. In Mumford, art is first posited as a condition of a balanced, humanized life. But then gradually the arts become instrumentalized—imagined as a balancing and humanizing force in society as a whole. Finally, the arts becomes a more individually transformative force, one that can create changes in particular readers. Inadequate "creative thought" (European humanism, American pragmatism) can then be blamed for failing to transform, balance, humanize society and individuals. And new forms of thought, called for by Mumford, can be imagined as the right kind of thought to work the needed transformation. We should, by now, recognize this logic as extremely Whitmanian.

The deployment of a multiply powerful art is at the heart of *Art and Technics*. In this book, a later Mumford, confronting the world of the 1950s, not the 1920s, directly describes the need for transformation in relation to the need for art to counterbalance technics. His claims about art are always in relation to his claims about technology—art becomes all that is necessarily missing from a world that is becoming increasingly mechanistic and impersonal.

Art has a purpose—"to widen the province of personality, so that feelings, emotions, attitudes, and values, in the special individualized form in which they happen in one particular person, in one particular culture, can be transmitted with all their force and meaning to other persons or to other cultures." Art functions to deepen personality, and to store and share that personality. As Mumford summarizes: "The work of art is the visible, potable spring from which men share the deep underground sources of their experience" (16).

The power of art to work across time and space is the highest stage of the development of art. Mumford suggests that art moves from self-identification to exhibitionism to a final, mature stage, where art "becomes capable of begetting fresh forms of life: when the work of art becomes itself an independent force, directly energizing and renewing those who come into contact with it, even though they may be separated by time and space from the original culture, now vanished, or the original person, now dead" (25).

Now, for Mumford, the work of art is an independent force, one that has the power to directly energize and renew the viewer across time and space and culture. Art, in general, becomes "great symbolic structures which reveal and enhance every dimension of human experience—extending man's memory, deepening his sense impressions, rousing his hopes, making more sensitive his feelings, widening the range of sympathy and understanding and loving reciprocity with his fellow creatures" (34).

Borrowing from his original scheme, Mumford continues to develop and attribute diverse powers to "true" art. It becomes the necessary intervening variable that causes the individual and social transformations Mumford seeks. True art has tremendous capacities for individual and social renewal, he believes, but it is being ignored, displaced, and destroyed in an increasingly mechanized and dehumanized world.

Mumford critiqued, at length, the acquisitive accumulation of art objects in *The Golden Day*. He attacks the Gilded Age predilection for turning culture into a religion by incessant "hunting for pictures, statues, tapestries, clothes, pieces of furniture, for the epidermis and entrails of palaces and cottages and churches" (*GD*, 107). Collecting for the home, or for the museum, was the same empty, acquisitive enterprise: "It was the triumph of the American conquistadors to make the museum, filled with the scraps of other cultures, the repository of an irrelevant and abstract conception of culture for our own day—quite divorced from history and common experience" (*GD*, 108).

This useful (and prescient) critique of museums and collecting drops out of his analysis in *Art and Technics,* as does the emphasis on connections to community, history, and common experience. In its place is an attempt to both accept and dismiss modern art—to accept it as an authentic artistic expression of despair, and to dismiss it as an inadequate "counterpoise" to mechanization.

> We find that the symbols that most deeply express the emotions and feelings of our age are a succession of dehumanized nightmares, transposing into esthetic form either the horror and violence or the vacuity and despair of our times. Violence and nihilism: the death of the human personality. This is the message that modern art brings to us in its freest and purest moments; and that, obviously, is no counterpoise to the dehumanization wrought by technics. (*AT*, 7)

So Mumford has moved from his earlier position calling for a shared, communally based, science-linked art (where he has much in common with Dewey) to a middle position of art as a form of creative thought which can build better individuals and societies, and finally, to a view of art as aesthetic expression that can transcend time and space to energize and renew individuals.

These are substantially different definitions of art's power. They are also, I believe, increasingly less wise, and so less valuable. In Mumford's intellectual development we can see what was lost as he adopted an increasingly instrumental view of the social role of the arts.

For Mumford, the creative act is the most human, personal, emotional act of man, "source of human feelings and human values." The absence of art would be the absence of what makes life worth living: "The opposite of art is insensibility, depersonalization, failure of creativity, empty repetition, vacuous routine, a life that is mute, unexpressed, formless, disorderly, unrealized, meaningless" (*AT*, 140).

Art becomes, for Mumford as for the 1990s NEA boosters, the arena in which all the aspects of life that he values (the sensate, personal, creative, full, new, expressive, formed, orderly, realized, meaningful) are embodied. The artist celebrates and shares these things in the act of creation, making them available to others in the community, to offset the allegedly dehumanizing deformations of an overly technics-driven society.

But before art can redress these distortions, "we must put ourselves in the mood and frame of mind in which art becomes possible, as either creation or re-creation . . . we must recover our own capacity for living; to detach ourselves sufficiently from the daily routine to make ourselves self-respecting, self-governing persons" (*AT,* 157). For art to fully work on us, we must ourselves become ready for its renewing function.

This is a modern version of Whitman's Divine Literatus, where art and artist operate as a transforming medicine that will heal our distorted lives and spirits, if and when we become willing and able to receive it. In both Whitman's and Mumford's instrumental perspectives, artists live a more fully expressive and humanized life. Their work can help the rest of us (numbed, mechanized, enslaved by routine) recover our humanity.

The Limits of Counterbalance

Mumford's view of modern life as mechanistic and impersonal is a particularly twentieth-century dystopia. It mobilizes visions of modernity as unconscious dehumanization—unbeknownst to us, we are becoming less alive, creative, full, balanced. Much of twentieth-century social criticism draws from this perspective, one that presumes that "we" are succumbing to a siren song.[23]

For Mumford, modern life is not merely "diseased" (as it is for Whitman), it is deformed—the leviathan of technical development has not only been unbridled, it has warped people and social relations so completely as to offer a society barely worth living in. What Mumford sought in his optimistic early years was a synergistic equilibrium, where creativity is both technical and artistic, where society connects technical with artistic development, where personal life has found a balance between material and ideal, public and private, intellectual and imaginative. Even in balance, dichotomies regulate the argument.

In this image of a deformed society, where one half of the equation has run roughshod, art must serve as a massive counteractant. Art must offer alternative visions as well as a powerful counterforce to the unbridled forces of mechanization. Art must become for Mumford, and for those who use this counterbalancing logic, the container for all that is being eclipsed, apparently permanently, by technology.

Mumford's "true art" is a rarified and individualized expression of artistic sentiment, one that cannot be widely disseminated without being ruined. He moved from a position that trusts the art of the communally based craftsman to one that idealizes only the art of the individually creative rebel. Mumford's view of the true artist is one who sees and feels so deeply that he can create works that offer us, the viewer/reader, access to our own alternative modes of conceiving of the world.

Therefore art can be revolutionary, but only as it offers a "true" expression of the experience of those most deeply debilitated by modernity (modernist art), or by those rare few who can understand and express a new, alternative vision (intellectuals like Mumford). Art is for the special few who offer it to the needful many, who may *then* use it to heal the wounds that modernity inflicts.

Interpreted ungenerously, Mumford ends up arguing that we, his readers, should prepare ourselves for the passing on of elite wisdom: those of us who are neither artists nor social critics must become able to respond to the meanings that artists and critics make available so us. Mumford can be seen as saying that we must reorder our lives so that we can appropriately respond to the transforming powers of true art.

Rhetorical Dramas Reconsidered

The art/technics dichotomy did not serve Mumford well. Yet his dichotomy is now ours, and we need to recognize its limits. We end up, too often, where he ends up. It is far too easy to reify the arts as human and liberating, damn technology as mechanistic and constraining, and anoint ourselves as seers and sages. We can then imagine ourselves, especially in the universities, as keepers of the flame. We in the arts and humanities believe we must relentlessly protect our fragile treasure while the forces of mechanistic evil—be they imagined in capitalism, in the marketplace, in corporate life, in new technologies, in business and engineering programs—assault us at every turn.

This is a rhetorical drama—one that casts us as the heroic figures who must stem the rising tide of mediocrity and corruption. It is a rhetorical drama absent in Tocqueville, and central in Whitman and Mumford.

As I detail in the following chapters, it is a rhetorical drama that requires, and follows from, an instrumental perspective on the arts. This perspective is developed in various forms by early and mid-twentieth-century critics, and becomes fully played out by the mass culture critics of the 1950s and 1960s. In the mass culture debates, critics function as a brave band of intellectuals struggling to protect the fragile arts from the perceived onslaught of the mass media.

Contemporary arts discourse draws from Whitman and Mumford, not from Tocqueville. It includes artists, critics, academics, and intellectuals as an "us" that must work together to protect art from "them"—the pollution of the mass media, the corporate world, and the crass, materialistic, philistine anti-art forces that seek to destroy all that is good, beautiful, and true. Art, as understood by "us," can and should redeem everyone else, by offsetting all that is wrong in contemporary life. This is a heroic and therefore appealing rhetoric, but it is one that precludes exploring—and enacting—a more valuable expressive perspective.

NOTES

1. All references to *Democracy in America* are to Alexis de Tocqueville, *Democracy in America*, vols. 1 and 2 (New York: Random House, Vintage Books, 1990). This is the Henry Reeve text as revised by Francis Bowen, and further corrected and edited with an introduction, editorial notes, and bibliographies by Phillips Bradley, and a new introduction by Daniel J. Boorstin. Copyrights are Knopf 1945, renewed 1972, and introduction copyright 1990 by Daniel J. Boorstin.

2. Betsy Erkilla, *Whitman, the Political Poet* (New York: Oxford University Press, 1989), 318.

3. This and the following quotes are from Walt Whitman, "Democratic Vistas," in *Walt Whitman, Prose Works 1892*, vol. 2, *Collect and Other Prose*, ed. Floyd Stovall (New York: New York University Press, 1964), 361–426. I cover the essay in order; page numbers will be included after every extensive quote.

4. See Milton Hindus, *Leaves of Grass: 100 Years After* (Palo Alto, Calif.: Stanford University Press, 1955), 18–20, for how this interpretation needs to be made very carefully. Whitman is neither a sunny apostle nor a dark skeptic of Americanism, but rather someone who struggled, successfully, to overcome his own despair.

5. Whitman reviewed Carlyle's major works in the *Eagle*. Newton Arvin, *Whitman* (New York: Macmillan, 1938), 182–84, argues that Carlyle's work made an early, "ineffaceable impression" on Whitman, in spite of Whitman's later impatience with Carlyle's disdain for the people, and contempt for democracy.

6. See Erkilla, *Whitman, the Political Poet*, 247–59, for an account of the origins of "Democratic Vistas," its relationship to Carlyle's essay, and its Hegelian characteristics.

7. Stovall, *Whitman*, vol. 2, fn. 667, 383.

8. This use of *swarms* recalls Carlyle's sardonic *swarmery*, referring to the idealistic crowds of reformers, to hordes of workers, to trendy ideas. Here Whitman, intentionally or unintentionally, makes the "swarm" that of popular literature.

9. I consider aspects of the "authenticity critique" in relation to contemporary culture in the final chapter of Joli Jensen, *The Nashville Sound: Authenticity and Commercialization in Country Music* (Nashville, Tenn.: Vanderbilt University Press, 1998).

10. Lewis Mumford, *Interpretations and Forecasts: 1922–1972, Studies in Literature, History, Biography, Technics and Contemporary Society* (New York: Harcourt Brace Jovanovich, 1979).

11. Obituary of Lewis Mumford, *New York Times*, 28 January 1990, 21.

12. Paul Goldberger, "A Steely Humanist," *Harper's*, July 1989, 88–91.

13. Several of Mumford's works are in a genre that could be called prophetic autobiography; see especially *Faith for Living* (New York: Harcourt, Brace, 1940); *Values for Survival* (New York: Harcourt, Brace, 1946); and *The Conduct of Life* (Harvest Books, [1951] 1960).

14. Donald L. Miller, *Lewis Mumford: A Life* (New York: Weidenfeld & Nicolson, 1989).

15. For an insightful reconsideration of the critique of Mumford as a middlebrow prophet of doom, see Wilfred M. McClay, "Lewis Mumford: From the Belly of the Whale," *The American Scholar* 57, Winter 1988, 111–18, as well as Michael Zuckerman, "Faith, Hope, Not Much Charity: The Optimistic Epistemology of Lewis Mumford" and other essays in *Lewis Mumford: Public Intellectual*, ed. Thomas P. Hughes and Agatha C. Hughes (New York: Oxford University Press, 1990) 361–76. A number of valuable interpretations of Mumford's work and legacy are also in *Salmagundi* 49, Summer 1980.

16. The book that first drew me to Lewis Mumford was his *Interpretations and Forecasts*. I happened upon it (through the serendipity of library shelving) while looking for a collection of Dwight Macdonald's essays. Up to that point, I had dismissed Mumford as a pompous windbag, based on one overblown excerpt from *The Myth of the Machine* (New York: Harcourt Brace and World, 1967–1970). The essays in *Interpretations and Forecasts* are a valuable introduction to the range of his thought; Mumford was an eloquent early voice, offering all kinds of still-interesting insights on virtually all the social, political, and cultural issues that still bedevil us.

17. Lewis Mumford, *The Story of Utopias* (Gloucester, Mass.: Peter Smith, 1959; originally published in 1922).

18. Mumford begins chapter 10 of *The Story of Utopias* by cheerfully saying, "Now that we have ransacked the literature of ideal commonwealths for examples of utopian vision and the utopian method. . . ."

19. Mumford, *The Story of Utopias*, 230. The contemporary reader cannot help but compare the paper-driven world of Megalopolis to the computerized digital age, where electronic highways are imagined to link vast numbers of people in a clean and tidy world of information circulation.

20. Lewis Mumford, *The Golden Day* (1926; reprint Westport, Conn.: Greenwood Press, 1983).

21. Robert Westbrook, "Lewis Mumford, John Dewey and the Pragmatic Acquiescence," in *Lewis Mumford: Public Intellectual*, 301–22, offers a convincing account of how and why Mumford misreads Dewey here. This missed opportunity for fruitful interchange between Mumford and Dewey is further considered in Robert B. Westbrook, *John Dewey and American Democracy* (Ithaca, N.Y.: Cornell University Press, 1991). I might add that Mumford's rhetorical style requires that he set up his vision as a unique and oppositional one, so he inevitably risks simplifying the positions of his "opposition" to make his argument.

22. Lewis Mumford, *Art and Technics* (New York: Columbia University Press, 1952).

23. See Joli Jensen, *Redeeming Modernity: Contradictions in Media Criticism* (Berkeley, Calif.: Sage, 1990), 57–100, for the implications of this "ideology of the modern" for beliefs about the power of the mass media.

Chapter Two

Arts for Renewal, Revolution, Conservation, and Subversion

Virtually all of what are now believed to be postmodern themes appear in the discourse of early twentieth-century critics—social fragmentation, mobility, capitalism, the cult of the new, mass communication, and technology were aspects of a developed critique of modern life. To drastically simplify, debates centered on the connections between art and criticism in the 1910s, art and social renewal in the 1920s, and art and political action in the 1930s. Discussions about the necessary role of art in the modern age were simultaneously discussions of the role of the artist—the abstract became concrete, and by the 1930s, intensely personal.

PASSIONS AND CONVICTIONS

The world of this new intelligentsia seems both contemporary and distant. It is contemporary because we are now used to American critical discourse. We are familiar with groups of writer/critics who offer claims about the nature and worth of contemporary life, who refer to each other in their arguments, and who draw on assumptions about the deleterious consequences of technology and capitalism, and the possibilities of particular alternatives to it.

This world seems distant for two reasons. The first has to do with theory—Freud and Marx were then new in American intellectual circles. What now seems hackneyed appears freshly minted in the jargon, slogans, and knowing asides of the period.

The second reason this period seems distant has to do with its passion. The faith and fervor of the participants is startling, especially in
comparison with today's more subdued theoretical discourse. The
combination of theory and emotion makes much of the writing seem
dated. Mike Gold's fervent essays have far less resonance today than
does the more measured work of, say, Randolph Bourne.

The Freud that influenced Greenwich Village in the 1910s and 1920s
was a romanticized Freud. Freudian thought became popularized as
the advocacy of personal freedom through the recognition of neu-
roses, and the throwing off of social repression. The bohemianism and
radicalism of the 1910s and 1920s now has a blustery sweetness, as
writers intently argue for sexual and emotional liberation in the name
of mental health.

Similarly, the Marxism of the period, especially by the 1930s, can
seem quaint—although, given subsequent events, it can also seem
dangerous. For some, Marxism as science becomes the answer to all
possible social and personal dilemmas, for others a form of artistic discipline, for still others a map of the future they were to create. The language of artistic action becomes martial and grandiose, and, in some
cases, startlingly naive.

So passion and hope animated intellectual discussions—passion
for new experiences, new living arrangements, new literatures; hopes
for new people, new societies, new futures. Essays were filled with exhortations, and books ended with calls for action, exclamation points,
and claims about the possibilities of a glorious future. There is an adolescent quality to the rhetoric, both in the passion of the exhortations
made, and in the totalizing nature of the explanations used.

Many of the critics in the 1910s, 1920s, and 1930s dismissed their
earlier convictions, and their fellow writers, in just those terms—as
"adolescent." The notion of "maturity" haunts memoirs of the period.
The 1930s became "adulthood" for bohemians of the 1910s and 1920s;
the 1940s and 1950s became the "adulthood" for the radicals of the
1930s. As the century wore on, the level of intensity diminished, and
debates took on a bookish air—arguments among gentlemen in book-
lined studies rather than polemics in front of crowds on street corners.
This is a shift in the imagined social location (but not the gender) of intellectuals during the period—from the streets to the study.

The relationship between art and society served as a touchstone for
intellectual debate from the 1910s to the 1940s; in reviewing books, es-

says, and memoirs, I found four distinct instrumental perspectives on the social role of art. These are simplifications, but offer us accounts that can be compared against each other, and against the expressive position I recommend instead. The differences among these positions fueled criticism throughout the period; what they have in common, in spite of their profound differences, is the shared presumption that something called art has great social power.

FOUR PERSPECTIVES

The first position can be called a *renewal* position. Associated with little magazines, experimental living, and Greenwich Village, a group of (mostly) men wrote, argued, and disagreed about the appropriate ways for art to energize, renew, and restore the promise of American life. The position is best characterized by the Young American critics who (drawing explicitly on Whitman) argued that a new art was necessary for a social renaissance.

Their view can be contrasted with a more radical view of art as a revolutionary weapon. This *radical* view, with roots in the prewar years, became the major intellectual force in the 1930s, the so-called Red Decade. During this period of American economic and social upheaval, a range of intellectuals understood themselves and their role in response to versions of Marxism. What defines the radical position is a belief that art can and should be used as a direct weapon for social change.

During a revolutionary period, a 1930s Marxist perspective holds, the artist must align himself with the proletariat, and find ways to further revolutionary aims, to bring about a new society, where all people, and true art, can finally flourish. While individuals made different connections with the Left throughout the period, the radical position, at its most fundamental, maintained that art had revolutionary power in conjunction with the forces of history.

Neither the renaissance nor the revolutionary approach to art went unchallenged. The clearest alternative to both claims about the social role of art and artists was offered by the New Humanists. This group argued that art was a repository of higher values, to be sustained and protected, and judged by standards other than immediate personal or social effect. For Humanists, uses of art for personal or social liberation were misuses of culture.

In this *conservation* position, art, especially in a modern, industrial-izing age, must remain a repository of humane values, values that help men discipline and civilize themselves. To deploy art for libera-tion was to misunderstand its true value and power—to embody and sustain civilization. Art functions to maintain what makes individuals moral, our common life worthy, and civilization's advance possible.

A fourth position in early twentieth-century American social thought was that of the *avant-garde* of the 1910s and 1920s, which be-came, in a transformed version, the position of *Partisan Review* critics in the 1940s. It is a view that art and criticism are inherently challeng-ing to the dominant culture. Their role is to challenge the stagnant sta-tus quo. This means that whatever true artists and critics do is salu-tary, since it undercuts the dominant culture, presumed to be hollow, regressive, and false.

This *subversion* view of art's social power is extremely useful. It log-ically meshes with any other available version of art's supposed pow-ers, and puts the artist/critic in an enviable position of always work-ing toward the social good, simply by doing art or criticism. The artist/critic is always, everywhere, making things better, by restoring the world (the renewal position), or changing the world (the radical position), or maintaining truth in the world (the conservation posi-tion) through art's implicit or explicit power to challenge "what is" (the subversion position).[1]

By the 1940s, the definition of art/criticism as inherently subversive allowed intellectuals to make their peace with the contradictory pas-sions of their youth and the differing assumptions of their elders, while giving them a justification for doing the intellectual or academic work they wanted to do. It also served as an animating framework for the mass culture debates of the 1950s, when the mass media, rather than social change, became the center of intellectual debate.

RENEWAL—THE SEVEN ARTS GROUP AND FRIENDS

The Young American critics, including Randolph Bourne, Waldo Frank, Van Wyck Brooks, and the early Lewis Mumford, offered a vi-sion of the arts as social renewal—a medium in and through which a new America could be created. Their project is most closely identified with the journal *Seven Arts* (1916–1917) and various books that were written during the same period, including Van Wyck Brooks's *Letters and Leadership* and Waldo Frank's *Our America*.

These critics defined themselves against the central dichotomy they found in the American cultural heritage: a sterile choice between genteel culture and technocratic growth. They felt trapped between an elite Puritan high culture and a commercial Philistine machine culture—both soul killing. For America to live up to its promise, a new form of culture must be developed, one that is neither genteel nor commercial.[2]

The Young American perspective draws heavily on Whitman's logic. Like him, they imagined a new form of culture that would be democratic, American, liberating, enlivening, soul-building. Through it, new, freer, more robust personalities could develop, and more authentic, organic, and restorative communities could be built. The renaissance would be a transformation of personality and so of society—new selves would grow from the new culture, to make possible a new society.

The new society was related to the best aspects of the past, and of the people. These aspects were, the Young Americans argued, choked and deflected both by genteel *and* by commercial culture. The elite culture of the universities and museums was desiccated, unable to offer the energy needed for personal and social change. The tawdry culture of the emerging media was an extension of the machine age, offering only false pleasures.

The goal of the *Seven Arts* critics was the creation of a new, more grounded, more organic, and more experienced culture, one that allowed "mature" personalities to develop and flower. This culture was imagined as synthesizing dualities that had divided men's experience since the Enlightenment. In *Wine of the Puritans,* for example, Brooks critiqued an American heritage he found laden with unnecessary divisions—reason separate from emotion, the arts from everyday life, the present from the past, the moral from the practical. These divisions are destructive, he argued; if American society, and the American people, are to recover, it and they must create and sustain a new, unifying culture.[3]

The nature and dimensions of such a culture remain strategically vague, and vary over time and across critics. Bourne's essay "Transnational America" is still being read for its call for a vivid cosmopolitan culture, making use of the forces of immigrant arts already at work (but deflected) in modern American life. Such a cosmopolitan culture would not be a melting pot, but a way to release a synergistic plural-ism that could offer integrity and purpose to American life.[4]

Brooks, in his essay "Young America," sought a culture that could become a common ground between intellectuals and their generation, where all could develop matured sensibilities and strengthen their re-sistance to the developing commercial culture.[5] Frank, in *Our America*, offers a more radical version, where creative culture can fire the imag-ination of the people whose modern existence is transforming them into a complacent herd.[6]

The defining aspect of the Young American critics is their engage-ment in self-transformation through cultural criticism. They saw themselves as enacting the personal and social change they called for. They saw themselves as part of a new generation that had the poten-tial to bring into existence America's true promise. As a group, they were engaged in an act of simultaneous creation and reclamation. To-gether, they could create a new culture, drawing from a "usable past" and enacting its best characteristics in a new, unique present. This was the way toward a social renaissance.

This is a cultural approach to social change, and it gives these crit-ics contemporary resonance. Culture is the medium through which we change how we think and feel, and *thereby* change how we live. Since culture is humanly created, we can make new forms of culture that will energize and transform us.

The Young American critics were idealists, not materialists, in their beliefs about social change. Their critique of the consequences of cap-italism was in relation to its spiritual and social costs; their calls for re-form were only vaguely economic or political. Since the quality of our common life is determined by institutions and practices that depend on beliefs and values, we can change the quality of our civic life by changing what we believe, value, and therefore enact.

This perspective—personal transformation leading to social change—is different from the more radical approach of Marxists and other Left intellectuals of the period. Waldo Frank ends *Our America* with the statement that "The men who listen to Steiglitz have not yet quite joined him in their mind with the example of Bill Haywood. In other words, the impulse of New America is still unfused." In 1919, for Frank, the necessary fusion was a creative act, one that is nonintellec-tual and proceeds from "love of life and love of being. It animated the Russian Revolution. It is the spiritual substance which will move mountains." Frank ends his book by exhorting the reader toward necessary social change:

> Whitman foresaw it and sang of it and warned us. We must go through a period of static suffering, of inner cultivation. We must break our impotent habit of constant issuance into petty deed. We must begin to generate within ourselves the energy which is love of life. For that energy, to whatever form the mind consign it, is religious. Its act is creation. And in a dying world, creation is revolution.[7]

THE APPEAL OF 1930s RADICALISM

The social renewal imagined by the Young American critics was an extension of the more general Progressive spirit of the era, one that found the possibility of new syntheses between science and art, man and machine, old and new. The Progressive perspective placed great faith in human abilities to find new connections, new fusions, new harmonies among disparate forces. Those connections were usually contingent, designed to function well for now, always available for rethinking and revision. The Progressive era, with its pragmatist heritage, valued the flexible over the rigid, the relative over the absolute.

To more radical critics it looked, therefore, like an ameliorative perspective. It seemed a perspective that was open to corruption through compromise. To understand how Marxism charmed a generation of intellectuals (most of whom later repudiated their intense faith) we need to explore why a rigorous revolutionary perspective seemed preferable to a renewal view.

One way to illustrate this is through *Intellectual Vagabondage,* Floyd Dell's 1926 critique of his own generation, whom he characterizes as childlike, self-indulgent bohemians.[8] In his analysis, a nineteenth-century heritage of "art for art's sake," becomes the excuse for Dell's generation to "play at life" as mere onlookers. The literature of the period, Dell argues, supported "the essentially homeless and childless and migratory life to which capitalism had largely condemned us."[9]

Artists adopted and protected their role as idlers and onlookers, Dell argues, treating the world as mere spectacle. This means they are intellectual vagabonds, "cut off from the world of reality by a magic circle," so that they "looked outside into the chaos of meaningless accident with a kind of divine scorn."[10]

This detached, distanced, immature attitude was first challenged, Dell claimed, by the work of H. G. Wells, and the sense that an old world was dying and a new world was waiting to be built; "nothing in the world was so calculated to throw the glamour of righteousness over our impulsive follies as the notion that we were the servitors of the Future."[11]

But, Dell implies, his generation cannot serve the Future, since it cannot free itself from the vagabond attitude. Instead, it responded to the World War and the Russian Revolution by continuing to bemoan the chaos and spiritual emptiness of the times, to "foist off our own muddlement upon the universe itself."[12] What is needed instead? A new generation, one that is not "shell-shocked" by world events, but who can instead scientifically explore the real reasons for them.

Here we come to a key intellectual trope of the period—the "muddlement" and "chaos" of the 1910s and 1920s is giving way to the "science" and "laws" of Marx and Freud. The next generation, Dell believes, will have good working theories of the unconscious, and of society.

Unlike previous generations, they have found "a definite kind of order . . . to correlate and explain all sorts of bewildering and painful discrepancies in outward conduct, previously inexplicable; they have created an intelligible and practically demonstratable theoretic unity out of just those aspects of human life which have for fictional and other artistic purposes seemed in the past a hopeless jangle of contradictions."[13]

This new theoretic insight has not yet met with wide response from the intelligentsia because "it would be a reproach to us for our own failure."[14] The lessons that the Russian Revolution could and should teach to intellectuals—the values of "dull matters" like honesty, sobriety, responsibility, duty—are ignored in American life. There is no actual social relation between artists and the masses, since artists have repudiated it through their isolated onlooker role. In fact, they've left the masses to be "fed" by the movies, the comic strips, and a literature that, Dell argues, undertakes only to "solace its audiences with simple wish-fulfillment of a quasi-infantile nature."[15] But the new generation will be different!

The new generation, Dell believes, will "take themselves and their responsibilities more seriously and at the same time more joyously."[16] They will find "the political terms upon which they can accept and serve and use a machine civilization." And "it may be quite natural for them to think of the arts as a means of communication rather than merely opportunities for irresponsible self-expression."[17] With this new understanding, and definition of the arts, they can create a literature that will "help them to love generously, to work honestly, to think clearly, to fight bravely, to live nobly. . . ."[18]

In Dell's analysis we see the appeal of 1930s radicalism: it offers certainty over muddlement, the power of theory to correlate and explain, the chance to be responsible and disciplined, and the charge to create a new art that would help artists, and the masses, be generous, honest, brave, noble, and clear-thinking. Heady stuff, indeed.

Dell did not go on to become a Marxist intellectual; his later works focused on "adult" responsibilities rather than political and social action. But he offers a critique of intellectual isolation that pervades the period; the same critique is used by Granville Hicks to position radical writing against that of the humanists and what he calls "the impressionists"—Young American critics.[19]

Hicks critiques the impressionists by arguing that art "not only expresses something but also does something, has consequences as well as causes."[20] If only, Hicks says, there had been someone to say, "This is the situation of society today: these are the forces that have shaped that situation; here is the power that can bring change." Then novelists and poets might not have "stumbled quite so blindly or taken such a precipitate flight." If only someone had said, "You need not stand alone in your fight against the corruption in and about you, for here are your allies," then "artists of every kind might have faced with new confidence the task of creation."[21]

Radical writers, artists, and critics offered, by the early 1930s, a way to avoid being muddled, timid, uncertain. Instead, the Marxist analysis of history offered clear causes, known cures, and particular forms of collective action. For intellectuals, this included a central role for art and artists in the coming revolution.

REVOLUTION ROAD: NEW MASSES AND FELLOW TRAVELERS

The Depression offered final proof to intellectuals that the old order was in decay; the most captivating and thoroughgoing critique of the old order, and plan for the new, was Marxism. While economic "muddlement" reigned at home, the Soviet Union was apparently enacting a clear and certain version of a new order. Marxism also offered, in some version or another, a clear and certain role for artists in the struggle for revolution.

That role was, however, contradictory. Artists were important to the revolutionary process, but their exact function was unclear. Were writers, critics, intellectuals serving the revolution only as they allied with the working class, or were they more useful as distinct voices of truth, in an age of capitalist lies? At the heart of the dilemma was the problem of trust in individual aesthetic insight: could and should artists trust their own aesthetic choices?

The problem, basically, had to do with ideology, although it wasn't addressed in those terms. Are artists of all kinds *by nature* revolutionary, or must they become so through some form of reeducation and insight? Once artists recognize the need for revolution, and are supportive of particular routes to it, must their work reflect that commitment? The 1930s are haunted by various assumptions on the Left about how artists should participate in a revolutionary process that depended, in theory at least, on the proletariat.

The issue of social location was a difficult one—where, in the class struggle, could intellectuals and artists position themselves? How can they think, write and act in appropriate alliance with a class they barely know and rarely emulate? If intellectuals form, instead, a separate class, how can they appropriately think, write and act toward the creation of a (predestined but still unformed) new society?

"Appropriate" alliances and "appropriate" actions suggest another aspect of the problem: that artists must form allegiances and behaviors that conform to particular perspectives, and that these perspectives are not, necessarily, "natural" ones. This becomes the problem that bedeviled committed Marxist intellectuals during the period—the perceived need to reeducate, discipline, and reimagine the self, in order to play the appropriate role in society. Radical intellectuals and artists felt the need to transform themselves, to be more than, or different from, a class of dilettantes.

One way for artists to maintain loyalty to artistic things, while continuing to serve the cause of social change, was to consider themselves "brain workers." In this way, artists could define themselves as members of an intellectual class, able (unlike the bourgeoisie) to think independently of the business class, and therefore free to ally themselves with their true comrades, the working class.

This is the logic of "Culture and the Crisis," a pamphlet issued by fifty-two artists and intellectuals in 1932.[22] The argument goes like this: we as intellectuals can think for ourselves, and "hence, to a degree, can think for our time and our people." All that is "orderly, sane and useful" in society has been created by either "brain workers" or "muscle workers" and their alliance in the "frankly revolutionary Communist Party, the party of the workers," will reject the "lunacy spawned by grabbers, advertisers, traders, speculators, salesmen."

By this logic, artists are members of an intellectual class that, along with workers, is responsible for all that is valuable (orderly, sane, useful) in society, and, along with workers, is the enemy of the pawns of capitalism—grabbers, advertisers, and so on. This alliance is logically an alliance with the Communist Party. Artists here do not claim to share the ideas, experiences, and values of the workers, only the same enemies, and an equally vital role in the coming revolution.

The question of "right action" remains. What should the intellectual class be doing—what kinds of work, in what kinds of settings, toward what kinds of ends? Here is where the nature of the relationship to the Communist Party is at stake—should art be connected to a particular party line? And is such ideological discipline a temporary condition, necessary now, but unnecessary once the new social order is in place and (it is assumed) creativity can flow freely and "naturally"? But if art is a revolutionary weapon, is it then propaganda? If so is it capable of whatever "true" art is capable of? In this debate over the value of revolutionary art, we find a variety of beliefs about what art can and should do.

The issue of allegiance to a Communist Party line was finessed by deploying terms like "responsibility" and "discipline." By 1937, at the second meeting of the League of American Writers, Earl Browder (then general secretary of the Communist Party) shaped his remarks to writers in relation to the need for unity against Fascism. He extended the same assurances he had made at the first Congress, in 1935, that there was no official Party line, that Communists simply wanted writers to write "as well as they could." This point of view was often shorthanded by saying that the revolutionary cause needed good writers, not bad strike leaders. The problem remained, however: what constituted "good" writing, or other forms of art, from a revolutionary vantage?

In the 1937 address, Browder claimed the revolutionary struggle as the source of all strength and value in art, and emphasized the necessity of "higher discipline to the whole struggle for democracy." Writers must "make their own decisions on the content and methods of their work; but they are responsible to their fellow-men that their work does in truth serve the common cause. The freedom which every writer demands cannot become irresponsibility. *Every writer is responsible to his associates and to the people for the results of his work*" (my emphasis).[23]

Browder defines culture as "the social organization of the search for an ever higher truth," a definition that would also please New Humanists. Such a search "is the creator of organization and discipline, it is the instrument whereby the progressive and democratic forces consolidate themselves, it is the hallmark of our camp as opposed to that of the fascists."[24] In this way, then, disciplined and responsible artistic creation fights fascism. In the logic of the times, the reverse also obtains: undisciplined and irresponsible art supports fascism.

A 1934 exchange between Mike Gold, exemplary 1930s radical writer, and John Howard Lawson, radical playwright, painfully illustrates the difficulty of personally negotiating "disciplined and responsible" creativity.[25] In this exchange we sense the dilemma of the 1930s radical artist who attempts to create the kind of work that is appropriate in its allegiances, messages, and role.

Mike Gold was an early and sustained voice for a new proletarian literature, beginning in the early 1920s with his work on the *Liberator*, and continuing into the 1930s as editor of the *New Masses*. Gold was the prime spokesman for "proletarian realism," a form of literature that was both revolutionary in influence and representative of the new kind of art that a revolution would allow to flourish.

According to Gold, proletarian literature deals with "real" conflicts, not "sickly, sentimental subtleties" (à la Proust) but rather "the suffering of the hungry, persecuted and heroic millions." Proletarian literature must have a social theme, otherwise it is "merely confectionery." Assuming that a worker's life is dull and drab is a bourgeois notion—proletarian writers will portray the horror, but include the "revolutionary elan" that will sweep it all away. True proletarian realism does away with all "lies" about human nature; instead, as "scientists" proletarian writers "know what a man thinks and feels." Since life itself is the "supreme melodrama" there need be no straining for effect or verbal acrobatics; intensely felt life will result in a new "poetry of materials"—"swift action, clear forms, the direct line, cinema in words."[26]

This is the critical sensibility that Gold brought to the ouvre of John Howard Lawson, whose experimental and radical credentials were strong.[27] In the 1920s, Lawson had been involved in the formation of the Workers' Drama League and the New Playwrights, whose new experimental social theater presaged the 1930s social drama. Yet Gold, in the *New Masses*, attacked Lawson as "A Bourgeois Hamlet of our Time," lost in his "inner conflict" "between two worlds," indulging in "adolescent self-pity," which is why, for Gold, Lawson's work lacks maturity and "esthetic or moral fusion."

The problem, Gold says, is in the man himself—a problem that cannot be solved until Lawson has "honestly faced himself, and found out what he actually believes." It is only through this process that Lawson can free himself from his delayed adolescence, and bourgeois sentimentality, because:

> To be a "great" artist, one must greatly believe in something. When a man has achieved a set of principles, when he knows firmly he believes in them, he can, like the Soviet diplomats, make compromises, box office or otherwise. Until then, a man or an author is forever betraying the fundamentals. This is what Lawson and the liberals always do; he has no real base of emotion or philosophy; he has not purified his mind and heart.[28]

Lawson's response to Gold's attack is remarkable—respectful and apologetic, rather than defensive. It begins by "admitting the truth of 70% of Mike's attack," but arguing that he himself is painfully aware of his own faults. "I would not be worth my salt as an author if I were not acutely familiar with the problems facing me in breaking away from bourgeois romanticism and being of some genuine literary use to the revolution."

Gold accuses Lawson of writing plays where a troop of ghosts wander around asking "where do I belong in the warring world of two classes?" Lawson says, "You're dead right, Mike," and thanks him for the "clear statement of a problem confronting myself and hundreds of other writers." What Lawson wants Gold and *New Masses* readers to remember is that he has repeatedly confessed that his work to date is "utterly unsatisfactory in its political orientation, that the left tendency in my plays has been clouded and insufficiently realized, and that the only justification for my existence as a dramatist will lie in my ability to achieve revolutionary clarity."

Lawson describes his recent plays as part of a transitional period, and suggests that it is never easy to make compromises. Instead, "it takes hard courage and hard thinking to accept a revolutionary line and stick to it." The condescending phrases Gold uses to describe Lawson and his work would be justified only if "Mike made out any real case against me as being counterrevolutionary, drifting toward any sort of liberal betrayal of the working class, sympathizing with any reactionary or reformist tendency, or answering confusion in terms of social-fascism." If his work exhibits any of those tendencies, he'd like it "thrashed out." But Gold's charges boil down into a claim that Lawson's question "where do I belong in the warring world of two classes" is monotonous. Lawson concludes by saying he is sorry that Mike finds the question boring, but that he intends to make his answer "with due consideration, and with as much clarity and vigor as I possess."

What we see in the exchange between Gold and Lawson is the human cost of Browder's call for responsibility and discipline: that artists can be charged with betraying the cause even as they struggle desperately to eliminate any tendencies that can be seen as reactionary, reformist, counterrevolutionary, liberal, and/or bourgeois. Lawson and Gold agree that these tendencies must be eliminated if artists are to justify their existence and create the kind of art that is of "genuine . . . use to the revolution." In the Gold–Lawson exchange we see that the social role of the artist is valuable only after he has "achieved revolutionary clarity," after he has purified his mind and heart, disciplined himself to a firm set of principles, and extirpated all bourgeois tendencies. Then and only then can he create work that will have good social effects—supporting the revolution and fighting fascism.

This purification, discipline, and extirpation is, in Lawson's case, a process he continued long after others left Marxism behind. At the time of this exchange, Max Eastman was criticizing such self-abasing responses in *Artists in Uniform*.[29] As a former editor of the *New Masses*, Eastman was incensed at the enthusiasm with which editors of the *New Masses*, and of a short-lived journal *Left*, responded to "Moscow-based" criticism. He sees, in the relentless self-scrutiny of radical writers, a humiliation and spinelessness. "Underneath these exaggerated acts of abnegation something serious is the matter."

He calls such writers "sickly and unsound" and suggests that "the American masses are quite right not to trust them," because they "do not believe either in science or art or in themselves." In a memorable paragraph, Eastman administers a stinging salvo: "When the time comes to change the foundations in this country there will be suffering masses of the people looking for a leader. And they will be looking for him on the level of their own eyes. They will not expect to find him kowtowing toward Moscow in a position which leaves nothing visible to the American worker but his rump."[30]

Lawson's painful dilemma about the appropriate role of the artist in the class struggle becomes, for Eastman, a repellant obsequiousness to Communist Party beliefs. Such men cannot possibly lead a revolution. For Gold, Lawson's dilemma is evidence of adolescent and sentimental bourgeois romanticism. For both Lawson and Gold, such muddlement cannot result in literature that serves as an effective revolutionary weapon.

What no one suggested, in these endless debates on the Left, is that art had no direct revolutionary role—that art was *not* a socially potent weapon. The instrumental perspective was taken for granted—completely naturalized.

The radical artists of the 1930s were deeply committed to social change, and believed that their work, somehow, could bring about a new society. Whether it would be through an alliance of artists with workers (as proposed in "Culture and the Crisis") or through work that represented "social truth" (as in proletarian realism) was never settled. Whether it was necessary for the artist to transform him/herself into a pure, vigorous, and creative revolutionary (as advocated by Eastman, Gold, and Lawson, in spite of their differences) was never clear. For our purposes, the dilemma of artists committed to revolution demonstrates a particularly intense and doctrinaire version of faith in art as social medicine. Like Whitman and the Young American critics, 1930s Marxists believed that art is a weapon for social change, and that artists are, in Dell's ironic phrase, servitors of the Future.

THE SEARCH FOR CERTAINTY—
THE NEW HUMANISTS AND ASSOCIATES

The fervently argued dilemmas of Left writers and artists was not the only intellectual game in town. The Humanist position grew in certainty and strength during the 1910s and 1920s and was at the apex of its influence by 1930, when Norman Foerster edited a series of essays, *Humanism and America,* including key figures in New Humanism like Irving Babbitt and Paul Elmer More.[31]

In introducing the essays, Foerster makes a clear connection between the ills of modernity and the necessity of an alternative system of belief. As with the two previous perspectives, the fundamental problem is perceived to be the modern condition. The key difference in the New Humanist perspective is that the presumed solution is *not* to build a new kind of society, either through a renaissance or a revolution. The solution is to begin with personal cultivation and discipline, in relation to a higher system of morals and beliefs. Troubling as it would be to both the New Humanists and the Marxists, there are surprising similarities in their calls for self-purification, responsibility, and disciplining the self to align with concrete principles.

Foerster introduces the book by suggesting that "the modern temper has produced a terrible headache," that "the noise and whirl increase, the disillusion and depression deepen, the nightmare of Futility stalks before us." People, he argues, are tired of the stale skepticism of the postwar era, and are "looking for a new set of controlling ideas capable of restoring value to human existence." Foerster offers Humanism as the new set of "controlling ideas," ones that can "mak[e] for order and new objectives."[32]

Much like Marxism, New Humanism offers order and goals, via self-discipline, in relation to larger truths. The differences between the two perspectives are profound, but they share a common response to the perceived aimlessness and chaos of modern life: the possibility of order, direction, discipline, and, finally, certainty. This is why both Marxism and Humanism are appealing—they offer a definite version of life, one that suggests a particular mode of conduct, in relation to a particular vision of a good society. This distinguishes them from the other two major positions available in the period. Neither the energetic pluralism of the renewal approach nor the subdued cynicism of the subversive stance clearly delineates how to be, or what to work toward.

We get a sense of what the New Humanism offers, in relation to other perspectives, through the debate between J. E. Spingarn and Irving Babbitt about the relationship between genius and taste—the relationship between artistic creation and criticism.[33] In his essay "The New Criticism," Spingarn develops an argument for art as individual expression. In his response, "Genius and Taste," Babbitt ridicules this notion of art as "unchained emotion" and offers his alternative—art as the utilization of the "ethical imagination" in the service of a "super-sensuous truth."

Spingarn wrote his essay (originally published in 1910) to "clear the ground of Criticism of its dead lumber and its weeds." He lists this critical detritus bit by bit: invoking rules, discerning genre, using abstract conceptions or rhetorical terms, and, finally, applying moral judgments to art. "We are done with these," Spingarn thunders, and so "we" are also done with the division between genius and taste.

If we return, via Croce, to art as expression, Spingarn argues, then the role of the critic becomes to understand what the poet tried to express and how he expressed it. That understanding involves the critic momentarily "becoming" the creator—"taste must reproduce the work of art within itself in order to understand and judge it" (*NC*, 43). At this moment, genius and taste merge. This means that criticism can be finally freed of its self-contempt, because it realizes that "esthetic judgment and artistic creation are instincts with the same vital life" (*NC*, 44).

Babbitt's response to Spingarn's blend of naturalism, romanticism, and modernism is a classic statement of the principles of New Humanism. Babbitt begins by pointing out that Spingarn's perspective, offered as "ultra-modern," can be traced to the eighteenth century, with its exaltation of spontaneity and free expression and its definition (via Diderot) of genius as calling for something "enormous, primitive and barbaric." He labels Spingarn and his followers as "primitivists" who see genius as "purely expressive, a spontaneous temperamental overflow."

This allows the critic to vicariously anoint himself with genius:

> According to the primitivist . . . the genius has simply to let himself go both imaginatively and emotionally, and the whole business of the critic is to receive so keen an impression from the resulting expression that when it passes through his temperament, it issues forth as a fresh expression. By thus participating in the creative thrill of genius, the critic becomes creative in turn, and in so far genius and taste are one.[34]

In contrast with this "intoxicating" view of the linked roles of artist and critic, Babbitt offers a more restrained and judicious alternative. Babbitt does not believe that genius and taste merge, but that the critic, always, criticizes—the critic must constantly ask if the poet's aim was intrinsically worthwhile. The critic answers this question with reference to some standard set above his, and the poet's, temperament.

This is the defining element in all New Humanist criticism—belief in the need for standards above, and distinct from, individual situation and experience. These standards can and should guide human conduct, and therefore should also serve as criteria for the creation, and criticism, of art. These standards serve, too, as the "inner check" that separates man from animal, because they bridle passion and, through imagination and insight, orient man toward the good.

The New Humanist perspective relies on a dual vision of man's nature—he is both "natural," in flux, at the mercy of his animal nature, and "human," with an unchanging element , a higher self, a *frein vital* that he holds in common with all other individuals.[35] It is this element, the ethical will, which restrains desire and keeps the natural self "in check." Babbitt argues that "the two great traditions," the classical and the Christian, offer us appropriate checks—the classical tradition offers decorum and a sense of proportion; the Christian offers humility. These checks can mitigate against "the two root diseases of human nature, conceit and laziness."

Babbitt predicts dire consequences if Spingarn's "expressionistic-impressionistic view" triumphs: "To repudiate the traditional Christian and classical checks and at the same time fail to work out some new and more vital control upon impulse and temperament is to be guilty of high treason to civilization."[36]

The definition of a New Humanist is as a standard-bearer against barbarism, through the invocation of classical or traditional virtues that operate as inner checks in the lives of men. Humanism is defined against a Rousseauian romanticism, evidenced in Spingarn (and the Young American critics, and the surrealists), as well as against Jamesian pragmatism and Darwinian naturalism. Against visions of life as spontaneous, in process, instinctive, chaotic, and in flux, the New Humanism offer a vision of human life as disciplined, decorous, poised, and virtuous.

The role of art, in such a view, is to offer examples of imagination disciplined by intuition and tradition. It is the role of the critic to evaluate these offerings in relation to the successful achievement of this goal. The artist's imagination is "disciplined to reality," rather than gushing forth in emotional excess. "Genius" is not the eruption of self-expression, but, in the Greek sense, the ability to see life with imagi-native wholeness. The critic uses this standard when evaluating works of art, and helps make available those standards for others to use. Art operates with inner checks; criticism deploys inner checks; we, the people, can learn from art and criticism the nature and value of these higher standards.

New Humanists are deliberate elitists. Their vision is unapologeti-cally aristocratic—they believe that only some men have the poise, wisdom, and imaginative wholeness to lead. This is tied to their dual-istic notion of human nature, where lower, animal nature must be kept in balance, in check, by a higher self. Modern American democracy re-lies on a falsely romantic belief in the natural goodness of man. Con-temporary democracy is precarious, Humanists believe, because it cannot offer the necessary institutions, checks, and restraints that fos-ter better men, and therefore a better society.

Paul Elmer More, in *Aristocracy and Justice*,[37] refutes the claim, asso-ciated with Dewey, that "the cure of democracy is more democracy." His response is almost an exact opposite—the cure of democracy is *better* democracy, democracy that protects and advances the interests of the gifted few. These gifted few could develop and enhance institu-tions, laws, and processes that could offer necessary restraints on the natural excesses of the people.

The role of artists or intellectuals in such an enterprise is interesting. They become repositories for tradition—transmitters of the selected wisdom of human experience. In this way, they offer a stabilizing in-fluence; they become crystallized versions of the higher selves of the past, available to restrain the excesses of the present.

They offer a bulwark against the tide of meretricious modern cul-ture. Frank Jewett Mather Jr.[38] suggests that the arts transform those who might otherwise succumb to the blandishments of mass culture, evident as "the chicken and lobster eating motorist, the radio fan, the devotee of the 'talkies,' the sycophant artist who bows to base author-ity, and the behaviourist artist who admits nothing but his own glands."

Mather asks if it is audacious to assume that a "humanised art" can "make a man who is a friendly critic both of himself and of society in which he moves, a man who accepts the growing complexity of living as offering him fascinating and profitable problems of adjustment." Yes, but "we . . . have actually seen a few humanists made, have helped a little to make them perhaps; and we are dealing with spiritual values which transcend ordinary statistics. A few thousand genuine humanists in America would make our society humanistic; a hundred humanist painters, sculptors, architects, musicians, and men of letters would make our art solidly humanistic."[39]

We see, then, how a New Humanist conception of the arts as "civilizing" is connected to a belief in man's dual nature, and the need for restraints on excess. These restraints are individual, but also, in Humanist social theory, institutional. The arts function at the individual and social level as repositories for traditional values of wisdom and restraint. The few who know and understand these values must lead, and transform, a modern society at risk.

The New Humanists begin with a more Tocquevillian concern with how democracy can be protected from the dangers of despotism, anarchy, and barbarism. The modern risk, from the Humanist perspective, is unchecked, unrestrained democracy, based on a false faith in the natural goodness of man. A society based on such faith is at risk for anarchy or despotism; the barbarism of modern culture is evidence of how necessary humanistic values are to a truly civilized society.

COMPARING PERSPECTIVES

If we compare the renewal, revolution, and conservation perspectives on art in society, we find unexpected commonalities. Both the New Masses critics, and to a lesser degree the Young American critics, see art as a communal activity, demanding allegiances to other artists and to a particular social vision. Such a communal view is antithetical to the individualism of the New Humanists.

The unabashed elitism of the New Humanist position is tempered but not effaced in the Young American's beliefs that they will be the ones who create the culture that will lead to social renewal. The elitism of the New Masses position is complex—there is belief in a necessary alliance with the working class, but that alliance involves being able to "think for our time and for our people" (as claimed in "Culture and the Crisis").

The need for personal self-transformation is, interestingly, important in all three perspectives. The Young Americans believe that they should live and work in ways that enacted the culture they were hoping to create. The New Masses critics demand of themselves a discipline and purity that would allow them to create work that could serve the revolution. The New Humanists seek discipline and purity, in order to act, live, and think virtuously, in concert with higher standards.

The "machine age" is the enemy of the New Humanists, half of the equation for the Young Americans, and the future for the New Masses critics. But in spite of this variation in attitudes toward technology, there is agreement about another of the key aspects of modernity: for all these critics, mass culture is inadequate culture.

The predominance of new forms of mass entertainment figures into, but does not orient, the work of all three groups. During this period, movies, radio, records, comic books, paperbacks, and mass circulation magazines are permeating American life. The Young American critics see new mass forms as energetic, but not, unfortunately, the truly transformative democratic culture they yearn for. The New Masses critics dismiss commercial forms of culture as evidence of capitalism's hold on the middle classes, and as forms of propaganda that keep workers chained to their own oppression. The New Humanists see the media fare as further evidence of civilization's corruption.

But there is not, among these critics, a focused or thoughtful critique of mass communication, the media, modern entertainment, or mass culture.[40] These appear in the argument as asides, or as "obvious" examples of some larger point about the nature of modern life. A full-blown critique of mass culture does not develop until the 1950s, but its origins are partly in the critical turn taken in the 1940s by writers for the *Partisan Review*. We find in them, also, an ingenious way out of the critical dilemmas posed by the other three positions.

LEGACIES OF 1930s RADICALISM

It was much easier to believe in the inevitability of revolution, the virtues of the Communist Party, and the potential wonders of proletarian art in the early 1930s than it was by the late 1930s. By the end of the decade the revolution seemed to be ever-receding, the Communist Party self-serving, and proletarian art limited, even laughable. The fervent faith of various intellectuals wavered and in most cases foundered, as Stalinism and fascism loomed, and factions on the Left bickered endlessly among themselves.

The classic accounts of intellectuals' loss of faith in radical politics are the essays in *The God That Failed*.[41] In each case, the writer tells of the initial discovery of pattern, order, certainty, the joy of being part of a larger, noble cause, followed by a period of uncertainty, ending in disillusion and loss of faith in the Communist program.

Arthur Koestler describes "the mental rapture of the convert," when "the whole universe falls into pattern like the stray pieces of a jigsaw puzzle assembled by magic at one stroke. There is now an answer to every question, doubts and conflicts are a matter of the tortured past— a past already remote, when one had lived in dismal ignorance in the tasteless, colorless world of those who *don't know*"[42] (his emphasis).

Stephen Spender notes a common vice in people: "to regard their own cause and their own supporters as real, and all other causes and their exponents as abstract examples of outmoded theoretical positions,"[43] and argues that the Communist theory of society encourages this vice. The excitement of being a part of history, certain of how things work, and how it will all come out; the heady sense of being in the know when others are not, of being for the oppressed, against the oppressor— these are what drew converts, and what embarrassed the apostates.

These traits of true faith come, later, to be evidence of blindness and naivete at best, of conscious manipulation at worst. As Louis Fischer, a journalist who lived in the Soviet Union during the period, writes, "Hope distorted judgment. Seeing did not interfere with believing."[44]

Koestler calls faith in Communism "the great illusion of our time," and a "moral and intellectual debauch." In a memorable phrase, he says "We lost the fight because we were not fisherman, but bait dangling from a hook."[45] Those who were once captivated by Communism could either give themselves to some new, opposing addiction or pay with a "lifelong hangover."[46] An opposing addiction would be manifested by intense faith in some *other* closed system, and hatred for the one left behind, the hangover in a shift to less totalizing, less fervent, and less certain pronouncements.

Koestler's two options (between new addiction or hangover) were surely not the only ones available. But they offer us two poles between which to locate a post–1930s radical sensibility. Social criticism in the 1940s was at least partly a reaction against the fervent social commitment of the 1930s. Even for those intellectuals who did not actively ally with the Party, the discourse of the period presumed that artists could and should band together, to foster radical change through their work.

In the 1940s there were reactions against Communism as a doctrine, against fervent belief as a critical stance, and against collective action as necessary for artists and intellectuals. Yet even when challenging these key elements of 1930s thought, no one challenged the underlying faith in the power of art to change the social order: art remains a medicine, to be prescribed for the social good.

Many apostates developed a more personal and individual approach to social understanding, and the "abstraction" of Marxist social theory was critiqued. For Richard Wright, 1930s radicalism offered "an organized search for the truth of the lives of the oppressed and the isolated," but it was a search, he believed, that had not yet found a language. "In their efforts to recruit masses, they had missed the meaning of the lives of the masses, had conceived of people in too abstract a manner."[47] Wright goes on to realize, after a vicious excommunication, that "in all the sprawling immensity of our mighty continent the least known factor of living was the human heart, the least sought goal of being was a way to live a human life."

A call for a return to the particular, and the human, characterized many postconversion accounts. Fischer argues "all goals . . . are nothing in the abstract. They only have meaning in relation to the interests of living men, women and children, who are the means through which everything on earth is achieved."[48]

This attitude offers a very different agenda for arts and for criticism. Art and criticism cannot and should not demonstrate the virtues of the proletariat and the necessity of revolution. In fact, from this more individual and personal perspective, all totalizing theories, all sweeping explanations, all doctrine is suspect. It is a position that suggests that individual lives, individual actions, and individual perceptions of particular experiences are what count. It involves, then, a mistrust of those who are most certain, most sweeping, most doctrinaire. It is this new perspective, and this mistrust, that characterizes intellectuals in the 1940s, especially those who had been most captivated by the faith of the 1930s.

THE INTELLECTUAL AS SUBVERSIVE—*PARTISAN REVIEW* II

By the end of the 1930s, intellectuals had tried, and found wanting, a range of possible roles for themselves and for their work. The renewal perspective had not worked out—an energetic generation of writers and artists had not ushered in a vibrant, transformative, democratic culture.

New Humanist faith in certain overarching standards, based in the past, had a suspiciously totalitarian ring (although their sense of the arts as repositories of culture resonated as the cultural centers of Europe fell). The radical insistence on connecting art and politics had been repudiated.

So how could artists, critics, writers work for the social good? By the early 1940s, past efforts seemed to many to be unsuccessful (Young Americans), reactionary (New Humanists), and misguided (New Masses). One way out of the dilemma of past failures is to imagine a role for artists and critics that overcomes many of the perceived weaknesses, while maintaining the perceived strengths, of previous perspectives.

A new stance on the combined social role of arts and intellectuals should not presume a direct positive result. That was the weak point of the Young American and New Masses positions, because when history did not cooperate with their predictions, and neither a renaissance nor a revolution materialized, their perspectives were undermined. A less easily disproved effect for art on society could withstand the possibility of disproof by history.

A new stance on the social role of art and intellectuals should also avoid connection to organized doctrine, which would circumvent the perceived weaknesses of the New Humanist and New Masses perspectives. The authoritarian elements of both the radical and conservative approaches were now mistrusted. Was there a way to be radical, but not in thrall to any particular political program, a way to be conservative, without invoking narrow, absolute standards?

Finally, a new stance should be less demanding and distracting. It would not call for self-transformation or collective action. It should not expect artists and critics to organize and ally with nonintellectuals toward social change, since this had proven to be complicated, contentious, and unrewarding. A new stance should allow intellectuals ample time to do their intellectual work, without asking them to connect with nonintellectuals.

So an ideal new stance on arts and intellectuals in society would transcend the weaknesses but make use of the strengths of past perspectives, would allow individual freedom, promote critique without reference to absolutes, and require no social outcome. *The doctrine of art/criticism as subversion does all of this*. It is the ideal way to maintain faith in the power of artistic and intellectual practice to promote social good, while supporting all kinds of intellectual work.

A key aspect of the subversion perspective is that the artist/critic has a special consciousness, a particular gifted insight, and that the circulation of that consciousness will challenge the dominant culture. Good art, by its nature, is radical art, because good art is always in opposition to the status quo. And the status quo is known to be inadequate, oppressive, and deserving of subversion. The chronic critique of modernity (which characterized the previous three positions) is now wedded to a new subversive spirit. In this perspective art and artists have the power—even the duty—to challenge and disrupt modern life.

Notice how the subversion perspective is amenable to very different definitions of art. It offers the "empty set" definition we find in contemporary discourse—the category "art" can conveniently mean good stuff of any stripe. Art can be an inspiring, robust, invigorating force; it can also be a container of standards and virtue; it can also be a radical, destructive weapon. It can be all of these or something else—all that is certain is that, as art, it will be "challenging."

By this discursive logic, 1940s intellectuals could consider themselves a force against the dominant culture, and could count on being socially useful, no matter what they produced or what they believed, as long as it was nonmainstream, nondominant, non–status quo. They were doing "art" as long as they said so, and it was neither popular nor commercially successful.

Philip Rahv and William Phillips exemplify this new critical stance; their long editorship of the *Partisan Review* was a major means of its promulgation. Both were active supporters, in the early 1930s, of proletarian literature, and of the need for the intellectual to point the way toward a new, revolutionary art and criticism.[49] The *Partisan Review* of 1934–36 was a complement to the *New Masses*; the editors saw proletarian literature as "the visible edge of the future, a projection of the time when political revolution would dramatically sweep away archaic capitalist institutions and bourgeois culture."[50]

And yet, even in this first incarnation, editorials suggested some ambivalence about art as a mere vehicle for politically expedient beliefs, and suggested instead that literature had a role in reflecting the permanence of the past as well as the potentials of the new. As Gilbert argues persuasively, these ideas became the rationale, two years later, for rejecting proletarian literature, and for significantly reshaping the critical premises it engaged.

Another move away from the *New Masses* perspective was the argument that literary criticism was "a weapon of literature, not of politics."[51] It was seen as an activity by and for intellectuals, who were most influenced by literature. This removes art and criticism from direct engagement in social struggle—it keeps it as the property of an intellectual class, whose role involves defining and maintaining social values rather than defining or maintaining revolutionary activities.

Such a shift in the location and purpose of art and criticism did not go unnoticed by other radical intellectuals. Mike Gold accused the *Partisan Review* writers of a "terrible Mandarism."[52] Newton Arvin characterized their writing as "prosaically analytical." If criticism was for other intellectuals, not "the people," then it could take on the exclusionary characteristics so despised by those committed to proletarian art.

The *Partisan Review* folded for a year, and when it returned, it was solidly anti-Communist. Rahv and Phillips had moved from skepticism to a position of open opposition to Communism as a cultural and political force. The first editorial of the new *Partisan Review* announced that it would represent "a new and dissident generation in American letters."[53] The revolution had become literary rather than social.

This is confirmed most clearly by the importance placed on the role of the intellectual in social life. As Gilbert argues, "stripped of a dependence on a political movement, the artist, the intellectual, alone was the meeting place for radicalism in art and politics." The "site of struggle" was in the individual and in his or her work, to be written for, and read by, other intellectuals and artists. This gave the intellectual a new relation to politics and the social world: "The estrangement of the intellectual was the justification for his withdrawal from real politics, but it was also an explanation for his ability to rise above the mundane and reunite art and politics into the vision of a revolutionary culture."[54]

The "new generation" that the revived *Partisan Review* represented was a generation whose artistic and critical activity was automatically, in itself, radical. This is an avant-garde sensibility with roots in aesthetic modernism. It awards the artist a vital personal and social role—to remain pure in the face of social contamination, so that his or her art can challenge and undermine the supposedly suffocating influences of the age.

As Rahv argued in 1939, "the dissident artist, if he understands the extremity of the age and voices what it tries to stifle will thus be saved from its sterility and delivered from its corruption." Artistic expression becomes, thereby, personal salvation—a way to protect the self from the "sterility" and "corruption" of the age. By implication, those who are not dissident artists, who do not "voice what [the age] tries to stifle," become, or remain, sterile and corrupt.

Phillips and Rahv changed the focus of their concern from the relationship of intellectuals to the proletariat to the role of the intellectual in the modern age. They offer a discursive logic that presumes an intellectual's ability to rise above the mundane, free from that which limits, constrains, deadens, and numbs others. It is a position that anoints the critic and the artist as having abilities that are not widely shared. It offers, therefore, a reassuring sense of superiority to the times, and to the rest of society. It also offers a stunning (if indirect) disparagement of those who are not artists or intellectuals— they are, by implication, trapped, blinded, sterile, corrupt, as are their times.

SOCIAL CRITICS AND 'THE PEOPLE'

That artists and critics are specially gifted, and so can and should serve a special social function, is presumed in all four critical positions. A thorough analysis of the imagined social role of the intellectual in American thought would require another book. Here I simply note how faith in the instrumental power of art supports heroic assumptions about the social role of intellectuals. It also presumes that "the people" need the aesthetic and critical ministrations of intellectuals.

At stake in the debates among early twentieth-century American writers, critics, and artists was their appropriate social role—what should they be doing for the wider society? Underlying this question are a multitude of presumptions about what they *could* do for society— in dreams begin responsibility. We can imagine a circular continuum of possible social positions: from a Babbitt–More "guardian" of cultural values, to a Dell-described vagabond "onlooker," to a Bourne–Brooks "catalyst," to a Gold–Hicks "participant" to a Phillips–Rahv "subverter" who is also, at least in the abstract, a guardian, onlooker, and critic.

The "guardian" position presumes that cultural values are being challenged, effaced, diluted, corrupted. It is the role of the critic to point this out, by maintaining scrupulous attention to the standards available in "classic" culture. There is a conservative impulse in the guardian position, as well as an inherent respect for the cultural works of the past. The people are perceived as being swept up in emotionalism and greed as their barbarian traits are being catered to. The critic becomes a spokesman and bearer of besieged cultural values. It is through him and his fellows that the lamp of civilization is kept burning.

The "onlooker" has a less exalted role—he or she is more of a journalistic commentator, in but not of the society being watched. The people are being foolish and amusing, chasing after endlessly trivial delights that have little appeal for the spectator. This role has only modest responsibility for civilization—the onlooker can comment, critique, harangue. This is a social role of bemused disengagement.

The "catalyst" is more passionately connected to the society he or she is seeking to change. While sharing with the onlooker the desire to comment on the current scene, it is in connection with a more intense vision of what could and should be. The critic seeks the inchoate potential in the current situation, and through his work, tries to make it real. The people are unaware of the possibilities of their situation—with the critic's articulation, they can begin to imagine and work toward them.

The "participant" inserts himself into ongoing social activity, acting in and through his beliefs and values, in concert with others. He engages, if possible, with "the people," with the hope of building a better future. This position presumes that the intellectual has an obligation to ally himself with those less fortunate, and that their mutual alliance will lead to social change.

The "subversive" position, as we have noted, can comfortably include all these other positions. It assumes that any "good" artistic or critical work is challenging to the current situation and that the status quo automatically deserves undermining. As the critique of mass culture and mass society developed in the 1950s, the role of the intellectual became a more complex kind of guardianship—of an avant-garde as well as of a traditional sensibility, of anything that was alternative to the mainstream. The role of the intellectual was to know, see, and celebrate that which was increasingly unknown, unrecognized, and unappreciated in modern American life.

When we analyze various roles for American intellectuals, we find a surprising range of assumptions about "everyone else." For the guardian, the people are rude, uncivilized, undeveloped. It is only through the guardian, and the art he values, that those who want to can become more refined, civilized, worthy. This is a relatively straightforward form of superiority—with disciplined and rigorous aesthetic engagement, "the people" can become better.

For the onlooker, "the people" are a semipermanent exhibit, a tourist attraction. They are not assumed to be particularly barbaric, or misguided, or even in need of the ministrations of the critic. They are zoo animals doing things that can amuse, irritate, or surprise the onlooker. The onlooker leads a very different life, one that he believes is far more intelligent, interesting, rich and meaningful. But the onlooker has neither pity for, nor obligation toward, his fellows—just bemused disdain.

For the catalyst, the sense of obligation is much stronger—other people are in need of, and are searching for, the insights he can offer. This position assumes that the critic is a more articulate and sensitive version of everyday people, and so he has an obligation to express his pain, and his understandings, in ways that can benefit the less articulate versions of himself. He can know and see what others might only guess and glimpse. The people will recognize their own situation through his work, and will be galvanized into action.

The participant, if he has doctrinal alliances, will already know what needs to be done—his role is to get others to see and understand as he does. His job is to connect his deeper understanding with others' lived experiences. His is a difficult position of having better understanding but worse credentials—his goal is to bridge the perceived gap between himself and those he seeks to speak for.

The subverter believes that the people are hopelessly mired in a repugnant society—evidence of their oppression is their apparent (and baffling) contentment with the situation. The subverter's task is to offer a challenge to the times. Unlike the multitudes, he understands and appreciates the best works of the past, present, and future. Unlike them, he can keep the lamp of civilization burning, and/or comment with amusement on the antics of the common man, and/or articulate an alternative world that would be better for himself as well as them. But he feels no obligation to connect or ally with "them"—the subverter works for social change through maintaining connections to other intellectuals, and doing intellectual things.

These positions represent carefully developed, if often implicit, beliefs about people's abilities, needs, and relationship to intellectuals. I want us to be wary of the consequences of these positions, positions which proceed from (and are dependent on) an unquestioned faith in art's instrumental power.

CONCLUSION

In the early twentieth century, an American intellectual class was defined and celebrated, one that assigned particular roles to artists and social critics. The connections to academic life were present but not predominant. What most characterized this group was a Spingarnian loyalty to the presumption that "genius and taste are one," that to do "art" and to do "criticism" were both creative acts with social power. Intellectuals became a self-identified class that could include artists, critics, commentators, professors, all the "brain workers" who thought of themselves as up to something aesthetically oriented.

The "something" they were up to was often connected to a more systematic approach, as represented by Freud or Marx. In this way, the intellectual could claim special knowledge, since he or she was familiar with what supposedly underlies individual behavior or history. We can see how the presumption of deeper and more scientific understanding might be synergistic with a presumption of a deeper and more aesthetic sensitivity, and contribute to an overweening sense of the intellectual's special capacities.

Through faith in the truth of certain theoretical positions, the intellectual presumes that those who know the theory know more about how the world really works. Those who don't know or understand Freud or Marx are in the dark, unable to understand that which is obvious to those who have the necessary theoretical sophistication. Similarly, those who don't "know" certain books or music or paintings are in the dark. The ability to know deeply, to see clearly, to feel fully— these are traits that intellectuals are presumed to have, and others are presumed to lack. Criticism becomes a way for the socially committed to help others know, see, feel with the depth, clarity, and fullness that intellectuals claim for themselves.

The first thirty years of this century were marked by tremendous faith in the likelihood of major social transformations, and so writers, critics, artists focused on a central question: What is our role in the changing society? In doing so, they relied on an unquestioned belief in the instrumental power of art. This faith allowed them to imagine themselves as having special social powers and obligations, and they spent decades arguing about just what kind of work was most valuable, and what kinds of connections to the world were most appropriate. Left unaddressed was the possibility that art was *not* socially potent, and that intellectuals might not be the ones best able to change the world.

NOTES

1. This "subversive" view continues to be mobilized in current claims that scholarly criticism, circulating in learned journals and operating to secure institutional positions, is a form of political intervention. A critique of the consequences of this in contemporary media studies is in Joli Jensen and John J. Pauly, "Imagining the Audience: Losses and Gains in Cultural Studies," in *Cultural Studies in Question*, ed. Marjorie Ferguson and Peter Golding (London: Sage, 1997), 155–69.

2. This Philistine/Puritan dichotomy is effectively located in particular biographies of Young American critics by Casey Nelson Blake, *Beloved Community: The Cultural Criticism of Randolph Bourne, Van Wyck Brooks, Waldo Frank & Lewis Mumford* (Chapel Hill: University of North Carolina Press, 1990). His discussion is an excellent introduction to the group and period, and offers an insightful discussion of the weaknesses and potential of their critical perspectives.

3. Van Wyck Brooks, *Wine of Puritans: A Study of Present-Day America* (New York: B. W. Huebsch, 1924; originally published in 1915). Note Brooks's critique of counterbalancing dichotomies, as opposed to early Mumford, who later adopted them.

4. Randolph Bourne, "Trans-national America," in *The Radical Will: Randolph Bourne Selected Writings, 1911–1918*, ed. Olaf Hanson (New York: Urizen Books, 1977), 248–64.

5. Van Wyck Brooks, "Young America," *Seven Arts* 1, December 1915, 144–51.

6. Waldo Frank, *Our America* (New York: Boni & Liveright, 1919).

7. Frank, *Our America*, 231–32.

8. His account is also a good illustration of how Freud, Marx, and H. G. Wells figured in the heady brew of early twentieth-century thought. See Floyd Dell, *Intellectual Vagabondage: An Apology for the Intelligentsia* (New York: George H. Doran, 1926).

9. Dell, *Intellectual Vagabondage*, 176.

10. Dell, *Intellectual Vagabondage*, 214.

11. Dell, *Intellectual Vagabondage*, 227.

12. Dell, *Intellectual Vagabondage*, 247.

13. Dell, *Intellectual Vagabondage*, 248.

14. Dell, *Intellectual Vagabondage*, 249.

15. Dell, *Intellectual Vagabondage*, 258.

16. Dell, *Intellectual Vagabondage*, 259.

17. Dell, *Intellectual Vagabondage*, 260.

18. Dell, *Intellectual Vagabondage*, 261.

19. See the analysis in Granville Hicks, *The Great Tradition: An Interpretation of American Literature since the Civil War* (New York: Macmillan, 1935).

20. Hicks, *The Great Tradition*, 249.

21. Hicks, *The Great Tradition*, 25.

22. University of Tulsa Special Collections (New York: 1932); also quoted in Gerald Rabkin, *Drama and Commitment: Politics in the American Theatre of the Thirties* (Bloomington: Indiana University Press, 1964), 22.

23. This address becomes Earl Browder, "The Writer and Politics," in *The Writer in a Changing World,* ed. Henry Hart (Equinox Cooperative Press, 1937), 48–55.

24. Browder, "The Writer," 54.

25. This exchange is well worth reading in its entirety for the insight it offers into the 1930s concern with correct political thought. It can be found in Joseph North, ed., *New Masses: An Anthology of the Rebel Thirties* (New York: International Publishers, 1969).

26. Mike Gold, "Proletarian Realism," *New Masses* 7, September 1930; quoted in Daniel Aaron, *Writers on the Left* (New York: Avon Books, 1965), 225–26. The Aaron book is an essential introduction and overview to the thought and work of radical writers of the period.

27. Biographical information on Lawson is drawn from Rabkin, *Drama and Commitment*, ch. 6.

28. North, ed., *New Masses*, 223–24.

29. Eastman cuts a jaunty path through the period—see Max Eastman, *Artists in Uniform: A Study of Literature and Bureaucratism,* and *Art and the Life of Action, with Other Essays* (New York: Alfred A. Knopf, 1934).

30. Eastman, *Artists in Uniform*, 27–28.

31. Norman Foerster, ed., *Humanism and America: Essays on the Outlook of Modern Civilization* (Port Washington, N.Y.: Kennikat Press, 1967; originally published in 1930).

32. Foerster, *Humanism and America*, v–vi.

33. This debate can be found in Irving Babbitt, *Criticism in America: Its Function and Status* (New York: Haskell House, 1969; originally published in 1924). The two essays are J. E. Spingarn, "The New Criticism," first published by Columbia University Press, 1910; and Irving Babbitt, "Genius and Taste," originally published in *The Nation,* 7 February 1918.

34. Babbitt, *Criticism in America*, 156.

35. There is an especially good discussion of this view in *The New Humanism: A Critique of Modern America 1900–1940,* ed. J. David Hoeveler Jr. (Charlottesville: University of Virginia Press, 1977), 34–37. This book offers an original and insightful analysis of the Humanist perspective that greatly informs my analysis here.

36. Babbitt, *Criticism in America*, 164.

37. Paul Elmer More, *Aristocracy and Justice* (New York: Phaeton, 1967; originally published 1915).

38. Frank Jewett Mather Jr., "The Plight of Our Arts," in *Humanism and America,* ed. Foerster, 116–26.

39. Mather, "The Plight of Our Arts," 115–16.

40. Gilbert Seldes offers a noteworthy counterexample. Seldes was a wise and prescient commentator on the nature and value of early twentieth-century popular media forms; my thanks to Art Kaul for reminding me of this. For how Seldes thinks differently about these things, see Michael Kammen, *The Lively Arts: Gilbert Seldes and the Transformation of Cultural Criticism in the US* (New York: Oxford University Press, 1996).

41. Richard Crossman, ed., *The God That Failed* (New York: Harper & Brothers, 1949), including essays by Arthur Koestler, Ignazio Silone, Richard Wright, Andre Gide, Louis Fischer, and Stephen Spender.

42. Koestler, in *The God That Failed*, 23.

43. Spender, in *The God That Failed*, 254.

44. Fischer, in *The God That Failed*, 211.

45. Koestler, in *The God That Failed*, 44.

46. Koestler, in *The God That Failed*, 55.

47. Wright, in *The God That Failed*, 120.

48. Fischer, in *The God That Failed*, 228.

49. James Burkhardt Gilbert, *Writers and Partisans: A History of Literary Radicalism in America* (New York: John Wiley and Sons, 1960), offers a thoughtful and suggestive account of the *Partisan Review* group.

50. Gilbert, *Writers and Partisans*, 121.

51. Gilbert, *Writers and Partisans*, 136.

52. Quoted in Gilbert, *Writers and Partisans*, 143.

53. Gilbert, *Writers and Partisans*, 159.

54. Gilbert, *Writers and Partisans*, 185–86.

Chapter Three

Art as Antidote:
The Mass Culture Debates

Today's popular commentary on media and the arts still depends on distinctions developed during the mass culture debates of the 1950s. These debates were the first sustained attempt by intellectuals to analyze the social consequences of a flourishing mass media. Film, radio, comic books, records, and television had combined to form what Adorno and Horkheimer described as a "Culture Industry."[1] The mass culture debates were about what this new culture industry meant, for America, for democracy, and most of all, for the fate of high culture.

The premise of the debates is that the mass media, in a mass society, are bringing into existence a mass culture. In a mass culture, true art is drowned out, contaminated, or turned into something else. As with Whitman nearly a century before, 1950s intellectuals saw the real being threatened by the fake, valuable and worthy cultural forms and habits being swamped by "gaud and fraud." What was most frightening is that the audience didn't even seem to care—ersatz middlebrow art was being welcomed as the real thing. Intellectuals felt surrounded by people apparently unable to tell the difference between serious art and entertainment, or to understand why they must remain distinct.

At first glance, the mass culture debates may seem a naïve and dated parlor exercise in describing cultural capital. Some of its central essays spend an inordinate amount of intellectual energy distinguishing highbrow, middlebrow, or lowbrow, much like today's list of "what's hot and what's not." But there is much more to the debaters' need to label, and distinguish, different kinds of cultural forms. The mass culture debates are struggling to address the consequences of cultural commercialization.[2] In doing so, they are raising concerns that still trouble us, especially in relation to cultural globalization.

What mattered to the debaters was not the content of the categories, but the importance of maintaining distinctions *between* categories. Beneath the endless debate about cultural levels are much more difficult (and interesting) questions about cultural quality—how to distinguish between good culture and bad. Connected to notions of good and bad culture are concerns about cultural traditions, cultural autonomy, and cultural virtues—still vital questions in today's cultural politics.

Concern with authenticity and commercialization explains the mass culture debate's insistence on distinctions between different forms as well as levels of culture—distinguishing high art from folk art, from popular art, from mass art. High and folk and (in some accounts) popular art have their own "authenticity," and are therefore valuable, and to be protected. In contrast, mass art is commercial and therefore perceived to be dangerous. What seemed vital, then and now, is the ability to distinguish the worthy, and protect it from being displaced or polluted by unworthy forms.

In the terms of the mass culture debate, there were many threats to true art's survival. First, the artist can be seduced by the commercial marketplace—"sell out" and produce tripe. In addition, the audience can become seduced by the ersatz formulations of the commercial marketplace, coming to seek and accept tripe as art. And finally, true art forms can simply be overwhelmed, crowded out, drowned out, by the perceived onslaught of false art forms.

In the 1950s mass culture debates (and in the 1990s NEA debates, as we shall see) something called "art" meant the good, true, and worthy, and it was always perceived to be under siege. The goal of the debates was to discern how "good culture" (seemingly so threatened by mass society, mass media, mass culture) could be preserved, and flourish. Yet because instrumental rather than expressive assumptions about the arts prevailed, the results were a set of pernicious notions that continue to haunt us. Among these notions are simplistic definitions of "good" culture; ownership of high culture by intellectuals; patronizing assumptions about the mass audience; and unquestioned belief in media toxicity.

INTELLECTUALS AND THE PEOPLE

Separating social criticism from academic life was a presumed necessity for cultural renewal in the 1920s and 1930s. In the 1940s there was a shift toward university affiliation by social critics and intellectuals, and by the 1950s "separation" arguments were essentially over—criticism was a form of art and art was a form of criticism, and both were increasingly connected to academic intellectual life.

There are profoundly undemocratic consequences in equating art and criticism, and in assuming that both are academic intellectual enterprises. If criticism is art, and art and criticism are socially powerful, and intellectuals are the people who do art/criticism, then intellectuals (now mostly located in universities) "own" the arts; the arts are their responsibility. What is most unsavory in this formulation is that it ends up defining nonacademics as nonintellectuals who live, inadequately, in a nonaesthetic and noncritical realm.

The definition of intellectuals as a particular social group whose special charge is aesthetic and critical activity too easily becomes a presumption that other people are not engaged in (or capable of) aesthetic or critical work. Once intellectuals are in charge of the arts, and the arts are deemed to be socially powerful, then intellectuals are in a complex relationship to nonacademic people. The democratic public is imagined as an undifferentiated mass, all of whom lack the critical and appreciative capacities needed to understand art or criticize society. This formulation supports, finally, the specter of the mass audience—crude, dull, easily fooled—that haunts the mass culture debate.

From the point of view of the 1950s intellectual, true art is not merely at risk—it is under siege. In spite of the obvious unworthiness of mass culture, it is ever more widespread and influential. In spite of the obvious worthiness of "highbrow" culture, it is commercially unsuccessful, therefore at risk of disappearing altogether. When confronted by the popularity and financial success of media fare, intellectuals struggle (then and now) with the mystery of why "the people" persist in buying, and apparently liking, trash.

The structuring absence in the mass culture debates (as in earlier discussions) is the problem of "the people." How can the American people (seemingly eagerly!) choose and enjoy unworthy material? Several possible explanations emerge in the debates: some people are innately less critical and less aesthetically sensitive; people have been prevented from developing the necessary critical or aesthetic skills; people have been brutalized and transformed by exposure to bad art. The possibility that media fare may actually offer something of value is never considered.

The mass media plunge 1950s intellectuals into the conceptual bind we found in Whitman—democracy relies on the people, yet the people are enjoying repugnant cultural forms, and acting in repugnant ways. Under these conditions, how can the critic keep faith in democracy? To presume that the people are *inherently* repugnant is much less comfortable than assuming that the people are either being deprived of good art or have already been corrupted by bad art, and are therefore redeemable with healthy doses of good art. These more palatable assumptions require an instrumental view of the arts—unquestioned faith in the power of good art to ennoble and uplift (if it only were available), and bad art to brutalize and degrade (since people's tastes are obviously so bad).

The alarmist tone of the debate is because all the participants assume that the dominance of bad art threatens the survival of good art, and that for some reason intellectuals are the only ones who notice or care. They alone recognize how at risk the mass audience is. As the so-called mass audience cheerfully engages in obnoxious media fare, 1950s intellectuals feel forced to respond. Discussions of the consequences of mass culture for "the people" end, almost always, in calls for intellectuals to find ways to look after—protect and defend—"their" culture, the arts.

The divergent perspectives of the 1920s, 1930s, and 1940s on art-in-society consolidated, in the 1950s, in the identification of a particular class—intellectuals—and the association of that class with a particular intellectual activity—criticism. This makes the arts the property of the class deemed best able to evaluate and discuss them, and makes the intellectual responsible, in a variety of ways, for the powers of the arts. In this way, intellectuals can believe themselves to be the only group of people that can recognize, articulate, defend, and nurture the socially potent powers of the arts. This heritage has made things particularly difficult for today's arts supporters, who continue to seek ways to justify the social role of the arts in nonelitist, nonintellectual, nonacademic terms.

The 1950s debates incorporate both Whitmanesque rhetorics of redemption and Mumfordian rhetorics of counterbalance. The arts can supposedly save us *and* they can counteract the supposedly pernicious effects of the mass media. Since American culture is seen as increasingly anti-intellectual, anti-critical, and anti-aesthetic, the artist/critic must find some way to survive in this new mass-mediated environment, while finding a way to mitigate against the presumed powers of the media for social harm. The arts must be protected so that they can counteract the harm being done by the mass media.

OUR COUNTRY AND OUR CULTURE

The presumption that intellectuals must protect and defend good culture in an era where bad culture is coming to triumph informs the array of comments gathered in a 1952 *Partisan Review* forum called "Our Country and Our Culture."[3] This forum contains all of the emerging characteristics of the debate, including how art and intellectuals were both believed to be under siege in a new mass culture.

The premise of the *Partisan Review* editors is that there has been a dramatic post–World War II change in the attitude of writers and intellectuals toward America. Intellectuals have moved from a position of American rejection to a position of conditional acceptance: "More and more writers have ceased to think of themselves as rebels and exiles. They now believe that their values, if they are to be realized at all, must be realized in America, and in relation to the actuality of American life."[4]

But this "affirmation," the editors warn, must be equivocal. In addition to the remaining faults in economic and political institutions, mass culture offers "a tremendous obstacle." It leaves the artist and intellectual feeling like an outsider; in fact "its increasing power is one of the chief causes of the spiritual and economic insecurity of the intellectual minority."[5]

After this caveat, the editors quote Ortega y Gassett, invoking "the mass" that crushes everything that is different, excellent, individual, qualified, and select. Mass culture, they continue, has serious cultural consequences—it weakens the artist and intellectual by "separating him from his natural audience." Further, it "removes the mass of people from the kinds of art which might express their human and aesthetic needs." This mass culture excludes whatever does not conform to popular norms, and it "creates and satisfies artificial appetites in the entire populace." It has grown into "a major industry which converts [true] culture into a commodity." "Its overshadowing presence cannot be disregarded in any evaluation of any future of American art and thought."

Note the animating assumptions here—that there is a "natural" audience for art that is being lost to "artificial" appetites being created by
the mass media, and that the media (unlike the art world) transform
culture into a product. An "entire populace" is at risk. In this version,
as in earlier versions of counterbalancing rhetoric, art is natural, media artificial.

The questions that the editors put to the twenty-five contributors to
the symposium were drawn from this perspective.[6] The first question:
Has the attitude of intellectuals changed? was an invitation to sketch
histories of attitudes toward America and Europe. The second was a
question of orientation: Must the American intellectual and writer
"adapt himself" to mass culture? This is followed by a question that
returns, explicitly, to Tocqueville: Does "a democratic society necessarily lead to a leveling of culture, to a mass culture which will overrun intellectual and aesthetic values traditional to Western civilization?" The last two questions were: Where can intellectuals look for
"strength, renewal, and recognition" now that Europe isn't a viable
cultural example? and, Can a tradition of "critical non-conformism"
be maintained?

Not surprisingly, most of the contributors begin by taking issue
with some aspect of the questions. Norman Mailer, for example, is in
total disagreement with the assumptions of the symposium, and insists that the writer always works best in opposition to society, even
when he "loses the sharp sense of what he is alienated from."[7] But
most contributors use the questions to address some aspect of the intellectual's relationship to America, the nature of mass culture, and the
appropriate role of writers, artists, and critics in contemporary (1950s)
American life.

Lionel Trilling eloquently restates the *Partisan Review* premise that intellectuals were becoming more affirmative of America, writing that "an
avowed aloofness from national feeling is no longer the first ceremonial
step into the life of thought."[8] The world has changed, and "America is
not to be conceived a priori the vulgarest and stupidest nation in the
world," Arthur Schlesinger Jr. argues: "The depression was the first im-
petus to a revaluation of America. Then the rise of fascism abroad thrust
the problem of American culture into a new dimension. Next to Himm-
ler, even Babbitt began to look good. For all its faults, the United States
was an open society, unfinished, with a plenitude of possibilities, while
fascism meant the death of culture."[9]

Sidney Hook notes that American intellectuals "are limited in their effective historical choice between endorsing a system of total terror and *critically* [his emphasis] supporting our own imperfect democratic culture with all its promises and dangers."[10] This becomes the context for most of the contributors to the *PR* symposium—their concerns are with the dangers of the imperfect democratic culture, even as they support it against the alternatives they see in the postwar world.

The editorial introduction warns against unequivocal affirmation of America *because* of mass culture. In his individual contribution William Phillips suggests that there has been an "overadjustment to reality," that intellectuals are discovering "the blessings of the most philistine aspects of our political and cultural life."[11] As William Barrett puts it: "The trouble is that these periodic movements of the Zeitgeist always go too far, and the first thing we know the intellectuals, in the course of whipping up their enthusiasm for America, begin to show some of the appalling traits of conformism which *Time* magazine discovered recently in the undergraduates of the nation."[12]

Barrett characterizes the American psychology as dominated by "speed, facts, know-how, our positivism, our extravert [sic] and technological mentality." This leads to the dominance of the "mass art par excellence," what he calls "streamlined mass journalism." He argues that journalism "takes over everything, novels, plays, movies (which become increasingly more topical), and eventually everybody's mind." The result is more knowledge, but it is superficial knowledge that becomes a "deafening roar" that drowns out "the quiet wisdom of the sage."[13]

This vision of vast contemporary hubbub of mass culture that engulfs the quiet and good is shared by other commentators. Jacques Barzun describes the "whirring machinery" of commercial imperatives that immediately sucks in the artist who finds popularity.[14] C. Wright Mills, quoting Hans Gerth, describes how mass culture penetrates one's inner life and fantasies;[15] Philip Rahv suggests that mass culture's success depends on its ability to "cultivate a kind of strategic unawareness of meaning and consequence."[16] The noisy, boisterous, new mass culture obliterates the quiet, contemplative, and imaginative possibilities of true art. The quiet and natural is being overrun by the noisy and artificial.

Contributors struggle over the appropriate relationship between the intellectual and mass culture. The "guardian" position is argued by some: Rahv claims that it has been the business of the avant-garde, since the early nineteenth century, to "preserve the integrity of art and the intellect amidst the conditions of alienation brought on by the major social forces of the modern era."[17] Preserving the integrity of art, Irving Howe argues, involves recognizing how kitsch, "the mass culture of middlebrows" is "smothering" art. "There is culture-hunger, culture-talk, culture-guilt, most of it dry, dead and dutifully obedient to each twist of the Zeitgeist. The vast culture industries are parasites on the body of art, letting it neither live nor die."[18]

If art is to be preserved from hubbub, smothering, and parasitic enervation, then intellectuals must act in particular ways. Delmore Schwartz puts it directly: "It is obvious enough that the intellectual is necessary to sustain the traditional forms of culture amid the rank and overpowering growth of mass culture."[19] Since we can't stop "the ruthless expansion of mass-culture," Rahv argues, "the least we can do is to keep apart and refuse its favors."[20]

Others argue for intellectuals as participatory representatives of more worthy forms. James Burnham suggests that intellectuals continue to serve what he calls "their traditional role"—to "apply the spiritual tools of traditional Western civilization to the finishing and refining" of the raw materials of modern life.[21] Newton Arvin argues for an even more directive engagement with mass culture; he argues for a conscious attempt by intellectuals to "master and fertilize" mass culture.

Louis Kronenberger offers the most direct statement about appropriate intellectual engagement with mass culture: "The real problem is to avoid contamination without avoiding contact. For if American intellectuals are to be of use, they must—without adapting themselves to mass culture—yet associate themselves with American life."[22]

In the end, the symposium became a collection of suggestions on how intellectuals could associate with American life without celebrating the mass culture that all agreed was deplorable. "America is a nation where at the same time cultural freedom is promised and mass culture produced,"[23] the introduction states; the implicit, endlessly troubling question is why American culture is "squandering" its cultural freedom by turning out trash?

CULTURE FOR THE MILLIONS?

The mass culture debates result in a disturbingly precious and narrow definition of the arts. To critique the media, 1950s intellectuals deploy definitions of art that had been dismissed as elitist and outmoded by earlier generations. In dreaming of a new democratic art, Whitman had ridiculed traditional, exalted, genteel art. Similarly, the Young American critics distanced themselves from notions of the arts as canonical, refined, or sublime. The 1930s Marxists imagined a powerful, robust proletarian art and assumed that the avant-garde was designed to question the sacred tradition of museumized art. Yet, in the mass culture debates, "art" becomes a virtuous "empty set" that contains all that is nonmedia. This wonderful "art" is simultaneously traditional and avant-garde, conservative and subversive, but it is mostly instrumental high culture—a way to uplift and refine the people. By demonizing the media, the mass culture debate defines a simplistic alternative: unproblematic highbrow art counteracting problematic middle and low mass culture.

The mass culture debate also deploys an odd (but still current) calculus to consider what happens with American popular culture. It answers yes to the question that haunted Tocqueville's contemporaries—does democracy bring with it an inevitable "lowering" of standards?[24] In the mass culture debates, it is assumed that, as culture becomes more various and inclusive, it becomes somehow *diluted*, less able to do what it needs to do. This vaguely liquid argument is intertwined with a mathematical one, the assumption that commercially based material succeeds because it appeals to the "lowest common denominator."

On examination all these claims are problematic—how exactly does culture get high and low, thick and thin? And just what *is* this lowest common denominator—this barbaric component—to which the media supposedly cater? Do our "lower" natures prevent us from appreciating the arts? Is this lowest common denominator some anti-art fraction in ourselves that we must extirpate? Assumptions (articulated by intellectuals in the 1950s) that culture comes in high and low categories, in thick and thin versions, and appeals to various higher and lower common elements in us, continue to inform discussions in college classrooms.[25]

Concern that cultural dilution and decline are necessary components of a democratic society is complicated by definitions that conflate democratic society with commercial, industrial, capitalist, mass-mediated society. The mass culture debate offers an elaborate reframing of faith in "the people"—cultural decline is occurring *not* because the now-included people are inevitably barbarians, but because some aspect of commercial, industrial, mass-mediated society has made them into, or kept them from changing from, barbarians. By this logic, democracy is still worthy, the people can still be admired, and cultural freedom can still be supported, but only if we find some way to mitigate the evils of commercial, industrial, mass-mediated modernity.

In this formulation, art becomes the vital vehicle of mitigation. In much the same way that Mumford imagined art as a counterbalance to technics, the participants in a 1959 symposium sponsored by *Daedalus*[26] imagined true art as a valuable resource offering an alternative to the dominant order. Art was a resource and alternative from which the mass audience was being unfairly excluded. What began in the 1952 *Partisan Review* as attempts to assess the impact of the mass media on various forms of culture became in the 1959 symposium a requiem for, and repudiation of, the public as audience.

The *Daedalus* symposium drew on figures in academe, criticism, and the arts, with Frank Stanton, then head of CBS, as the lone media representative. In his introduction to *Culture for the Millions?* the edited collection of essays presented at the symposium, Paul Lazarsfeld notes the presence of "professional historians of prominence" like Oscar Handlin, Arthur Schlesinger Jr., and Stuart Hughes; philosophers Ernest Nagel, Charles Frankel, and Sidney Hook; "social scientists who are professionally concerned with the analysis of the social scene" such as Edward Shils, Ernest van den Haag, and Hannah Arendt; and artists—poet Randall Jarrell, novelist James Baldwin, composer Arthur Berger.

Lazarsfeld defines the symposium's topic as the consequences of a new mass society, with special attention to two questions: What happens *to* highbrow culture in mass society? And What does the great increase in middlebrow culture *do* to people? (his emphasis)[27] Lazarsfeld defines true art as both traditional and new, both "enduring works of art and the contemporary efforts of avant-gardists who deserve respect because of the seriousness of their intentions." For him, middlebrow is the "average movie, the family magazine, the respectable television program"; and lowbrow "such things as comics, detective stories and vaudeville."[28]

Again, this construction of levels was more than just a parlor game about "brows." It was about believing that there are distinctions among these levels that need to be maintained. While participants in these and other symposia and collections[29] often offer their own personal versions of what goes into each category and why, there is general agreement that there are three levels of culture—high, middle, low—and that they are distinguished by decreasing levels of sophistication, seriousness, complexity, subtlety—and, *as if naturally*—social value.

Edward Shils makes the case, in his keynote address, for a historically varying "cultural dissensus," with differing amounts of superior, mediocre, and brutal culture available in any given historical period. What he terms "superior or refined" culture is always serious, shows acute penetration, and is coherent in its perceptions; it has subtlety and a "wealth" of expressed feelings. He insists that "it goes without saying" that superior culture refers to the truth and beauty of the work, not the social status of its creators or consumers.

In Shils's account, mediocre culture simply does not measure up to superior culture—it is less original, more reproductive, and creates novel genres like the musical comedy that are "not yet fully incorporated into superior culture." Brutal culture shows a "grossness of sensitivity and perception," lacks depth and subtlety, involves games and spectacles as well as the genres of the other levels. It expresses action more directly, with "minimal symbolic content."

Each level calls for different "cognitive, moral and appreciative capacities" in its audience. Shils argues that people inherently differ in their cognitive capacities, which is why, throughout history, there have been these three different levels of culture. This dramatically hierarchical argument is combined with a more Tocquevillian claim about mass society incorporating more people into society, and allowing a wider dispersion of civility. Surprisingly (and in ways virtually ignored by later commentators and discussants), Shils suggests that mass society offers more people the opportunity to experience an "efflorescence of sensation and sensibility." Yes, a part of the population still "lives in a nearly vegetative torpor,"[30] but mass society offers the possibility of learning to value "the pleasures of eye, ear, taste, touch, and conviviality."

Other commentators ignored Shils's Tocquevillian assumptions about civility and Deweyan interests in efflorescing sensibilities. Instead, they deployed the same high-middle-low categories and elaborated on the conviction that people vary, through either nature or culture, in their capacities to appreciate the truth and beauty found in high culture. Shils's argument that mass society liberates sensual and empathic capacities disappeared, as commentator after commentator developed the differences between genuine and spurious art, and bemoaned the "vegetative torpor" of the mass audience.

RECOGNIZING GENUINE ART

One of the most interesting elements in the debates of the 1950s (and later of the 1990s) is the importance of the desire for "natural" or "uncontaminated" art. "Natural" art emerges for artistic rather than commercial reasons. It is created, shared, appreciated for its own sake, without reference to popularity, or the market, or the desires of an audience. Uncontaminated art is art that has remained distinct and separate from other, lesser forms—it is *never* merely entertainment. High art is always presumed to be both natural and uncontaminated.

Naturalness, genuineness, purity are all connected to the problem of authenticity, which is a primary theme in criticism of modernity (and now postmodernity).[31] Whether a cultural form or an activity is "authentic" is not problematic until there is the possibility of inauthentic art or action. Once technology allows reproductions, imitations, and fakes, the original and genuine become important.[32] Once urban life allows estrangement and so duplicity, once everyday experience includes elaborate created encounters, once "the natural" becomes demarcated as special and at risk, then authenticity matters even more.[33]

Authenticity takes on special resonance in relation to the arts because there is a presumed connection between the authenticity of the object and the authenticity of the experience it engenders. True art yields true experience. False art yields false experience. In the mass culture debates, it is taken for granted that middle and low levels of culture offered cruder and more degraded forms of experience. Mass culture cheats the mass audience because, in the logic of the debates, they are being blocked from experiencing the truth and beauty offered by genuine art.

Linking art to experience is the defining feature of the expressive view that I am arguing for. Yet it is dangerous to assume, as mass culture debaters do, that certain kinds of culture *automatically* result in certain kinds of experiences. In the mass culture debates, there is no attempt to explore the experience people have with forms of culture, no matter what their supposed level. It is simply assumed that genuine art contains and offers genuine experience, while "unnatural" and "impure" media forms do not. In this way, their arguments remain instrumental, even as they attempt to address aesthetic experience in their arguments.

In the mass culture debate, the contrast between true art and mass art is almost always glossed as a contrast between art and entertainment. Art is serious, while entertainment is fun. The experience of art is mental, difficult, and valuable; the experience of entertainment is emotional, easy, and not worth much. The mass culture debates define art as being utterly different from entertainment in both its nature and its influence.

Hannah Arendt's contribution to the *Daedalus* symposium does this quite thoughtfully. Arendt distinguishes art from entertainment by arguing that art is a phenomenon of the world, and entertainment a phenomenon of life. Art can transcend time and space, it can "continue to grasp and move the reader or spectator, across the centuries."[34] Entertainment, on the other hand, is designed to be used up, to be consumed; it is a metabolic contribution to daily experience.

In Arendt's formulation, true art can also be used for social purposes. Genuine works of art can function as "social coinage," as commodities used to give status to patrons. While such usage degrades art, it does not destroy it. Art's destruction, she believes, comes when art is turned into entertainment: "There are many great authors of the past who have survived centuries of oblivion and neglect, but it is still an open question whether they will be able to survive an entertaining version of what they have to say."[35]

Arendt insists on the maintenance of a distinction between art and entertainment; the very survival of art depends on it. The mass media, with their voracious need for content, are "ransacking the past" for art objects to popularize, and are permanently destroying true art. She paints a frightening picture of a world that has used up art by making it entertaining. Hers is the most apocalyptic account of the permanent consequences of art's contamination through popularization.

Other contributors made more familiar claims about the differences between art and entertainment. The comparison is between work and play, and between what is believed to be true of intellectual activity, in comparison with other forms of allegedly less strenuous forms of cognition. Most presume, with Shils, that art is serious, subtle, complex, while entertainment is light, broad, simple. They also assume that true art deals with weighty, substantive matters, placing mental demands on the audience, while entertainment is light, easy, and emotionally seductive in its effects.

Once again art and intellect are conjoined, in relation to beliefs about the differences among cultural levels, and the differences between art and entertainment. Cultural levels mirror cognitive levels: the higher the level, the more cognitive effort is required. True art is presumed to involve difficult and strenuous mental activity; entertainment is presumed to be more visceral, as well as easy and effortless. Art is complex and inaccessible; entertainment is easy and accessible. Art requires intellect; entertainment does not.

Entertainment then becomes the antithesis of intellectual activity. Stanley Edgar Hyman assumes that the foremost danger of mass culture is its "overpowering narcotic effect, relaxing the tired mind and tranquilizing the anxious."[36] "Genuine art is demanding and difficult, often unpleasant, nagging at the mind and stretching the nerves taut. So much of mass culture envelops the audience in a warm bath, making no demands except that we all glow with pleasure and comfort. . . . Homer knew all about this effect, at various times calling it Lotus Eaters, Calypso, Circe, and the Sirens. . . ."

So in Hyman's perspective, entertainment is bad not only because it is somehow "consuming" true art, but also because it is simultaneously diverting and numbing the audience. Many other critics concurred—the mass audience isn't just being misled by the media, but being narcotized and degraded, too.

True art, Charles Frankel argues in the followup discussion, is not designed to make people happy. One measures the worth of art in terms of "the increased intensity of our consciousness, increased self-awareness, increased ability to make discriminations."[37] Again, true art is presumed to have direct and beneficial effects on consciousness, self-awareness, discriminating capacities: on the mind. But mass art is presumed to have a direct effect on the mind, too—only this time, like a narcotic.

This is how the mass culture debate moves from a concern with content to a concern with effects. The earlier *Partisan Review* symposium asked, "Can intellectuals find ways to live with, ameliorate, reverse, survive the consequences of mass society?" The subsequent *Daedalus* symposium asks, "How can intellectuals ensure that the mass audience is protected from the bad effects of mass culture, and (if possible) exposed to the good effects of art?" Both these debates elaborated on an unquestioned instrumental perspective on the social power of the arts, and resulted in patronizing assumptions about the mass audience, and the ways in which it is being manipulated.

THE MANIPULATED MASS PUBLIC

Discussions of mass culture, in the 1950s and today, take for granted that we have moved from a community of publics to a society of masses.[38] In this new society, the individual is more loosely connected to others and to society—mass man (in the terms of the times) is atomized, alienated, fragmented, and therefore anomic.

In mass society, the argument goes, the individual is less and less defined by custom and tradition, and, it is implied, less protected by them. Unstuck from the "cake of custom," he must find his own way in the modern world, without the foundation and guidance that tradition can offer. In this way, mass man is presumed to be vulnerable. He is exposed, disconnected, unprotected by the bonds of community, and is thus easy prey.

This is an intriguing twist on the rural–urban metaphor that dominates mass society theory. Just as the past is represented as an agrarian community, and the present as an urban society, the mass man is represented as a yokel from the sticks, wandering the urban streets uncertain of who he is, what he wants, whom to trust, what to believe in. The atomized, narcotized, deracinated mass man is imagined as an immigrant to the modern world, one who can easily be swindled and fooled.

In this scenario, the media become the hucksters who offer blandishments and enticements to the unsuspecting yokel. The seduction is always a betrayal, since what the media offer is never fully satisfying, never what the audience really wants or needs. The media create and sustain artificial appetites—like a drug, they create demands they can never fully satisfy. And the media audience is easy prey, because modernity has stripped them of the resources they need to counter the forces of the modern.

The irony of mass society theory is that it is the mirror image of liberal hope. In classical liberalism, freedom from tradition was freedom from bondage—the individual was not stripped and vulnerable, but free and strong. Modern society was expected to offer unfettered development of individual talent and ability. As Tocqueville described so enthusiastically, new, flexible, voluntary social ties, ties of choice not bonds of tradition, were the promise of modernity.

American deliberations about the public are best understood against this contrast in American thought—a dialectical tension between the optimism of classical liberalism and the pessimism of mass society theory. The mass culture debate articulates this dialectic in relation to the mass media and the postwar world, and in relation to the twentieth-century heritage of American beliefs about the arts traced here. This means that the mass culture debates share what I take to be the defining element of American social criticism—concern about the possibilities of democracy.

Democracy's possibilities depend on "the people," and this is where the mass culture debates become both murky and simplistic. Do the people know what they are doing? How can they? As a mass audience of the new mass media, they are doubly damned—they are choosing adulterated, mediated forms, while being denied anything other than these adulterated, mediated forms.

The arguments proceed like this: the media don't offer people art because the people don't want art, but they don't want art because the media don't offer it. The people have appalling taste, but then again, they haven't had a chance to develop good taste. And perhaps their good taste (evidenced in the existence of past genuine folk and popular art) is being deformed by mass art. No matter these contradictions, what is clear to the critics is that the mass audience, awash in mass culture, is not the active, engaged, discriminating, democratic citizenry that America needs.

We have already found these contradictory arguments in Whitman, Mumford, and a variety of early twentieth-century intellectuals. What the mass culture debates add to this heritage is the belief that the audience has become a "mass," atomized, numb, and narcotized—"not yet people, no longer folk."[39]

James Baldwin eloquently expresses the betrayed possibilities of modernity: "We are very cruelly trapped between what we would like to be, and what we actually are."[40] He believes that the "amorphous people are in a desperate search for something which will help them to re-establish their connection with themselves, and with one another."[41] Can the "amorphous people" be helped? Only if the truth is told—it is the job of the creative artist, he believes, to "ask . . . just why the lives we lead on this continent are mainly so empty, so tame and so ugly."[42]

The artist has different interests, abilities, and social purposes from the rest of the people, Baldwin believes, so it is unreasonable to wish that "the great bulk of the populace embark on a mental and spiritual voyage for which very few people are equipped." That is the job of artists, who disturb the peace in order to improve the mind. Yet Baldwin also speaks of the "overwhelming torpor and bewilderment of the people," and says that he is "less appalled by the fact that *Gunsmoke* is produced than I am by the fact that so many people want to see it."[43]

Baldwin's recognition of the distance between hope and reality, his belief that few people can serve the social function of artist, and his reaction to people wanting to watch *Gunsmoke* remain key elements in our cultural criticism.

THE INADEQUATE PUBLIC

The American dream, in all its many versions, includes faith in the possibility that everyday people can govern themselves. Details about the nature of self-governance vary, of course, and our heritage of debates about the proper role of government is evidence of how difficult it continues to be to sort out the conditions under which "the people" govern best. But the underlying faith, no matter what the democratic scheme, remains the same—at some point "the people" know what they are doing.

This means that weaknesses or flaws in people's abilities to think and act wisely are extremely troubling. If the people are not, for whatever reason, capable of political wisdom, they are not capable of wise self-government, and America is at risk. America can destroy itself from within, through the foolishness of the public, and it can be destroyed from without, through the foolishness of the public.

In the post–World War II world, dangers from within seemed particularly acute. What intellectuals saw when they looked around was a nation on a buying spree,[44] eagerly "consuming" goods and services and television shows. The appalling spectacle of people actually wanting to watch *Gunsmoke* was everywhere.

The *Partisan Review* editors clearly stated their dilemma in 1952—cultural freedom, the reason they could finally "choose the West," resulted in mass culture. The social hopes for art—the cultural renaissance imagined in the 1920s, the new proletarian literature imagined in the 1930s, a widespread familiarity with the classics longed for by the New Humanists—had not developed. Instead, new commercial forms of culture, dependent on advertising, were becoming ever more popular.

This postwar culture, uniquely American and incredibly successful, was far different from Whitman's imagined democratic art, and Mumford's desired counterbalance to technology. The new American media did not, for intellectuals, fulfill Whitman's long-deferred dream of a new democratic culture, one that was specifically American, specifically connected to American conditions and dreams.

Instead, according to the logic of the mass culture debate, it was a cheap imitation, pablum, drivel, trash. It was neither the pure and authentic folk art presumed to exist in the past, nor the traditional and uplifting high art of the previous centuries, nor the serious and challenging avant-garde art of the present. It was a new form of culture that had dangerous consequences for public life.

Hopes for a new and vibrant democratic culture are always linked to hopes for a new and vibrant democratic society. The critique of mass culture is always a parallel critique of mass society, and of the habits and practices of the modern. Just as cultural freedom becomes mass culture, for intellectuals the dreams of modernity are defiled by shopping malls. As intellectuals critique mass culture, they also critique the consumer ethos they believe has come to dominate the hearts and minds of the postwar public.

Consumption, the "danger from within," became a major theme in the following decades. Intellectuals from both the political right and the left agreed that Americans were (and are) becoming transformed from citizens into consumers. The public, it was presumed, falsely believed that goods buy happiness. The American dream had become an American nightmare of endlessly shopping, trying to make material objects fill an ever-increasing spiritual emptiness.[45]

Thus, unwittingly, we lead (in Baldwin's terms) tame, empty, ugly lives. What Randall Jarrell calls The Medium casts a spell on us, tells us to buy, buy, buy, and keeps us coming back for more. Jarrell's analysis draws on the common assumption that people are on a quest for meaning, but, sidetracked by consumption, seek fulfillment endlessly through semisatisfying mass culture, and end up, in his words—starved for truth, stuffed by lies.[46]

Here, then, is what critics believe has happened to the public, under the influence of the media and modernity: They are narcotized and numbed by the sea of mass culture in which they float, besotted by prosperity, eagerly consuming goods and culture that cannot possibly give them true pleasure, insight, or wisdom. The more optimistic intellectuals assume that the mass audience still wants good culture, and hopes that people's desire for cultural junk is an indication that they still have as-yet-unmet needs for more real, satisfying, challenging, serious, and uplifting fare.

MEDIA-CHALLENGING ART

In this scenario, the public needs intellectuals to create the kinds of work that will "wake them up," put cold water in their warm bath, stretch their nerves taut and challenge them to higher levels of consciousness and discrimination. The art that intellectuals call for is an art that explodes mythologies, challenges the status quo, breaks the spell. The new mass audience needs, therefore, new avant-garde artists, and they also need intellectuals to explain how and why avant-garde art is so important.

Avant-garde art is self-defined as art that challenges, and what avant-garde art was originally intended to challenge was mainstream or traditional art. Yet in the terms of the mass culture debate of the 1950s, both traditional and avant-garde art is "high art." How did these two seemingly incompatible artistic forms become linked?

Once a narcotizing mass culture form has been imagined, one that casts a spell on a mass audience, then alternative forms must be imagined, ones that can "break" the spell. High art (if one believes that it contains truth, is serious, and even embodies classic values and virtues) is a candidate for spell-breaker. So is avant-garde art, since it too is deemed to be serious, and also challenging and subversive. So both forms share, it seems, the qualities that distinguish art from entertainment, and so both must have the power to challenge modern mass beliefs.

They are also both forms increasingly removed from everyday experience. Traditional forms, based in a receding past, are distant from contemporary instruments, techniques, habits. High art takes on an ever-more antiquated air, and concert halls and museums become symbolic sites to recreate imagined aristocratic habits. Simultaneously, avant-garde art becomes more abstract, self-referential, and arcane. In these conditions, intellectuals, already certain they are responsible for "good" culture, are also needed to explain high and avant-garde art to increasingly disrespectful audiences. So high and avant-garde art, in spite of their historical opposition, become synonymous in the mass culture debate—they are absolutely not mass culture, they are presumed to have the power to challenge modern beliefs, and they both need intellectuals to explain them to the uninitiated.

True works of art, even as they contain the ability to transcend time and space, are still inherently difficult. In the logic of the debates, only a small portion of the population has the aesthetic sensitivity or refinement to fully appreciate them. Shils can make his argument about the uneven distribution of aesthetic, moral, and cognitive capacities, and be joined by Arthur Schlesinger Jr., who believes there are only a few who are capable of intense aesthetic experience.

If only a small portion of the population has the capacity to fully experience or appreciate true art, then it is even *more* important that intellectuals (who are automatically presumed to be gifted with such capacities) have an influence on those unable to reap the benefits of aesthetic appreciation. Education becomes one way to ensure that a larger portion of the population is at least exposed to the benefits of art. As Irving Kristol argues, "We are not educating people to appreciate our high humanist, literary culture in this country. In order to appreciate this culture, you have to have certain years of training."[47]

The fate of high art—now fully defined as inaccessible to the everyday public, and therefore the special responsibility of intellectuals—is sealed. You need years of training, plus innate gifts, to have access to the transforming powers of true art. The rest of society, if not sunk in Shils's vegetative torpor, is still unable to appropriately respond to art's powers. Evidence of this is not just that they don't go to museums, galleries, and poetry readings when they have the chance, but that they persist in their affection for low art like Baldwin's *Gunsmoke*.

We return, then, to the mystery of mass taste. Why people like stuff that intellectuals detest is the most prevalent unaddressed aspect of the debate. As we have seen, one answer could be the Circe argument—the mass audience has been seduced or hypnotized into liking trash. Another version is the "lack of choice" argument—the media just aren't making the good stuff available.

It is also possible to assume, with Shils, that the audience is made up of people with inadequate moral, critical, and aesthetic capacities, but this is always an uncomfortable move for American social critics. Very few are willing to define the people as *inherently* inadequate. Instead, they imagine an intervening factor to explain why the people fail to live up to intellectuals' expectations.

Here again the mass culture and mass society debates entwine. The people have been seduced by the media because they have been made vulnerable by the forces of modernity. Like the rural immigrant, they are easy marks for the shallow glitter of the modern, urban world. If only they lived in authentic communities, or had traditional educations, or had stronger nuclear families, they would have the wherewithal to withstand the blandishments of advertising, mass culture, shopping malls, the ideology of consumption.

This seduction and betrayal logic[48] can operate to blame the media for causing the audience to have bad taste, or to blame the media for preventing the audience's achievement of good taste. Exposure to mass culture can be presumed to pervert and contaminate aesthetic capacities; it can also be blamed for the failure to educate and develop innate aesthetic capacities. The media become both poisoners and bad teachers, and the result is a public who likes to watch, read, and spend time with trash rather than art.

There is a deep desire, on the part of intellectuals, to believe that the public can somehow be salvaged. Few American intellectuals argue for final disengagement; instead they suggest a range of ways to protect the purity of "their" cultural forms while engaging (without becoming contaminated) with contemporary popular culture. There is a presumption that such engagement will amount to something—will allow the intellectual to challenge, or subvert, or somehow intervene in the social process in helpful ways.

The hope is that some larger portion of the population will realize what they are missing—will recognize that they don't really like what they think they like, that the cultural material they enjoy is not worthy or satisfying, that it may in fact be dangerous and destructive. Intellectuals see themselves as being able to warn the rest of the populace about what is being done to them, and what they are missing.

But how do intellectuals themselves manage to escape the deleterious effects of mass culture? Art has long been believed to be a guarantor of consciousness, insight, alternative awareness. This means that if an intellectual dwells in the world of high art, he believes he is dwelling in an environment that constantly increases his capacities to discriminate and understand. High art and avant-garde art become a world in which intellectuals can safely dwell, a world that is reassuringly distinct from the rowdiness, crassness, and commercialism of mass culture.

Depending on one's political preferences, that world can remain an elite and exclusive world. Or it can be offered to all who care enough to enter. Or it can be made accessible to as many as possible through attractive public programs. But this "good culture world" should not, the mass culture debaters agree, be diluted or popularized or dismantled. Artists and intellectuals need access to uncontaminated and undiluted good culture, and good culture needs their protection and care.

THE ROLES OF THE MIDDLEBROW

This logic is not something that intellectuals have invented by themselves, and then foisted on an unwitting public. Belief that "good culture" is something that only some people have, that it makes you more wise, insightful, and worthy, and that it is something that you can "get" if you have innate capacities and years of training, has a long and fascinating heritage in American popular thought.

The public's desire to be educated and cultivated is a parallel story to the one I am telling here about intellectuals' desire to educate and cultivate the public. Chautauqua, working men's clubs, women's study groups, the Delphian Society, the Book-of-the-Month Club, and of course public libraries and universities are all sites created because there was public demand for the "good" that "good culture" was believed to bring.[49]

Yet these forms of public engagement with "good" culture are dismissed as "middlebrow" by intellectuals in the 1950s mass culture debates. The attempts to locate, distill, and disseminate "good" art to an interested larger audience are forms of popularization that threaten the integrity and power of the original art form. In the era of television, when all forms of high art could be relatively easily broadcast, it became even more important to distinguish true art from its popularized versions.

Among the many charges against the mass media were that they failed to fulfill their unprecedented potential for public education. This condemnation linked up with a deep ambivalence about popularization in the mass culture debate. Is it still art if it is widely available and widely liked?

Popularization connects to the complex problem of art's role in social status. As Bourdieu has so effectively argued—art/taste functions as cultural capital, it distinguishes its participants from each other.[50] When something becomes popular, it loses its ability to define a particular group as exclusive. If art is the exclusive property of intellectuals, because they care about it, and have the training and capacity to fully appreciate it, then any mediated versions of high art have to be suspect. At best it is throwing pearls before unprepared swine, at the least a dilution of art's power, and at the very worst a transformation or destruction of art's meaning.

This makes a difficult problem for American intellectuals, convinced of art's power, and wanting to make the people better. If they really believe that the people will be better through exposure to good art, then they should be working wholeheartedly for the mass mediation of the arts. They should find the most popular outlets for their work, and work tirelessly to engage as many people as possible with their creations. But this is not the path recommended, in the mass culture debates, for "real" writers, artists, and intellectuals. To pursue popular approval is to doom oneself, inevitably, to middlebrow status.

In the mass culture debate, intellectuals are caught in a conceptual bind of their own making. They presume cultural levels, varying in the degree of difficulty of their content and of their "decoding." True art is by definition unpopular—very few can create it or enjoy it. Yet true art is also good for people—it challenges them, makes them wiser, uplifts them. An intellectual who cares about social progress should therefore support the widest possible dissemination of true art.

The mass media, particularly television, offer excellent venues for such dissemination. But, on the terms of the mass culture debate, the media are an inappropriate way to disseminate art. For intellectuals then and now, the media are absolutely inadequate cultural mechanisms—they pollute what they purvey.

In the mass culture debate, good art is incompatible with mediation, particularly by television. The reasons are diverse, but reveal much about beliefs about art, and beliefs about the media. Intellectuals' ambivalence about popularization depend on notions of art as pure, as complex, as requiring training, and as therefore appealing to a small fraction of the population. They also depend on notions of the media as automatically contaminating and inevitably simplistic.

For example, there is concern that the nearby presence of nonart contaminates the art itself. Broadcasting boxing or comedy or other lowbrow fare on nearby channels or on the same evening will trivialize good culture—opera, ballet, serious theater, symphonies. True art, displayed side-by-side with low art, is cheapened and contaminated. True art, interrupted by advertising, becomes commercialized. True art, supported by advertising, becomes a commodity. Television, in some arguments, is so inherently contaminated by the bulk of its fare that no art can survive on it.

Another reason that mediated art is deemed unsatisfactory involves the assumption that works of art, widely broadcast, will inevitably be simplified. Often this appears as the unexamined assumption that wide dispersion of an image is the "dilution" of it, and that spreading culture widely means that it has to become flavorless and unsatisfying—too diluted to do good.

A related concern is actual rewriting or editing—the fear that true art will be simplified by media hacks to appeal to the masses. Another concern is that the art form is "lessened," that recorded or broadcast performance is less thick and substantive than live performance. This is tied to the belief that the authentic is also the original and the face-to-face, and that all reproductions or transcriptions are more degraded versions of the "really real."

These claims about the dangers of popularization presume that the media have to ruin art in order to make it popular. This is because true art is, now by definition, extremely difficult to understand or enjoy. Here is a fascinating tautology: if art requires special gifts and training to appreciate, then art that is widely appreciated can never be art. Since much of what was in the media in the 1950s was widely enjoyed, it could not possibly be defined as art.

LEGACIES OF THE MASS CULTURE DEBATE

The mass culture debate moves beyond presumptions about art's powers into fears about the loss of those powers—it draws, therefore, on a legacy of elite concerns about democracy. The mass culture debate proceeds both in the name of high culture (in Lazarsfeld's summary, what happens *to* highbrow culture in mass society) and in the name of the people (what does middlebrow culture *do* to people?). The intellectuals engaged in the debates never, ever, explore, respect, or trust contemporary, commercially successful culture.

As we see in the next chapter, when arts supporters argue for public funding of the arts in the 1990s, they draw on the ideology of mass culture. When the National Endowment for the Arts offers arguments about how the arts are necessary for a good, full, rich life, it draws on the longer heritage of hopes for art's power, and also on the assumption that the mass media are a danger to art's survival.

So the first legacy of the mass culture debate is a *resurgence of genteel definitions of the power of the arts.* In disconnecting "true art" from popular, mediated forms, art becomes unproblematically combined with the avant-garde originally invented to challenge it. Belief in true art's purity, and its threatened contamination, thread through the mass culture debates. For art to do its uplifting work, it must not be mixed or blurred with entertainment, or with commerce.

Why is art poisoned if it becomes, or is mistaken for, entertainment? The mass culture definition of art presumes that humor is simplistic, and trusts pleasure only when it is cerebral, not visceral. Entertainment, presumed to be simple and emotional, will lower the complex and cerebral qualities of the arts. The masses, being more simple and emotional, will insist on such lowering, since most are incapable of understanding superior forms.

The fear of the commercial relies on this assumption that the masses will demand debased (simple, pleasurable, light) forms of art, since they are incapable of appreciating higher (complex, serious, heavy) forms. So part of the fear of the commercialization of the arts is tied to a fear that the masses—their tastes, proclivities, and demands—will lower art.

But fears of the effects of commerce on art are also based in a longer history of ambivalence about capitalism and market-based relations. In this discourse, art represents authentic or honest or spontaneous or humane relations, and the market represents inauthentic, dishonest, calculated, and mechanical relations.[51] Any combining of artistic and commercial purposes is doubly damned—it caters to the whims of a capricious mob, *and* it succumbs to the logic of an inhumane system.

To "sell out," to create in order to reach a wide audience and make a profit, is to betray all that makes art (supposedly) sacred.

What makes art sacred, in the mass culture debate, is a combination of its ties to past civilization, and its presumed basis in honorable human motives in the present. Here is another way that older forms of art, classical or European, can be "art," along with folk or "primitive" art, and avant-garde or modern art: they are all not-entertainment and not-commercial and not-media. Unlike commercially based entertaining media, the arts are presumed to spring from, and call forth, deep and authentic impulses of the human spirit.

This leads us to the second legacy of the mass culture debate—the presumption that *the mass audience is mired in shallow and inauthentic culture, and so its members lead shallow and inauthentic lives.* The ideology of artistic power, as imagined in the mass culture debate, presumes a mirror relationship between content and understanding, between text and reading, between cultural form and cultural experience: complex art creates complex understanding, reading, and experience, while true art creates true understanding, reading, and experience.

By the same logic, supposedly simple art creates simple understandings, light art produces light readings, false arts offer false experiences. The masses, whom intellectuals believe are swimming in a sea of mediocre culture, are therefore also swimming in a sea of inadequate understandings and experiences.

This is how the mass culture debate creates a vision of a narcotized audience, one that has been numbed into a half-life. The people of the modern audience, because it is being shaped by mass culture, are believed to be living lives that are less meaningful, less rewarding, less authentic, less challenging, less worthy than the lives of those shaped by high culture. By this logic, the people who choose mass culture are participating, unwittingly, in their own deprivation. They are debasing themselves, and becoming contaminated, and thereby putting at risk (in the future) the true values and worthy experiences still to be found in art.

Such a public is numbed, cheated, and (ultimately) dangerous. As disrespectful as this notion is, it is less harsh than the assumption that the bulk of people will *never* be able to truly understand art. A numbed and deprived public can learn to appreciate art, if they can find ways to shake off the hypnotic influence of mediocre, mediated culture. Contemporary art (challenging and subversive) is presumed to have the power to de-hypnotize. But any art can be imagined as an antidote to the narcotizing influence of the media, because, by definition, art "makes you think," forces you to be discriminating—helps you become more like an intellectual.

The third legacy of the mass culture debate is this parallel version of the ideology of arts power—*the ideology of media power*. If exposure to the arts makes you an intellectual, then exposure to mass culture makes you an idiot. No one worries about someone who spends "too much time" listening to Mozart, reading Proust, or watching modern dance. Everyone worries about someone spending "too much time" listening to rock music, reading comic books, or watching TV. The assumption is that mass culture is in itself harmful, especially in large doses. It is harmful because it has a powerful influence, it can make you into what intellectuals think mass culture itself is—dull, stupid, formulaic, repetitive, unoriginal.

The mass culture debate conceptualizes us as living in a new mass society which isolates us and makes us vulnerable, at the mercy of a commercial, entertaining mass medium that creates a sea of mediocre culture which numbs and stupefies us. The final legacy of the mass culture debate is *the vital role of the intellectual*—the few who are aware of the dangers of mass society and mass culture.

Intellectuals, as social critics, have long presumed that they have special insight, but the mass culture debate offers a particularly virulent version of the intellectual as sage and seer. In the logic of the mass culture debate, the bulk of the population has been seduced into liking mass culture, through the power of the media, in combination with the characteristics of modern society. Intellectuals, who hate mass culture, have been spared. Because of their own intelligence, skepticism, and insight, intellectuals are aware of the terrible influence that is spreading throughout modern life. Art not only reminds them of what used to be, it also protects them from what has already come.

The mass culture debate tells the following story: intellectuals are the possessors and protectors of a sacred, ancient, humane, and subversive substance: art. Intellectuals have a responsibility to defend art against onslaught and contamination. Their role is more than the canary in the coal mine—they must do more than simply warn of the poison gas. They must head for higher ground, circle the wagons, keep the fires burning, defend civilization from the barbaric hordes.

In this way, 1950s intellectuals draw on older versions of protecting the sacred and offer an updated version of "the saving remnant." This is not, obviously, a deeply egalitarian perspective. It is not fully aristocratic, in that it often leaves room for the salvaging of the public through some outside force—art, information, or education. But it is an extremely arrogant perspective, and it demonstrates a total mistrust of the understandings and experiences of nonintellectuals.

It is a perspective that flows directly from an instrumental belief in the power of art to shape people and society. It now also has become a bemoaning of how bad art misshapes people and society. The dreams and possibilities of previous generations have been lost, or corrupted. The reality of the American dream is that the public has been seduced by the media. This can happen over and over—while the critic stays as aware of, and protected from, the seduction of the media and the marketplace.

As intellectuals become more university-based, protection from contamination becomes ever easier, and is institutionally supported. Academic reputation depends on avoiding seduction by either entertainment or commerce. Serious scholarly work involves a rigorous disdain for all popular or commercially successful uses of one's work. This means publishing with university rather than trade or popular presses, as well as protecting curricula from the popular and the vernacular.

The final legacy of the mass culture debate may be *the penetration of cultural studies into the humanities*. For the "intervention" of cultural studies into intellectual life has become yet another decontamination of mass culture, this time by the trappings of scholarship. For the cultural choices of everyday people to earn respect and attention, they must first be processed in and through theory, proffered in sophisticated and nuanced discourse. Once popular forms of culture have been thus transformed, they are acceptable, more or less, in academic life.

Elaborated textual readings of a television show can be academically legitimate, especially if done in conjunction with some already canonized theoretical text. Nimble combinations of popular and arcane sources demonstrate that one is not brutish, or doltish, or barbaric. Appreciating the contradictions, richness, and subversive potential of popular culture is also possible, if that culture connects to an oppressed minority, or to the past. But cultural studies as it has emerged has almost no interest in understanding how mainstream audiences enjoy mainstream commercial culture.[52] Because of the legacy of the mass culture debate, it is wise to bring along maximum scholarly apparatus if one is doing work on popular or commercial culture.

The ideology of art as power, and bad art as bad power, finds an unexpected home in academic cultural studies with its supposed challenge to hierarchical notions of art. As the canon cracks, as genres blur, as divisions are defined as elitist and patriarchal, as new literatures and perspectives are welcomed and valorized, instrumental faith in art as social medicine remains secure.

Under the banner of cultural studies, we crack the canon so that we can expose students to the really "good stuff," now redefined as a non-canonical canon. And, as with Whitman, this stuff is neither the culture of dead white men nor current best-sellers. It is material that we have uncovered, revered, and been improved by.

In (post)modern life—fragmented, contradictory, ruptured, contained, repressive, celebratory, or whatever—it is still up to intellectuals to figure out what is "really" going on. We see beneath the surface, behind the signs, through the veils, across time and space. We can deconstruct and decode and theorize and analyze and intervene. We can tell people what they are really up to when they think they are just reading, watching, living, choosing. We can do so because we, as intellectuals, have the discrimination and insight that means we are not enmeshed in the same forces that enmesh others. We have critical ability, the talisman of the intellectual against modernity's murk.

Intellectuals in the 1950s made much of critical ability, long before the term came to stand for any work done by academics interested in cultural and social life. How much difference is there, really, between current celebrations of the powers of critical ability to subvert and intervene in the social formation and what Lionel Trilling argued in 1952: "The literary mind, more precisely the historical-literary mind, seems to be the best kind of critical and constructive mind that we have, better than the philosophic, better than the theological, better than the scientific and the social scientific"?[53]

Would any current critical theorists disagree with Sidney Hook when he suggests that the ability to discriminate is the "cardinal aspect of the life of thought,"[54] or argue when such a claim is combined with Howe's definition of an intellectual as "a critic of cant and convention whom the philistines will not cease to find destructive"?[55]

Contemporary academic intellectual life, even in its most radical form, does not challenge the instrumental ideology of art as medicine. Contemporary academic life does not question the exaltation of the intellectual's role that accompanies it. Today's climate of cultural criticism is a logical extension of our heritage of thought about the arts in America.

NOTES

1. Theodor Adorno and Max Horkheimer, "The Culture Industry: Enlightenment as Mass Deception," in *Mass Communication and Society*, ed. J. Curran, et al. (Berkeley, Calif.: Sage, 1977), 349–83.

2. The best analytical overview of mass culture debate themes remains chapter 1 of Herbert Gans, *Popular Culture and High Culture: An Analysis and Evaluation of Popular Taste* (New York: Basic Books, 1999; originally published in 1974).

3. The series "Our Country and Our Culture" appeared in three successive *Partisan Review* issues: May–June, July–August, and September–October 1952. Soon afterward it was published in what the promotional copy called "a handsome, paper-bound book" as *America and the Intellectuals, a Symposium* (New York: Partisan Review Series 4, 1953).

4. "Our Country and Our Culture," 284.

5. "Our Country and Our Culture," 285.

6. The twenty-five contributors: Newton Arvin, William Barrett, Jacques Barzun, Louise Bogan, James Burnham, Richard Chase, Allan Dowling, Leslie Fiedler, Joseph Frank, Horace Gregory, Sidney Hook, Irving Howe, Louis Kronenberger, Max Lerner, Norman Mailer, Margaret Mead, C. Wright Mills, Reinhold Niebuhr, William Phillips, Philip Rahv, David Reisman, Arthur Schlesinger Jr., Mark Schorer, Delmore Schwartz, and Lionel Trilling.

7. Norman Mailer, "Our Country and Our Culture," 299.

8. Lionel Trilling, "Our Country and Our Culture," 318.

9. Arthur Schlesinger Jr. "Our Country and Our Culture," 591.

10. Sidney Hook, "Our Country and Our Culture," 569.

11. William Phillips, "Our Country and Our Culture," 587.

12. William Barrett, "Our Country and Our Culture," 421.

13. Barrett, "Our Country and Our Culture," 421.

14. Jacques Barzun, "Our Country and Our Culture," 429.

15. C. Wright Mills, "Our Country and Our Culture," 446.

16. Philip Rahv, "Our Country and Our Culture," 310.

17. Rahv, "Our Country and Our Culture," 310.

18. Irving Howe, "Our Country and Our Culture," 578.

19. Delmore Schwartz, "Our Country and Our Culture," 595.

20. Rahv, "Our Country and Our Culture," 310.

21. James Burnham, "Our Country and Our Culture," 291.

22. Louis Kronenberger, "Our Country and Our Culture," 442.

23. Paul Lazarsfeld, "Our Country and Our Culture," 285.

24. Tocqueville's name appears, inevitably, in these discussions of cultural leveling. With a flourish, he is identified as the first person to make a case for the inevitability of cultural decline in a democracy. The orienting concern was Tocqueville's supposed claim that mass culture is "the price we pay for democ-

racy." See, for example, H. Stuart Hughes, "Mass Culture and Social Criticism," in *Culture for the Millions? Mass Media in Modern Society,* ed. Norman Jacobs (New York: D. Van Nostrand, 1961), 188. This misrepresents Tocqueville's position, which was a *response* to this fear. As discussed in chapter 1, Tocqueville substitutes the notion of illumination, *lumiere,* for uplift/leveling, and argues that, in democracy, more people are sharing in better, and more useful, cultural forms.

25. In teaching courses since the mid-1980s, I have used what I call the art/trash game. I ask students to list "high, middle, and low" versions of cultural forms like newspapers, magazines, music, painting, dance, literature, and architecture. A lively discussion ensues about what these categories mean, always mobilizing notions of dilution, commercialization, and the "lowest common denominator."

26. Papers from the June 1959 symposium, sponsored jointly by *Daedalus* and the Tamiment Institute, were published (with additional papers by Paul F. Lazarsfeld, Arthur Berger, and Leo Lowenthal) in *Culture for the Millions?* ed. Jacobs.

27. Paul Lazarsfeld, "Mass Culture Today," in *Culture for the Millions?* xi.

28. Lazarsfeld, "Mass Culture Today," xi

29. A number of essay collections appeared; the most representative, besides *Culture for the Millions?* were Bernard Rosenberg and David Manning White, eds., *Mass Culture: The Popular Arts in America* (Glencoe, Ill.: The Free Press, 1957); and their follow-up, *Mass Culture Revisited* (New York: Van Nostrand Reinhold, 1971). Mass culture, the touchstone of intellectual concerns in the 1950s, became academic coursework in the following decades.

30. Edward Shils, "Mass Society and Its Culture" in *Culture for the Millions?* 3.

31. See, for example, T. J. Jackson Lears, *No Place of Grace: Antimodernism and the Transformation of American Culture* (New York: Pantheon, 1981); Marshall Berman, *All That Is Solid Melts into Air* (London: Verso, 1983); and Bryan S. Turner, ed., *Theories of Modernity and Postmodernity* (London: Sage, 1990).

32. The classic discussion of this is Walter Benjamin, "The Work of Art in the Age of Mechanical Reproduction," in *Illuminations,* ed. Hannah Arendt (New York: Schocken, 1969).

33. This is especially obvious in arts tourism, which is learning how to market authenticity. Kimber Craine, communications manager for the National Assembly of State Art Agencies, says, "One of the greater interests among people who travel, and one that is growing, is the search for authentic experience. Many people who travel have done the theme parks, they've done Disney; now they want to go places where they can experience real life." Craine is quoted in Jennifer Halperin, "Crafting for Dollars," *Governing* 10 (July 1997): 48.

34. Hannah Arendt, "Society and Culture," in *Culture for the Millions?* 45.

35. Arendt, "Society and Culture," 48–50.

36. Stanley Edgar Hyman, "Ideals, Dangers and Limitations of Mass Culture," in *Culture for the Millions?* 133.

37. Charles Frankel, panel discussion on "Ideals and Dangers of Mass Culture," in *Culture for the Millions?* 194.

38. For an influential discussion of this notion during the period, see C. Wright Mills, *The Power Elite* (New York: Oxford University Press, 1956), especially chapter 13.

39. Hyman, "Ideals, Dangers," 132.

40. James Baldwin, "Mass Culture and the Creative Artist," in *Culture for the Millions?* 122–23.

41. Baldwin, "Mass Culture and the Creative Artist," 123.

42. Baldwin, "Mass Culture and the Creative Artist," 123.

43. Baldwin, "Mass Culture and the Creative Artist," 120–21.

44. See, for example, Leo Leonni's remarks about consumer society ("Man is always on a buying spree . . .") in "Mass Culture and the Creative Artist," *Culture for the Millions?* 178.

45. For a thoughtful social history about our ambivalence about materialism and consumption, see Daniel Horowitz, *The Morality of Spending: Attitudes toward the Consumer Society in America, 1875–1940* (Baltimore, Md.: Johns Hopkins University Press, 1985). For a summary of the critique of capitalism, and a developed alternative to it, see Tyler Cowen, *In Praise of Commercial Culture* (Harvard University Press, 1998).

46. Randall Jarrell, "A Sad Heart at the Supermarket," in *Culture for the Millions?* 97–110.

47. Irving Kristol, panel discussion on "The Mass Media," *Culture for the Millions?* 167.

48. This logic is explored in detail in Joli Jensen, *Redeeming Modernity: Contradictions in Media Criticism* (Berkeley, Calif.: Sage, 1990).

49. For scholarly analyses of aspirational culture and audiences, see, especially, Janice Radway, "The Book-of-the-Month Club and the General Reader," in *Reading in America: Literature and Social History,* ed. Cathy N. Davidson (Baltimore, Md.: Johns Hopkins University Press, 1989); and Joan Shelley Rubin, *The Making of Middlebrow Culture* (Chapel Hill: University of North Carolina Press, 1992). For a consideration of how divisions between high and low were developed and sustained in America, with Shakespeare as an exemplary case study, see Lawrence W. Levine, *Highbrow/Lowbrow: The Emergence of Cultural Hierarchy in America* (Cambridge, Mass.: Harvard University Press, 1988). For an insightful account of various historical forms of cultural uplift, see Helen Lefkowitz Horowitz, *Culture and the City* (Lexington: University Press of Kentucky, 1976).

50. Pierre Bourdieu, *Distinction: A Social Critique of the Judgment of Taste,* trans. Richard Nice (Cambridge, Mass.: Harvard University Press, 1984).

51. An interesting alternative to this demonization of commerce is the eighteenth- and nineteenth-century notion of *"doux-commerce,"* where self-interested commerce was imagined as a socially felicitous counterbalance to baser emotions. See Albert O. Hirschman, *The Passions and the Interests: Political Arguments for Capitalism before Its Triumph* (Princeton, N.J.: Princeton University Press, 1977). Tocqueville's analysis draws from this tradition.

52. See Joli Jensen and John J. Pauly, "Imagining the Audience: Losses and Gains in Cultural Studies," in *Cultural Studies in Question,* ed. Marjorie Ferguson and Peter Golding, London: Sage, 1997, 155–69.

53. Lionel Trilling, "Our Country and Our Culture," 324.

54. Sidney Hook, "Our Country and Our Culture," 573.

55. Irving Howe, "Our Country and Our Culture," 581.

Chapter Four

Art as Elixir:
Contemporary Arts Discourse

In the 1990s, in response to political efforts to cut funding to the National Endowment for the Arts, social critics and commentators, arts activists, political pundits, artists, and community organizers argued about the social value of the arts, and the necessity of funding them with tax dollars. In the NEA debates, the arts are portrayed as having the ability to make American life better. This is the contemporary version of the ideology I am questioning here—that art operates instrumentally, so it can serve as social medicine. But as arts supporters sought to defend the public funding of the arts, they made an important shift in arts discourse.

Rather than continue to define the arts as an extraordinary, elite, or sacred resource, as in the mass culture debates, many arts supporters in the 1990s sought to redefine the arts as commonplace, friendly, and communal culture. They "de-elited" the arts, disconnecting them from increasingly stigmatized notions of the arts as institutionalized high culture. In the 1990s, arts supporters made the arts more vernacular. But the vernacularization of the arts, and the reaction against this rhetorical strategy, indicate how unquestioned the faith in art as medicine remains.

Even when the arts are re-described as everyday practice, they are *still* presumed to be instruments for social change. In the NEA debates, the arts (whether folk, communal, ethnic, avant-garde, or high) are imagined as central to social improvement; offering antidotes to media and commerce; and as key aspects of democracy.

Why do we continue to believe that the arts have vast social power? When we examine contemporary arts discourse,[1] we find

themes, assumptions, and rhetorical strategies from previous generations—continuing attempts to address longstanding American concerns about democracy, progress, and commercial culture through an
instrumental view of the arts.

DEFINING THE ARTS

"The arts" are defined capaciously and inconsistently in the NEA debates. This is a problem with arts discourse throughout the twentieth
century—critics deploy the definitions that best suit their claims or arguments. In analyzing their arguments, it is best to try to decipher
what each critic means by "the arts," while continuing to recognize
that "the arts" function as an empty set. Each critic places into that set
his or her own notions of creative, expressive, aesthetic practice and
forms, including literature, painting, sculpture, drama, music, dance.

In contemporary arts discourse, when the arts are imagined to be sacred and uplifting, they are usually imagined as traditional high culture, the so-called fine arts, ensconced (not without controversy) in
museums, concert halls, and universities. When they are said to directly improve each of us, as well as our communities, they can be any
kind of creative endeavor, including handicrafts. When they are described as multicultural expression, they are most likely to be what the
mass culture debaters called folk art, or any cultural form that can
claim connection to ethnic identity.

It is important to note that the empty set demarcates what the arts
are *not*. As in the mass culture debates, the arts are *not* widely popular, mass-mediated, or commercially successful. They are imagined as
forms that are threatened by the "other" nonart culture found in modern life. The arts denote forms of nonmediated creative endeavor that
are assumed to be at risk, and under siege.

Categories of high culture, fine arts, crafts, and folk and ethnic art
can shift, often in mid-defense, so that ethnic arts are given sacred uplift potential for children, or communities are said to be strengthened
by some combination of fine arts, crafts education, and multicultural
participation. In contemporary discourse, as well as in previous versions of arts commentary, this imprecision is extremely useful.

In the 1980s in particular, proponents of government funding
worked to destigmatize the arts, showing critics and taxpayers how
the arts are neither exotic and elite, nor dangerous and pornographic.

The newly defined tame, desirable, vernacular arts are rhetorically positioned as democratic forms, connected to everyday life, while simultaneously being celebrated as ennobling *and* under siege. This contradictory rhetoric still maintains faith in the arts as social medicine, an elixir threatened by commerce, technology, and the mass media.

To redescribe the arts as familiar and communal practice is obviously a risky rhetorical strategy. The American heritage of arts discourse, especially the mass culture debate, offers important ways to distinguish good from bad, beneficial from harmful, progress from decline. Removing the conceptual boundaries that distinguish something called "the arts" from the mass media *and* from everyday life undermines the ways we think about culture, commerce, and democracy. The discussion sparked by this rhetorical move is wonderfully revealing of the contradictions in our current view of the arts, and in the role that the instrumental perspective continues to play.[2]

DEFENDING THE ARTS

Why would defenders of arts funding willingly abandon a definition of the arts as extraordinary creative excellence and replace it with a definition of the arts as uplifting, friendly, community-based craft? This move was made in direct response to the charge that the arts are the culture of the already privileged, imposed from above. The "art as uplift" perspective that defined the rhetorical position of mass culture debaters (and the New Humanists before them) is a patronizing one—it presumes that "good culture" (of the elite) will improve people who don't know enough to like it already (the masses).

As we have seen, cultural critics since Whitman have struggled with the realization that "the people" don't usually like the culture that the critic believes is best for them. The desire to understand why this is so, without blaming the people, has shaped the tone, logic, and direction of previous discussions of the arts and the media.

The late twentieth-century attacks on public funding of the arts drew on a heritage of mistrust of intellectuals and elites; defense of funding required somehow finessing the consequences of the lack of popularity of "good art." But hostility to public arts funding is an understandable response to the ways that the arts have been defined by critics and artists—from a variety of political positions—as "good for" people who don't like them very much.[3]

Maintaining a definition of the arts as the fine arts means that anti-NEA funding critics seem populist and reasonable when they ask, "Why should the taxpayers fund the cultural tastes of the privileged?" As long as the arts are defined as the fine arts, institutionalized in museums and galleries, created by an exotic cadre of exceptional, unusual people, then they are easy to stigmatize. And anti-NEA critics can then make an especially compelling case, as they often did, by using controversial cultural projects that artists defend as aesthetically valuable, while others see them as pornographic and/or sacrilegious.

So defining the arts as either classic high culture, or radical avant-garde culture, is rhetorically risky. Since the rise of modernism, the art-as-medicine perspective has been applied to all controversial new forms of art. The traditional fine arts are good for us, say conservatives, because they dispense essential, or time-honored, truths. New, difficult, upsetting works are *also* good for us, say radicals and progressives, because they challenge those truths. In this way, conservative, progressive, and radical positions on the arts share a definition of the arts as powerful (although in different ways) and beneficial (although for different reasons).

Supporters of both mainstream and avant-garde art make use of the same instrumental, medicinal logic. This puts defenders of controversial art in the difficult position of defining art as valuable *because* it is patently offensive, valuable *because* it is designed to destabilize the status quo. Avant-garde art is especially good for you when it upsets and disgusts. Obviously, this perspective on the medicinal value of high art is not particularly persuasive to taxpayers or their elected representatives.

The right will support traditional fine arts as vessels of timeless values, but will not support avant-garde art for the very reasons that the left supports it—its presumed ability to challenge and subvert. Supporters of NEA funding found themselves charged with defending exhibits by Mapplethorpe and Serrano, using arguments about the First Amendment, and art as purposely designed to challenge norms. These arguments were unconvincing to conservatives who might have otherwise supported the arts for their supposed ability to uplift individuals and support traditional values.

While some defenders of the NEA could dismiss critics as "know-nothing voices" that "need to be suppressed,"[4] others struggled mightily with ways to justify and defend arts funding. In that struggle, a number of beliefs about "how arts work" are evident. There are still critics willing to argue for art as intellectually sophisticated culture that will serve as beacons for the ignorant and aesthetically deprived masses. While such a pure New Humanist position can still be found,[5] it rarely dominates the discussion.

Instead, current commentary draws primarily on a diluted, displaced version of the 1950s antidote position—good culture counteracts toxic media. The counterbalancing perspective we found in Mumford, which continues among critics on both the left and the right, from the 1950s until today, presumes that "the people" have been hypnotized by the commercial media, and need to be awakened and/or uplifted, by the arts (high, fine, radical, or avant-garde) and the critical/academic apparatus that they have come to include.

This is still a patronizing rhetorical position, but it does not directly criticize the masses. This displacement of a critique of popular taste as being poisoned by the media, but redeemable through art, is also a longstanding characteristic of arts discourse. Mainstream tastes and interests (as they are represented in commercial culture) are being dismissed, while the tastes and interests of the elites *and* the radical are being extolled, and, if funding prevails, subsidized.

So how can arts supporters respond to hostility from people who resent being told that stuff they don't understand, don't like, and often find offensive is *still* good for them and for America, and should be funded by tax dollars? They found ways, however vaguely, to redefine the arts as a creative continuum and a creative heritage.

According to a typical example of arts-booster literature, the Campaign to Triple California State Funding to the Arts, support for the arts is about support for self-expression, healing, wisdom, diversity, and personal growth. To support the arts is also to support civic growth, safer neighborhoods, drug rehabilitation, and higher property values. To support the arts is to connect with the past, and make better prospects for the future. As their literature argues, "The arts enrich every aspect of civic life and contribute and enhance every citizen's ability to prosper and succeed, from cradle to grave."[6]

So something called "the arts" can benefit all of us, from birth to death, socially, economically, spiritually, and physically, no matter who we are or what our background is. This is a powerful version of the art-as-medicine perspective, developed to make it more likely that public funding would continue. The strategy was to define the arts in a way that no one could deny their value—who could possibly *not* support the route to such wonderful stuff? The instrumental ideology remains unquestioned, even as the arts are defined in more vernacular, everyday ways.

ELEMENTS OF VALUE

A major theme in this re-positioning of the arts is making a connection between the arts and local communities. Defining the arts as vital to community life can result in a kind of cynical functionalism, as Irwin Washington, executive director of the Lula Washington Dance Theater in south central Los Angeles notes, "They have to dress up what they do as something other than art. So a lot of groups have learned to define what they do as social service or as education. Or community development or economic development or health. They have to call it something else besides art."[7]

Rhetorically positioning the arts as community enhancement draws on the language of civic pride and urban renewal. The arts can be touted as ways to revitalize moribund downtowns and make urban neighborhoods better places to live.[8] Much is made of comparative rankings of support of the arts across nations or states or cities, mobilizing fears of "falling behind" if arts funding is cut.[9]

The literature supporting the Campaign to Triple California State Funding to the Arts[10] begins with the claim that "California is in danger of losing its image as a global leader in the arts," because it ranks forty-sixth out of fifty states in per capita arts support. It then develops a host of exemplary themes, to help would-be campaign members to persuade others of the importance of increased arts funding.

Support for the arts, the California campaign literature argues, "produces one of the best returns on any investment the state makes." This is because "not only do the arts generate substantial economic activity, create jobs and augment local and state tax coffers, the arts are vital to key industries which drive the state's economic engine—including the tourism, entertainment and high tech industries." The arts are said to "prepare students for the new global job market" because they promote "out of the box thinking," "team problem solving," and "creative approaches to complex problems."

Moreover, the arts are "also a cost effective approach to addressing a myriad of social issues—as gang intervention and drug reduction strategies . . . as a tool in the healing arsenal for people with AIDS and cancer, and as a life-affirming focal point for the elderly."

Here we have a laundry list of arts-caused good things, all of them available as counterevidence for the charge that the arts are either elitist frills or subversive trash. But the California campaign also gives some suggestions for directly countering particular charges. Is art pornographic and nonreligious? Let's not throw out the baby with the bathwater, says the "suggested response"; instead, point out that "public support of the arts funds better education, job preparedness, economic growth, and increases in home values, promotes tourism, and is a cost-effective means to deal with social problems such as crime and drug use." Yes, there may be controversy, but only in a tiny fraction of cases; and remember, "art is about creativity, and creativity is about pushing the envelope."

In response to the charge that the arts are elitist, the campaign literature suggests a strategy that sounds much like the "trickle-down" economic theories of the Reagan era: "Public monies spent on the arts filter throughout the community and directly benefit every class, every age group, every demographic."

And, in the following sentence, for those on the Left who might doubt this model, "the arts promote inclusion and bring people together." On the international front, the arts are claimed to "work as our ambassador to the world . . . they help sell our concepts of capitalism and democracy and as such are a vital part of our national defense. America is about freedom. Art is an expression of that freedom."

This particularly fulsome example of booster rhetoric shows how the arts can be endowed with all kinds of social power, and happily wedded to commercial success. In defending arts funding in the school system, the language is only somewhat less overblown.

Arts education is deemed "key to developing the competencies critical for work and life in the twenty-first century."[11] In interviews with various educators, a number of claims for arts-based improvements were made, including raising test scores, developing multiple kinds of intelligences, fostering "an appreciation for learning and working with people from different cultures," and "how to be better thinkers, how to be better workers, and how to live a higher quality of life." As several interviewees noted, "the benefits of arts education have not yet been effectively documented and disseminated," but no one seems to doubt that they soon will be. Lack of documentation for positive arts effects has never tempered the fervor with which the arts are supported.

Support for arts education is a direct legacy of the NEA debates. As National Public Radio's Robert Siegel noted, "In the debate over NEA's future, both critics and supporters of the Endowment have had praise for arts education. Supporters cited it as an example of the good work the NEA does. Critics presented it as an alternative to public funding of controversial artists. Foundations and corporations have also been putting more of their money into arts education."[12]

In seeking funding, arts supporters attempt to convince the hostile, the skeptical, or the indifferent that the arts deserve public financial support. In doing so, they define the arts in ways that explicitly or implicitly respond to particular hostilities (the arts aren't elitist, and need not be controversial), to skepticism (the arts are an investment, they make money, they stabilize communities), and to indifference (the arts aren't frills, or for someone else, they are vital ways to make life better for each and every one of us). The arts are vaguely defined as a melange of cultural forms, including what can be called traditional, classical, and avant-garde high arts, as well as folk or ethnic arts and crafts, while still being touted as powerful medicine for whatever ails society.

RESPONSES TO REPOSITIONING

Does it matter if the arts become defined as familiar, homey, ethnically diverse, community-building investments in our future? The response to this redefinition shows us what is at stake when we discuss the arts—that arts discourse is a way to address, however elliptically, our ongoing concerns about democracy, the public, commerce, the media, and modern life.

The exemplary document in the repositioning of the arts as vernacular culture is the 1997 NEA report *American Canvas*, written by Gary O. Larson.[13] It was seen by many as outgoing NEA head Jane Alexander's final commentary on the state of arts, after the bruising funding battles of the 1980s and early 1990s. It quotes from a series of meetings with community leaders, and offers a combination of commentary, critique, recommendation, and exhortation. The report directly addresses the problem of Americans who "fail to recognize the direct relevance of art to their lives." Some people "understandably view the arts as belonging to someone else," because they are the "product of an educational system that at best enshrined the arts as the province of elite cultures and at worst ignored the arts altogether."[14]

American Canvas repositions the arts as "not something that exists 'out there' in a world alien to many families, but . . . an essential part of the lives of most families." The report goes on to argue, "If we will look, we will find art all around us—in the things that we make with our words (songs, stories, rhymes, proverbs), with our hands (quilts, knitting, raw-hide braiding, pie crust designs, dinner-table arrangements, garden layouts)."[15] Such a homey redefinition is a way to convince those who, in the report's words, "look with suspicion at an 'arts world' that seems alternately intimidating, incomprehensible, expensive, alien, and, thanks to the generally poor job that the mass media have done in covering the arts, often disreputable."[16]

The report became an occasion to discuss the consequences of repositioning the arts as everyday activity, rather than extraordinary, exalted, or sublime creative expression. In "NEA Report Strikes at the Spirit of the Arts," Linda Winer summarizes *American Canvas* as "a notice to nonprofit arts and artists that their special role in elevating the spirit of civilization can no longer be assumed." She sees it as "a Trojan Horse of upbeat recommendations on how artists should stop being so darned concerned with such alienating and unwanted pursuits as the making of good art."[17]

Instead, she argues, they are being called upon to "devote more time to getting popular through cultural friendly service." They are being told that "if they want to survive in our hyped-up, sensation-crazy, profit-driven, pop-culture obsessed world, they'd better cut out that high-minded artsy stuff—nobody cares about that anyway—and prove their worth by solving the national crises caused by years of decaying schools and basic human neglect." Winer is arguing that repositioning the arts works *against* the making of good art, and that it encourages a marketing mentality of customer service, and expects art to cure community ills that have other causes.

Arthur Danto, in "Elitism and the NEA,"[18] makes a case for how the NEA's repositioning of the arts is *not* an effective way to argue for government funding. Why should taxpayers support gardening and proverbs? As he notes, "it is precisely because the advocates of art aim at enriching the lives of ordinary people that it will not greatly help to say that their lives are already enriched by art." Instead, he argues, "the problem is to explain the relevance in people's lives of the 'enshrined' arts, which have little in common with table arrangements and pie crusts." Danto does not, in this instance, describe what the actual differences are between enshrined art and everyday aesthetic activity, except to suggest that "the art in question" is more "distant and difficult."

The debate about repositioning the arts as everyday practice, catalyzed by the *American Canvas* report, foregrounds unresolved issues of distinction between "real art" and everyday activity. It also brings up important concerns about cultural democracy, the problem of choice, and the ways in which excellence can seem compromised by popularization. In a February 1998 forum, under the auspices of the National Arts Journalism Program (NAJP) at Columbia University, four panelists discussed the state of arts funding—Danto, described as an art critic and philosopher; Ron Feldman, art dealer and member of the National Council on the Arts; *New York Times* cultural critic Edward Rothstein; and NYU Dean of Graduate Arts and Sciences Catherine Stimpson.[19]

Earlier, Rothstein had made a stinging attack on the NEA's redefinition of the arts.[20] His arguments represent the "elite arts" defense, and demonstrate what seems to be at stake for those who want to continue to define the arts as exceptional. In a *New York Times* article, he charges that the NEA "has ended up becoming a multi-cultural clearinghouse." It is his contention that "the ideology of democracy leaves us with a vision of the arts that is pure pork barrel." As he explains, "without a homogeneous culture, without an education system that creates deep understanding, without a realization that art is more than entertainment, public patronage becomes a market phenomenon, responding to conflicting demands, competing bids, promises of influence." His ringing question was, "If the NEA is not elitist, what do we need it for?"

Notions of distinction become ways to critique the marketplace and the inadequacy of people's current tastes. Rothstein castigates democracy because he says it fosters an unwillingness to make distinctions, a leveling that is based in the great liberal idea of equality. He argues that "art is incompatible with this ideology" because art engages constantly in acts of discrimination. He goes on to claim that there is a premise in the "ideology of democracy" that the ability to create is distributed equally. He scoffs at this, using athlete Michael Jordan and chess player Gary Kasparov as incontrovertible evidence that "there are differences between us at birth that the civil order must ignore but the esthetic order is beholden to."

This definition of democracy as an abandonment of evaluation in the thrall of an ideology of sameness was directly challenged by other members of the panel. In contrast to Rothstein's characterization of democratic arts ideology as "no distinction is really possible, and one assertion is as good as another," the moderator, John Rockwell, as well as Stimpson and Feldman, clearly argue for discriminating choice as essential in a democracy. Stimpson argues that "political democracy sustains individuality . . . it sustains [it] in the voting booth, it sustains it in the marketplace." And Rockwell adds, "All kinds of political decisions are made, and it doesn't seem quite clear to me why choices can't also be made in intellectual and aesthetic areas." Similarly, Feldman argues that democracy is always about making choices; in a democracy "we are always burdened with making the choice, and privileged to make that choice."

But if choices are to be made, by whose standards should we judge? The problem of criteria of evaluation is a thorny one, and has become the crux of the so-called culture wars. When social critics talk about such disparate concepts as multiculturalism, deconstruction, and postmodernism, what they are struggling with is the crucial fault line between faith in timeless truths, and belief in pluralistic reconfigurations of contingencies. It is a fault line that has bedeviled philosophers since the Enlightenment, but it is now—through these kinds of public (mediated) discussions—becoming part of everyday political, social, and religious discourse.

The religious right worries about secular humanism; neoconservative critics worry about endless relativism; liberal commentators worry about totalitarianism and hegemony. If there aren't universal standards or timeless truths, then how are we to judge, and how are we to allocate? On what bases should we live our lives, choose our values, fund our arts?

Rothstein criticizes the NEA as a form of "bureaucratic patronage" that is now responsive only to "democratic demand." Thus, "instead of making decisions either on the basis of art or on the basis of some idea of the social good, or creating some kind of official art of a country, the artistic patron has to deal with this other force, the pressure of democratic demand."

What Rothstein is saying is that market or demographic criteria should not fund art. Why not, we might ask? The answer would involve understanding how and why arts discourse requires us to maintain a distinction between the arts and commerce, as well as the arts and popular taste. For Rothstein, the value of their arts is in their *separation* from market and taste criteria. But he does not explore the alternatives he call for: what exactly would "basis of art" criteria of evaluation be? There are many who would be rightly suspicious of art funded on the basis of a single "idea of the social good" or "official art of a country."

What is so bad about arts that are supported by "democratic demand"? Rothstein believes that the NEA wrongly sees the arts as entertainment, or as moral force, or as self-expression. In contrast, Rothstein wants the arts to be understood as a distinctive discipline, believing it is possible to make aesthetic judgments separate from social and political ones.

Stimpson most clearly questions his assumptions, and she is far less worried about the problem of consistent, coherent criteria for evaluation. She thinks we are living in "a marvelous period for the arts and culture. It is a period of multiple voices, great fertility, and, if you'll forgive the cliche, border crossings. It's messy, and we're not quite sure how to judge it, but there are enormous energies . . . this is a period of great fertility."

In contrast, Rothstein believes we are in a period where the citizenry "has absolutely no sense of the history or evolution of any art in the West." He asks, "How then are we to create a citizenry that is going to react to art in anything other than a journalistic, political, or ideological way, when no one has ever learned a language of art in any particular depth, when no aesthetic education has taken place?"

Rothstein directly addresses the specter that haunts American cultural criticism—the inadequately educated citizen. For him and many others, the lack of the "language of the arts" is a crucial lack. He calls for a national project, an "education in the language and discipline of the arts," and presumes that such an education would ensure that people choose the "right" arts for the "right" reasons. Obviously such an education, for Rothstein as well as for Danto, would *not* include the language and discipline of pie-making or gardening.

A definition of the arts as something extra-ordinary, beyond the everyday, is being protected. Like Danto and many others, Rothstein fears that the arts can't do and be what they need to do and be, in this fertile, messy period that Stimpson is so enthusiastic about. In contemporary arts discourse, the Arnoldian notion of a stable and easily located "best that has been thought and said" is being directly challenged by what the debaters gingerly describe as "the subtext of multiculturalism," as well as the redefinition of the arts as everyday aesthetic practice.

When the arts are simply imagined to be the beacons of excellence, to be created by the few for the edification of the many, they are clearly distinct from other, more popular forms. Current commentators may struggle with exactly how to determine the differences between them, based on content characteristics, but they insist on the need to prevent true art from being diluted, and to ensure that people have the training they obviously need to discern the best from the worst. This becomes much more difficult when the boundaries for "real" art are blurred.

To worry about being able to make evaluations is to worry about people's ability to choose their culture wisely, and few NEA commentators trust or appreciate the choices that people are currently making. This is especially evident when the mass media are discussed. Support for arts education, which also emerged in the NAJP panel, is a way for critics from a variety of political perspectives to once again call for an improved citizenry without directly criticizing people's current tastes.

What commentators hope is that, with the right kinds of arts education, the populace will finally know enough to appreciate the wonderfulness of the arts they currently disdain, mistrust, or are bored by. They will come to like the right kind of art, and thus be able to enjoy the benefits such arts are presumed to bestow.

THE PROBLEM OF COMMERCIAL MEDIATION

The much-dreaded "other" in arts discourse is modern commercial culture, conflated with the mass media. The arts, even now, when they are being defined as homey crafts or multicultural expression, are *still* positioned as nonprofit, as forms of culture that are, can, and should always remain, noncommercial. No matter how the arts are defined, they are always distinguished from, and preferable to, and able to be poisoned by, the marketplace and the media.

This is evident in commentary on why the arts need to be publicly funded, in explanations for why there is hostility to arts funding, and in arguing for why arts education is vital for the future.

In cultural criticism, "the media" are linked to technology, advertising, commerce, mass culture—all things believed to be anti-art, and therefore poisonous to the human spirit. When commentators imagine art as a form of anti-media, art is constructed as not-technology, not-advertising, not-commercial; it is therefore good for you, it is not-toxic.

In NEA chairman Jane Alexander's 1995 speech to the Economic Club of Detroit, she combines a number of media, commerce, and art themes:

> Like the loss of its pro-ball team or a landmark department store, the disappearance or diminishment of the arts signals an essential change in the character of a community and a civilization. The economy slackens. The spirit of our cities suffers. We turn inward—literally—to the succor of our homes, to our television sets, our video games, our cookie cutter shopping malls, our prefab culture. Is this what we want for our children, our grandchildren? The spirit and soul of a community will be damaged without this alternative to banality.[21]

This statement offers art as an antidote to the soul-destroying power of "our pre-fab culture," wherein television and shopping malls are banal. Notice, though, that Alexander compares the loss of art to the loss of a ball team or a department store—surely also modern, commercial, and prefabricated forms. But here she is defining the arts as soul-enhancing potions that draw us together in public space. Later she says "as technology, the TV, the computer and the World Wide Web serve more and more of our needs in the home and office, coming together in the community at arts events will become more and more desirable. These live events will begin to seem like some of the few authentic experiences we have." But such things as children's soccer games, pro-wrestling matches, skating rinks, and flea markets are also live events, no less authentic and public than museums and theaters. Do they offer an alternative to mediated, commercial banality? Should they also be funded by taxpayers?

Like most arts boosterism, Alexander's speech defines the arts as spiritual community enhancement. In calling for public rather than private funding of the arts, she asks, "Are all aspects of American life—from the nature of our government to a community's level of tolerance—to be decided by marketing-savvy special interest groups or by the voice of all of the people?" The final move in seeking support for the NEA is claiming a difference between the vox populi and special interests. But arts supporters are a special interest group, *and* they are becoming savvy marketers. What, then, is the essential difference between them and the groups that Alexander fears will decide "all aspects of American life?"

While things like marketing, the media, new communication technologies, and shopping malls are all imagined as not-art, the contemporary art scene is almost always dependent on them. In the abstract, and in booster discourse, the arts are imagined as antidotes or alternatives; but in the concrete, the arts are being marketed, mediated, sold in shopping malls, and used to develop corporate good will. This blurring of the divide sparks concern, too. Apparently, the only way that art can be trusted to do its magic work is if it remains clearly separate from media, culture, and commerce. Why?

The valuable social "work" that art is imagined to do is always contrasted with the seductive blandishments of mass culture. Some commentators believe that we can still use the media as conduits, to dispense the medicinal arts message. In his speech "Lifelong Learning in the Arts: We Need the Arts to Create Community and to Build Connections Across Generations,"[22] Ernest Boyer, president of the Carnegie Foundation for the Advancement of Teaching, argues that "if we do not educate our children in the symbol system we call art, we will lose not only our civility, but our humanity as well." He says "we need the arts to express ideas and feeling in ways beyond words . . . to stir creativity and enrich a child's ways of knowing . . . to empower the disabled . . . above all, we need the arts to create community and to build connections across generations."

This nonverbal, creativity-expressing, empowering, community-creating cultural form is utterly different from the symbolic material already extant. As Boyer argues, "we have 19 million preschoolers who watch television 15 billion hours every year. And wouldn't it be wonderful if we had a "Ready to Learn" cable channel with music and poetry and theatre and painting, a channel dedicated exclusively to arts programming for young children? After all, we have channels for news and sports and sex and weather and junk jewelry and kids' cartoons. Is it unthinkable that we would have at least one channel to enrich the aesthetic experiences of children?"

In Boyer's argument, only something called the arts can enrich children's "aesthetic experience." Television is a medium through which the powers of the arts *could* work, if only we had a channel devoted to dispensing this special elixir to kids.

PBS was imagined by its early supporters as some combination of a public forum, educational experience, and dispenser of high culture forms. The difficulties in meeting all these expectations, especially in a changing cable environment and in combination with the NEA funding debates, foreground the problem of the "artness" of PBS. Ambivalence surfaces about corporate underwriting, frustration with "culture lite," as well as ambivalence about television in general.

In support of the PBS principle, Jacob Weisberg argues that "the free market is a fine arbiter of many things, but aesthetic and intellectual value is not among them."[23] Like public education, the arts should be funded, Weisberg argues; but this need not include television, which he sees as socially destructive—"the real question is whether society can survive TV." He then argues that PBS has been unsuccessful in arts programming because it is dependent on corporate underwriting and "pander[s] ineptly to popular taste." "Middlebrow pabulum proliferates: cooking shows, reruns of Lawrence Welk, lightweight Anglophiliana of all kinds." He says that new cable channels like Bravo offer better fine arts programming, and A&E offers better documentaries, and he applauds the American Movie Channel and several planned independent film cable channels. The rationale for PBS needs to be reassessed, Weisberg argues, and "it's time to make some tough choices. Mine is to toss the preternaturally jolly dinosaur overboard, and sink or swim with Piss Christ."

By this logic, television is already offering some quality material and therefore does not need special funding, and yet television is still threatening society's survival. PBS, as an attempt to offer better-than-usual TV fare, is not successful in comparison with other channels. So—is television really anti-art? Or is it sometimes a good art distributor, but just not good enough?

Movies, radio, records, and television have all been dreamed of, initially, as potent distributors of high culture, and castigated for becoming, instead, distributors of "lower" forms.[24] As we saw in the mass culture debate, they have also been criticized for homogenizing or watering down both the high and the folk arts—of taking "authentic" culture and commercializing it.

NOTIONS OF AUTHENTICITY

When the arts are defined explicitly as the folk or traditional arts, it becomes particularly important that they remain untouched by commercial forces. In an NEA report, "Changing Faces of Tradition,"[25] Elizabeth Peterson explores the rationale for federal support of folk and traditional arts. As she says, "in ideal circumstances, folk arts as a living cultural heritage enable individuals and communities to shape and make sense of the world." Traditional arts are "doubly local": they are "both rooted in time and place, and expressions of the shared aesthetics, values and meanings of a cultural community."

This rationale connects well with Alexander's arguments for the arts as community-enhancing, while clearly separating these arts from mass culture. Quoting Peter Guralnick, the report argues that traditional artists speak from "a shared experience that links them inextricably not to the undifferentiated mass audience that television courts, but to a particular, sharply delineated group of men and women who grew up in circumstances probably very much like their own, who respond to the [art] not just as entertainment but as a vital part of their lives."

The "undifferentiated mass audience" who "responds to . . . entertainment" haunted 1950s American cultural commentators. Contemporary arguments for folk and traditional arts draw heavily on images of a modern, mass society, with rootless, atomized, aimless audiences entertained by media rather than "rooted in time and place, sharing . . . community." The folk arts, by this logic, offer ways to retain and enhance aspects of pre-mass life. From an essentialist perspective, they offer valuable, if vestigial, versions of the pre-mass-mediated cultural world. But aren't media audiences also "rooted in time and space"? Can't they share experience? Don't we still have face-to-face communities? And isn't "sharing aesthetics, values, and meanings" possible in modern life, too?

In the celebration of the folk or traditional arts we find, once again, the discourse of modernity, where a lost communal world is mourned, and a new, impersonal mass society is deplored. This critique lives on, most recently in the discussions surrounding Robert Putnam's influential analysis of "bowling alone."[26] But have we really become the atomized, anomic society that has so long been feared? Are cultural communities only being destroyed or are they also being constructed? And if so, are they somehow more worthy if constructed by the arts, and less worthy if constructed by the mass media? Why, exactly?

When the arts are defined as noncommercial, and combined with folk or traditional art, the concept of authenticity becomes a key rhetorical feature. There is an assumption that culture produced for profit, for large audiences, is less real and less worthy than that produced for love, for local kindred spirits. This draws on a romantic image of the folk, created and sustained through handicrafts, that has been historically constructed for specific purposes.[27] The idealization of the folk, and folk culture, continues in the ways that we imagine some forms of culture as "more real" and thus more valuable. This belief in a purer, more wholesome "primitive" people, creating virtuous culture, is being radically challenged in anthropology and museum studies. But in social commentary, we continue to mobilize a host of unexamined assumptions about the virtue and authenticity of noncommercial cultural forms.

The complexity of the relationship among high art, folk art, commerce, and media is evident in "market art," crafts made by native peoples expressly for the tourist market.[28] In Western Alaskan villages, the ideology of art/craft is evident as Eskimo carvers respond to increasing demand. To work faster, carvers specialize in particular designs, but "many of the objects, bought as mere souvenirs, are now looked up to as aesthetically significant works of art, even in terms of contemporary criteria and critical evaluation."

One carver says, "I see a lot of people working to meet demand. If I did that, I think I would lose my touch and my vision." The journalist reporting on the finding notes the tension between art values and money values—"Modern life means paying the bills. Villagers here must reach deep within themselves and find the talent and vision to create beautiful items admired by tourists and sought by collectors around the world. These artists excel because they have to."[29]

Now, where, in this as in many other examples, is the line dividing high art, folk art, craft, market demand, commercialization? Objects—carved bone, balleen, and ivory—are being made by native peoples to be sold to tourists, to make money. These objects are, it is said, aesthetically significant, as are many other objects of folk or traditional art, and are created, at least by some, in an explicitly high-art spirit. But how are they different from "mere" souvenirs? Or from kitsch? Are the hand-carved stones different from the mass-produced place mats and ashtrays using their image? How, exactly?[30]

Where does the "meaning" of the art object lie—in its origins? In its content? In its reception? These questions currently bedevil literary studies. But in public arts discourse, the meaning of an art object is in its membership in the empty set "the arts." The object has meaning if it can make something called "the arts" seem more virtuous and valuable than mediated culture. The social meaning of art requires the maintenance of a distinction between art and the commercial culture that most commentators believe is poisoning our lives.[31] But it is extremely difficult to maintain that logic and that distinction, once the high arts are rhetorically combined with folk arts and everyday practices, into some new, wonderful but familiar mix.

We are in a complicated rhetorical stance here, one that needs constant repair so that art can be kept sacred. Folk or traditional art can be imagined as medicinal only if we find ways to imagine it as emerging from, evoking, connecting with, and dispensing the meanings of a communal, pre-modern past. But this requires a hypodermic needle model of art-influence. It presumes that the origins of an art object somehow determine its effects. It assumes that art automatically transmits the values or meanings of its origins.

Some commentators explicitly point to the values allegedly represented in cultural forms, presuming that the arts dispense good values and the media dispense bad values. In this way, communities formed through the arts would somehow be more virtuous than those formed through the media. But are there really different values lodged deep in art and media? Can they be directly transmitted—sent to the audience—via the object?

And, given the contentious state of many local arts communities, does art really guarantee a community we want to live in? If we begin to question how art does its magic, we recognize that communities may not be so easily shaped, and values may not be so easily inculcated, by art.

ARTS IN THE MARKETPLACE

When commentators try to work out, in the concrete, their feelings about art, media, and the marketplace, their resistance to connecting them is clear. Art cannot operate as an alternative, redemptive force if it is sullied by the forces that are blamed for depraving us. Alexander calls for keeping "the arts" distinct from "marketing-savvy special interest groups,"[32] even though arts supporters are exactly that when they campaign for federal funding of the arts and when they seek it from the NEA.

In symbolic terms, "the marketplace" signifies corruption. This means money is anti-art when part of the marketplace, but good when it is distributed by some nonprofit agency, as in arts funding. But once again, by what alternative criteria should we fund art? Rothstein's question remains—are there other nonmarket criteria that we can agree on, and trust, that are preferable? What would these be?

Once the marketplace is defined as anti-art, it is automatically anti-spirit, anti-truth, anti-good. Such is the logic of Lawrence Russ's "Art and the Mad Machine: The Spirit of Addiction vs. the Spirit of Life."[33] The "addiction" in his essay is a contradictory amalgam: he begins by quoting William James (out of context) about "the bitch-goddess, success," then describes how advertising attempts to persuade people to buy products rather than to address their true needs, and then how these efforts make people more "insensitive, dependent, uncreative," so that they "crave larger doses, more extreme sensations, more extravagant symbols of status," until finally "the country spins downward in that widening, addictive spiral." What can save us from this downward spiral? Why the arts, of course.

"The arts throw their wooden shoes into the gears of that infernal machinery . . . good art offers ploughshares of revelation and pleasure, not sharper swords of competitive lust." He goes on to say that it is art's "implicit criticism of our destructive ways" that makes "the peddlers of worldly wealth and sway so scornful, angry, and even fearful in the face of the arts." He finishes his essay by claiming, "Our future is not saved or lost primarily in physical, economic or scientific combat, but rather in the war between the spirit of selfish desire and that spirit of irrepressible light that feeds—and shines from—our great works of art."

Well. This is an excellent example of the logic of counterbalance, where the arts are imagined as forces of light, opposed to and potentially triumphant over the forces of darkness. We found a more thoughtful example in Mumford's later career, and various versions of it in the mass culture debates of the 1950s and 1960s. In the abstract, this argument is invigorating, but in the concrete, it falls apart. This is evident whenever intellectuals try to justify liking something that is also commercial.

Take, for example, Rosenbaum's assessment of "The Danger of Putting Our Cultural Destiny in the Hands of Business,"[34] his meditation on the chain bookstore Barnes & Noble. Rosenbaum is clearly ambivalent about his affection for the new store in his Chicago neighborhood. It reminds him of his childhood public library in Florence, Alabama, in the 1950s, but he writes he's "not sure that all of what Barnes & Noble offers is an improvement." Sure, there's a wider and broader selection of reading matter, but the covers of the books are distressingly colorful and alluring. And the use of kiosks and staff favorites and purchasing incentives disturbs him.

And this connects to his ambivalence about corporate sponsorship of educational activities, which "have a totalitarian feel to them, in that they make it difficult to distinguish between true education and advertising." He supports government funding in the French model, which, he argues, avoids the intrusion of the marketplace on the "artistic integrity" of a work. He concludes, "There's no harm in checking out the magazines at Barnes & Noble over Starbucks coffee, but students should understand that, no matter how cozy, a bookstore doesn't replace a library."[35]

Well, yes. But libraries also struggle with the problem of patron demand vs. "other criteria" as they build collections. And Rosenbaum really *likes* the atmosphere in Barnes & Noble, and the selection, but he remains troubled by alluring book jackets and corporate funding of the arts. Why? What Rosenbaum is struggling with here is that Barnes & Noble is designed to make money, and does so by offering him (and many others) "good stuff" that he enjoys. But he also believes that the "good stuff" must be tainted, because it has corporate, money-based interests behind it.

The conundrum he is stumbling over is a desire for "disinterested" art or education or librarianship. Corporate interests are less trustworthy, for him, than the interests of teachers and librarians. But are they really? The real question is—*whose interests are the ones we should live by*? Whose values should count most? It is at *this* level that we can and should discuss culture, society, and commerce. Can capitalism serve the public interest? What are the consequences of particular economic arrangements for culture? What are the consequences of those influences for the quality of our individual and common life? But we can't get to that level of analysis from his argument. Instrumental logic prevents it.

Rosenbaum's ambivalence about his affection for Barnes & Noble is comparable to a widely shared ambivalence among intellectuals about contemporary culture. Yes, it offers us lots of stuff we like a lot, but surely it is poisonous, and not nearly as good for us as the worlds of our childhood. But we have been saying that for many generations now, and our decline (if it exists) has not been so simple or precipitous.

Rosenbaum's concern about corporate sponsorship is also widely shared. It is difficult for arts-supporters to sort out how they feel about the use of their "product" for corporate purposes. As alternative funding is being sought, it becomes unclear whether the arts are still "safe" and "good" if they also make money for someone else.

ARTS FOR COMMERCE

Many corporations are happy to use the arts as a public relations vehicle. For example, Mobil Oil "has built its public image as a caring, responsible and trustworthy company through the use of non-product advertising and sponsorship . . . [it] associates itself with quality by sponsoring PBS shows and arts events."[36] H. J. Heinz gave $450,000 for arts education, tied to a design contest for ketchup bottles. In response, a *New York Times* editorial says, "There does not seem to be anything inherently wrong with letting a company promote its ketchup if that is what it takes to generate money for arts programs in the schools . . . museums, performing arts groups and many other worthy causes would be nowhere without the benign self-interest of private companies." But is such self-interest benign?

In a 1997 conference "The Arts and Public Purpose," the "still tenuous alliance between for-profit and non-profit organizations" was the central concern.[37] The line between the two has been blurred, it was noted, but "audiences did not know or care if a play or opera was financed by nonprofit or commercial sources, *although that distinction still remains important to artists*" (my emphasis). In this perspective, money from any source is simply an opportunity to keep plays and operas available for audiences.

Another form of nonprofit/for-profit relationship was discussed, too—nonprofit arts as a "farm team," supplying the creativity that entertainment industries need. This concept was supported by examples of "fringe artists" who had become mainstream—in other words, commercially successful. It was noted that an appearance on Oprah Winfrey's television show could transform a book or singer. From corporate sponsorship to farm teams to success on *Oprah*—what now is the distinction between commerce and art?

When arts, media, and money become so obviously intermingled, the logic of the arts as antithetical to "the mad machine" is utterly challenged. When this intermingling is in conjunction with the vernacularization of arts, belief in the redemptive or counterbalancing power of the arts becomes even more difficult to sustain.

If the arts are also to include folk art, and then things like gardening and pie crusts, how can they still remain powerful and pure, available to save us? Once the arts are also souvenirs, or on Broadway, or get on *Oprah*, and/or become aspects of everyday life, it is difficult to see how they can operate to counteract all the bad stuff of the media and the marketplace.

In recent NEA-supporting material, the arts are made synonymous with nonprofit activities, done purely for love, not money. With this logic, however, all nonmarket activities are pure and redemptive, and deserve government support. And by this logic, artists should refuse any kind of monetary reward, since it would sully the redemptive power of their efforts. This, of course, is not where the rhetoric leads—it is apparently not money per se, but the market that is sullying.

The dichotomy between commercial culture—mediated, mass—and "good culture" is maintained. The arts are defined as noncommercial even as they relentlessly seek the funding they need to survive. They are imagined as being different from and vitally opposed to commercial culture, even as they use the same techniques (blockbuster museum exhibits), canonize past versions of it ("classic" movies, for example), and find success in it. In spite of all this, the arts still maintain an imaginary rhetorical role as antidotes to perceived cultural toxins in contemporary life.

PROTECTING THE INTERVENING VARIABLE

Arts commentators deploy a convoluted and inconsistent logic so that they can maintain their, faith and ours in art as social medicine. But recent attempts to desacralize the arts have made it more difficult to maintain faith in art's redemptive and/or counterbalancing power. How exactly is art different from the mass media, if it is commercially beholden and market driven? How is art different from what "the common people" do every day, for pleasure and not for profit?

Arts supporters, as well as academic critics, will not surrender the notion of the magic, wonderful "arts" even as the arts become redefined in ways barely distinguishable from the stuff they are supposedly antithetical to. So why maintain faith in the instrumental powers of art? Why not just give up the divide altogether, dispense with any notion of the arts as something special, and talk instead about expressive or aesthetic practice, or various cultural forms? *What would happen if we gave up all belief in the arts as social medicine?*

If we gave up notions of art as social medicine, the logic of American cultural and social criticism would come unraveled. The arts must maintain their conceptual distinctiveness so that they can still be invoked as a fudge factor in criticism. As distinct, sacred forces, the arts can serve as an intervening variable, one that guarantees that the people will become better, and society will be improved.

In American cultural and social thought, it is simply assumed that people and society will get better if the "right kind" of art is circulating. This allows critics to avoid directly blaming people for lousy tastes or lousy choices—it is instead the lousy culture that they are saturated in. If only they could have a bracing dose of high, folk, avant-garde, progressive, subversive, and/or communal art! In this way, critics maintain solidarity with democratic principles but not with actual people—they support "the people," just not these particular current people.

Invoking the arts as a fudge factor also allows us to avoid the hard work of directly defining what we value, and what should be done. To fill in the blank, to actually argue for what "art" now stands for, is to actually decide what you think is good and bad, important or trivial, necessary or unnecessary. And it is to call for specific, concrete action in support of those beliefs. Current arts discourse allows us to be for all good things, and against all bad things, simply by invoking the presumed good of the arts in opposition to the presumed bad of media, commerce, and the marketplace.

Such a discourse has significant costs. It guarantees that our social criticism is vague, overblown, insulting, and impotent. When we discuss our common life, what is wrong with it, and what can be done to improve it, we need all the directness, specificity, clarity, and compassion we can muster. Current arts discourse works against those qualities: an expressive, pragmatist view supports them

DREAMING DEMOCRATIC CULTURE

In the previous chapters I have explored a heritage of thought that continues to shape our beliefs, and discussions, of the social role of the arts. I compared and critiqued Tocqueville, Whitman, and Mumford as exemplary voices in a discussion that has included a variety of American intellectuals in the twentieth century, voices that we still hear today in our ongoing, unfinished discussion. I have done this to show both what is gained, and what is lost when we keep seeing art as having the instrumental power to make us better—when we keep believing in art as medicine.

American intellectuals struggle with a key dilemma—how to keep faith in democracy when the people seem so unworthy of it. In early hopes of a new democratic culture, and in later fears of mass-mediated culture, the same logic is deployed—faith in the ability of particular forms of culture to transform us into people worthy of democracy.

But our long-held faith in the instrumental power of the arts needs to be questioned. And that means that its potential redemptive role in democracy must be challenged. And that means we must rethink our demonization of the media, too, and that the role of the intellectual as a protector of arts-based virtue can also be challenged. And that puts a lot of what I—and many others—cherish at risk. But I also believe that such questioning allows us to reconfigure our democratic dreams in ways that are more realistic, more respectful, more powerful, and more practical.

NOTES

1. I interpretively analyzed approximately eighty-five editorials, essays, and articles, drawn from popular and trade media, from the 1990s. These were selected from a larger pool of material (more than three hundred articles) gathered through an electronic search using combinations of key words including *arts, funding, public, NEA,* and *society.* The selected articles addressed the question Why fund the arts? These pieces were analyzed rhetorically for their dominant themes and for their implicit assumptions about the social role of the arts.

2. Another revealing conversation worthy of interpretive analysis would be the coverage of the 1998 hiring of former Country Music Foundation director Bill Ivey to follow Jane Alexander as the head of the NEA. Coverage struggled with how to combine Ivey's country music connections with his academic ethnomusicology background and professorial demeanor in relation to the role of the NEA. Journalists ended up focusing on some version of Ivey's ability to "hang with queens and kings and talk to us good ol' country music boys, too," while carefully arguing that "Ivey's grass-roots background is no dumbing down of the nation's keeper of culture." See, as an example, Miriam Longine, "NEA Goes Country," *Atlanta Journal and Constitution*, 26 April 1998, 1L.

3. For histories and analyses of public funding of the arts, see Alice Goldfarb Marquis, *Art Lessons: Learning from the Rise and Fall of Public Arts Funding* (New York: Basic Books, 1995); Edward Arian, *The Unfulfilled Promise: Public Subsidy of the Arts in America* (Philadelphia: Temple University Press, 1989); Andrew Buchwalter, ed., *Culture and Democracy: Social and Ethical Issues in Public Support of the Arts* (New York: New Press, 1992).

4. Note the contradiction to avowed beliefs in free speech in this remark by New York State Senator Roy M. Goodman at the "The Arts and the Public Purpose" conference, May 1997, quoted in Mel Gussow, "Some Artistic Neighbors Try to Lower Their Fence," *New York Times*, 31 May 1997, section 1, 11.

5. New Humanist faith in art's essential ability to uplift and sacralize has contemporary versions, for example, Henry J. Hyde, "The Culture War," in *National Review* 42, no. 8 (30 April 1990): 25–27; Alexandra York, "Toward an American Renaissance in Art and Ideas," *The Humanist* 55, no. 1 (January–February 1995): 29–32; Kevin A. Hluch, "A Revolutionary Concept: The Aesthetic Scale in the Art World," *Ceramics Monthly* 46, no. 1 (January 1998): 98.

6. "Campaign to Triple California State Funding to the Arts" thecity.sgsu.edu/CALAA (June 1998). This Web site included sample letters, frequently raised objections, suggested support strategies, and action steps.

7. Irwin Washington, "Arts Education vs. Artists," on National Public Radio's *All Things Considered*, 15 September 1997.

8. A 1996 conference in Chicago, "The Arts and Humanities as Agents for Social Change" explicitly focused on using the arts for urban renewal; see Dirk Johnson, "Does Art Change Things or People?" *New York Times*, 28 September 1996, section 1, 15.

9. Bruce Weber, "Building on the Arts: Cities are Fostering the Arts as a Way to Save Downtown," *New York Times*, 18 November 1997, A1. Contemporary arts rhetoric on city rankings draws on images that have been evident in urban booster rhetoric since the nineteenth century. In an editorial that combines references to earlier philanthropic boosterism with a call for a new arts initiative in Boston to "keep it in the ranks of world-class cities," see Anne Hawley, "The Fate of Art in Boston," *Boston Globe*, 11 May 1998, A13.

10. California campaign, thecity.sgsu.edu/CALAA.

11. Getty Educational Institute for the Arts, "Educating for the Workplace through the Arts," national conference, excerpts published in *Educational Leadership*, November 1997, 12–14.

12. Robert Siegel, "Arts Education vs. Artists," National Public Radius *All Things Considered,* 15 September 1997.

13. Gary O. Larson, "American Canvas: An Arts Legacy for Our Community," report for the National Endowment for the Arts, arts.ednow.gov, 1997; excerpts published in National Arts Journalism Program Occasional Report No. 1, Columbia University, 1998.

14. Larson, "American Canvas," NAJP excerpts, 36.

15. Larson, "American Canvas," NAJP excerpts, 36.

16. Larson, "American Canvas," NAJP excerpts, 36.

17. Linda Winer, "NEA Report Strikes at the Spirit of the Arts," *Newsday,* 17 October 1997, B2.

18. Arthur Danto, "Elitism and the NEA, *The Nation,* 17 November 1997, 6–7.

19. "The Future of Public Arts Funding," NAJP Occasional Report No. 1, 1998.

20. Edward Rothstein, "Where Democracy and Its Money Have No Place," *New York Times,* 26 October 1997, section 2, 1.

21. Jane Alexander, "Our Investment in Culture: Art Perfects the Essence of Our Common Humanity," *Vital Speeches of the Day,* 15 January 1996, 210–13.

22. Ernest Boyer, "Lifelong Learning in the Arts," *Vital Speeches of the Day,* 15 October 1994, 15–18.

23. Jacob Weisberg, "Bullwhips Yes; Barney No: The GOP's Kulturkampf Will Force Liberals to Rethink What Kinds of Art the Government Should and Should Not Fund. PBS Doesn't Make the Cut," *New York* magazine, 6 February 1995, 26–27.

24. See Carolyn Marvin, *When Old Technologies Were New: Thinking About Electric Communication in the Late 19th Century* (New York: Oxford University Press, 1990); and Daniel Czitrom, *Media and the American Mind: From Morse to McLuhan* (Chapel Hill, University of North Carolina Press, 1982).

25. Elizabeth Peterson, "The Changing Face of Tradition: A Report on the Folk and Traditional Arts in the United States," NEA Research Report No. 38, November 1998.

26. Robert Putnam, *Bowling Alone: The Collapse and Revival of American Community* (New York: Simon and Schuster, 2000).

27. For a telling account of authenticity and the academic emergence of folklore studies, see Regina Bendix, *In Search of Authenticity: The Formation of Folklore Studies* (Madison: The University of Wisconsin Press, 1997).

28. Mike Dunham, "Subsistence Art: Traditional Crafts Surface in Gambell, but Some Artists Long for a Freer Spirit," *Anchorage Daily News,* 21 September 1997, 16.

29. Quoted in Dunham, "Subsistence Art," 16.

30. Walter Benjamin argues that reproduction removes the art object from "the fabric of tradition." Uniqueness and permanence—the aura—decays. The loss of the aura is simultaneously an emancipation; art objects are freed from ritual, and so can function more politically. Benjamin considers some consequences of this shift in relation to painting, poetry, Dadaism, film, and the aesthetics of fascism, in "The Work of Art in the Age of Mechanical Reproduction," in *Illuminations,* ed. Hannah Arendt (New York: Schocken Books, 1969).

31. On the nature and implications of making and maintaining distinctions, see Eviatar Zerubavel, *The Fine Line: Making Distinctions in Everyday Life* (Chicago: University of Chicago Press, 1993).

32. In calling for public rather than private funding of the arts, she asks, "Are all aspects of American life—from the nature of our government to a community's level of tolerance—to be decided by marketing-savvy special interest groups or by the voice of all of the people?" Jane Alexander, *Vital Speeches of the Day*, 15 January 1996, 210–13.

33. Lawrence Russ, "Art and the Mad Machine: The Spirit of Addiction vs. the Spirit of Life," *Omni*, July 1992, 6.

34. Jonathan Rosenbaum, "The Danger of Putting Our Cultural Destiny in the Hands of Business," *The Chronicle of Higher Education*, 17 April 1998, A64.

35. For an insightful analysis of how chain bookstores may *not* be destroying literary culture, see Charles Paul Freund, "Literature in Chains: Are Superstore Databases Turning Books into Pretzels?" *Reason*, November 1997.

36. "We're the Good Guys: Image Propaganda from Mobil Oil," *Business and Society Review*, Spring 1995, 33–35.

37. American Assembly–sponsored conference on "The Arts and the Public Purpose," Harriman, New York, in May 1997; quotes from Gussow, "Some Artistic Neighbors Try to Lower Their Fence."

Chapter Five

Art as Experience: John Dewey's Aesthetics

Dewey's perspective on the arts is a powerful alternative to the assumptions we have explored so far. Dewey does not imagine the arts instrumentally, as social medicine, although he values them deeply as social experiences. His perspective considers, simultaneously, aesthetic experience *and* democratic possibility. Yet, unlike the intellectuals and social critics we have considered so far, Dewey does not expect art to transform people so that democracy can flourish.

Dewey's vision of a democratic society depends on social action based in social inquiry. Dewey's faith is in intelligent social practice. His primary concern, throughout his career as a public philosopher, was how to make the best of people's inherent capacity for democratic life. His work in education, social philosophy, and cultural and social criticism is of a piece—it shows how we can change the ways we think and act, to make a better world.[1]

Dewey presumes that everyone has aesthetic impulses, and takes delight in aesthetic experiences. He does not presume that "the people" are deprived of intelligence and sensitivity, and therefore in need of doses of art, although he is painfully aware of the deprived conditions under which many people work and live. Nor does he presume that intellectuals are in special possession of traits that the general populace lacks, although he deeply values the habits of inquiry that good education can foster.

The key difference between Dewey and the other critics we have examined is that he does not presume that some essence called "the arts" must be injected into the populace to make them into better people.

This is why his perspective differs radically, both in logic and in tone, from almost all the other critics we have discussed.

A TOCQUEVILLIAN PREMISE

Tocqueville and Dewey share faith in the possibilities of rational, imaginative thought, and both value democratic experience. In contrast to the Whitmanian heritage that has suffused American social and cultural criticism, I propose that we begin with a more Tocquevillian premise, then develop a Deweyan perspective on the role of the arts in contemporary life. If we do so, we can escape the rhetorical bind of contemporary defenses of the arts, let go of the self-righteous heritage of the mass culture debates, and move beyond the sterile dichotomy of art/commerce, or art/industry, that characterizes twentieth-century American thought.

Like Tocqueville, we can compare the modernity we find in contemporary America with the alternatives that have existed and which currently exist. What are the possibilities in the society we already have? What are the true dangers to it? We can pay special attention to the benefits of individualism and voluntary associations, not in relation to utopian possibility, but in relation to actual alternatives.

With Tocqueville, we can focus not on the presumed evils of capitalism and commerce, nor on the lost promise of the American dream, but on the current good and bad in our common life. And, with Tocqueville, we can see and appreciate that which is extraordinary and beneficial in contemporary experience.

This is not a call for a sunny denial of all that is wrong in contemporary society, or a knee-jerk call for mindless patriotic fervor. A more Tocquevillian orientation would allow us to explore what the society we now have is already offering, and then evaluate it against the available alternatives. It may be that, overall, the supposed evils of individualism, commerce, and the media offer us much more than we realize. It is also possible that, with a Tocquevillian premise, we find that they offer some protection from tyrannies we have forgotten how to fear.

The concerns of contemporary criticism are the vapor trails of long-standing concerns about mob rule, fascism, revolution, fragmentation. If we no longer feel these to be clear and present dangers, then Tocqueville helps us appreciate our relative freedom from their likelihood. Contemporary critics of modernity bemoan the loss of traditional society, and seek faster progress toward a utopian version of it, without recognizing the value of what is already here, or the problematic consequences of the traditions they wish could return, or be reinvented.

We struggle over the continuing injuries of race, class, gender, and sexual orientation without remembering how incredible it is that we can articulate, much less become socially active about, these injustices. For all that is wrong in modern life, there is so much that is extraordinarily better, especially from the perspective of women, children, and minorities. Modernity is not just political, or economic, or social, or cultural. To distinguish one element of it as causal or curative is to lose sight of how the "modern formation" is one that operates synergistically (for good and ill) to sustain individualism, rationality, and relative freedom from many past evils.

A Tocquevillian orientation acknowledges trade-offs. To begin with his perspective is to begin by noticing what modernity makes possible, and what is worth protecting in it. Among the things he found in 1830s modernity were new forms of democratic culture, less refined and sophisticated, but also lively, varied, engaging, and appropriate to the society in which they emerged. Why is it still so hard for us to appreciate, as he did, the extraordinary and unprecedented creativity, variety, fecundity, and everyday delights of contemporary commercial culture?

Can we construct a social criticism that takes contemporary arts and media seriously, is concerned with the ways in which our actions and beliefs are culturally determined, and believes in the prospect of popular democracy, without extraordinary interventions? All the social critics we have considered rely on art—be it defined as high, traditional, popular, avant-garde, or subversive—to make us into what democracy needs us to be. What would American social criticism be like if it cared about democratic possibilities, and valued artistic experience, but did *not* imagine art as an "intervention"? What would happen if we let go of the presumption that art has the medicinal power to save or doom us?

ART AS EVERYDAY EXPERIENCE

Dewey defines the arts as forms of social practice; as such the arts share the possibility of all human practice to solve problems and make the world better. Adopting Dewey's pragmatic perspective on the arts has profound consequences. If we deploy his perspective, virtually all the assumptions about the arts with which we are now familiar come undone.

We can create an alternative discursive heritage for the arts when we combine aspects of Tocqueville and Dewey. With Tocqueville we appreciate modern culture's ability to "spread light" in engaging, lively, varied ways. We combine this with Dewey's perspective on the arts, public life, and democratic possibility. The result is a pragmatic social aesthetics, one that challenges the ideologies of redemption and counterbalance, treats the mass media as aspects of communicative practice, and expects social critics to respect the aesthetic experiences of everyday people. A pragmatic social aesthetics changes both the logic of American social criticism and the presumed responsibilities of intellectuals.[2]

Dewey's ideas about aesthetics, the arts, culture, and experience thread their way through all of his work, and are best understood as a part of his larger project. Dewey's perspective on the arts is most directly developed in his 1934 book, *Art As Experience*,[3] which is simultaneously a critique of mainstream aesthetic theory, an articulation of an alternative approach, and a definitive treatment of the notion that is central to Dewey's thought: experience. As Alexander notes, to understand how Dewey thinks about aesthetic experience is to illuminate the central themes of his whole philosophy.[4]

Dewey suggests that it is best to arrive at a new theory of art by way of a "detour," a path away from artistic products and toward "ordinary forces and conditions of experience that we do not usually regard as aesthetic" (*Art As Experience*, 4).[5]

It is Dewey's contention that:

> The sources of art in human experience will be learned by him who sees how the tense grace of the ballplayer infects the onlooking crowd; who notes the delight of the housewife in tending her plants, and the intent interest of her goodman in tending the patch of green in front of the house; the zest of the spectator in poking the wood burning on the hearth and in watching the darting flames and crumbling coals.[6] (5)

Here we have a more "vernacular" version of the arts—one that sounds much like the NEA defense of the 1990s. Contemporary vernacularization of the arts, in defense of continued public funding, leaves us in a rhetorical bind because it still relies on an instrumental logic. This logic forces arts supporters to seek public funding for everyday activities, claiming that, as "arts," these activities could do wonderful things for the young, the old, the handicapped, the oppressed, for individuals, neighborhoods, and communities.

Dewey writes against what he calls the "esoteric view" of art, a view that puts art on a pedestal, as something distinct from the everyday. But he also writes against all theories that isolate and compartmentalize art, that "'spiritualize' [art] out of connection with the objects of concrete experience." That is just what contemporary arts supporters are doing when they simultaneously vernacularize and spiritualize the arts. Dewey's goal in this book is to "recover the continuity of esthetic experience with normal processes of living."[7]

Why would Dewey want to do this? Dewey asks us to consider a work of art as something that "develops and accentuates what is characteristically valuable in things of everyday enjoyment."[8] In reclaiming aesthetic experience as an aspect of everyday life, Dewey is animating his philosophy of experience—giving it direction, purpose, and meaning. Aesthetic experience is, for Dewey, a clarified and streamlined version of general experience—"freed from the forces that impede and confuse its development."[9] It therefore offers the philosopher a way to understand experience itself, and it offers Dewey a way to argue for experience as organizing and animating intelligent social action.

For Dewey, "experience in the degree in which it is experience is heightened vitality."[10] It is "active and alert commerce with the world; at its height it signifies complete interpenetration of self and the world of objects and events." Aesthetic experience is one of the means by which individuals seek and maintain connections to the material world and to each other—it sustains the conjoint activity that is the ground and end of Dewey's philosophy.

Art is not the only means. For Dewey, education and science also offer experiences that animate and enlarge our lives, and that can support the kind of experience-based inquiry that allows us to change society. As with Tocqueville, the arts and the sciences are venues for forms of social interaction. They are therefore aspects of, rather than forces in, social life.

Exploring how art operates as experience is Dewey's opportunity to explore how experience operates overall. Aesthetic experience becomes the particular case that illuminates the general condition—the organization of human energies. Art operates, he argues, "by selecting those potencies . . . by which an experience . . . has significance and value. . . . [I]n art the forces that are congenial, that sustain not this or that special aim but the processes of enjoyed experience itself, are set free."[11]

He considers the arts as a form of connection among people, a connection that encourages "the expansion of sympathies, imagination and sense."[12] The arts, as experience, are forms of communication, and communication is for him the vehicle for community. As he argues in *The Public and Its Problems*,[13] community is another term for democracy. Here we can establish the necessary connection: for Dewey, as well as for our other critics, arts can operate as vehicles for democracy.

This is a difficult juncture in my argument. Dewey would seem, on a cursory reading, to be saying that arts (and maybe science and education) are what people need to be good citizens. But his argument is crucially different from that of Whitman and twentieth-century critics, because he is talking about aesthetic *experience,* not about art as a special commodity or force for good. He is talking about something that each of us is already engaged in.

Dewey is adamant that the arts are more intense, meaningful, revealing, and portable versions of things that happen every day. As objects of experience they offer intensified versions of what already connects us with each other. They can also offer "a manifestation, a record and a celebration of the life of a civilization, a means of promoting its development, and . . . a judgment upon [its] quality.[14]

The arts operate in this way *not* because they have special powers, or represent higher or better aspects of man, or contain essential wisdom. They do this because the arts *are* experience, they are the human practice of communication, and therefore they are examples of valuable conjoint activity. Put somewhat differently, for Dewey the arts are widespread human actions, actions that become forms of recognizing, recording, celebrating, encouraging, and evaluating themselves.

This means that the arts are intrinsically ours—they are cultural and communal—and they are thereby valuable. Dewey's perspective values the arts not by compartmentalizing them, but by restoring them to the concrete creative experience of all people. He argues that we must work to ensure that all people can sustain and develop lived experience in vivid, various, lively ways.

ART, COMMUNICATION, AND DEMOCRACY

Dewey's philosophy of art is grounded in his concerns about modernity and democracy. If we examine a key chapter ("The Crisis in Culture") in his *Individualism Old and New*,[15] in conjunction with his arguments in *The Public and Its Problems*, we see how his pragmatic aesthetics can address industrialization, commercialization, and democratic possibility.

The key term is *communication*, understood not as the transmission of ideas, but as the creation and maintenance of common meanings.[16] For Dewey, communication is the way that people come to share an understanding of the consequences of their combined actions; this understanding can "inform desire and effort and thereby direct action."[17] Free and unfettered communication is the way in which the public can become aware of itself, and so can create and sustain a true community. And Dewey believes "the clear consciousness of a communal life, in all its implications, constitutes the idea of a democracy."[18]

Where does art fit into this connecting of communication and democracy? *The Public and Its Problems*, published in 1927, is Dewey's account of the problem of a democratic public, written before he had fully developed an analysis of the ways in which art operates. In this early account, Dewey views art as a special form of social inquiry—a deeper and more compelling version of the knowledge that the public needs to become aware of itself.

The book is written to suggest the conditions necessary for the creation of an articulate democratic public, and the conditions necessary for the creation and maintenance of democratic communities. It is written *against* arguments, like Walter Lippmann's, for the necessity of elite, expert, intellectual opinion.[19] Lippmann is the shadow opposition against which Dewey offers his notion of social inquiry, based in concrete experience, shared, circulated, and made available for discussion and evaluation, as the necessary condition for democracy.

In this context, art appears briefly, almost as an afterthought, as a potent disseminator of the full scope of social inquiry. Artists have always been, he says, the real purveyors of news, "for it is not the outward happening in itself which is new, but the kindling by it of emotion, perception and appreciation."[20]

Dewey argues that "the highest and most difficult kind of inquiry and a subtle, delicate, vivid and responsive art of communication" can breathe life into the machinery of the transmission and circulation of knowledge. He ends his chapter on the search for the Great Community with these stirring words, even invoking Whitman: "When the machine age has thus perfected its machinery it will be a means of life and not its despotic master. Democracy will come into its own, for democracy is a name for a life of free and enriching communion. It had its seer in Walt Whitman. It will have its consummation when free social inquiry is indissolubly wedded to the art of full and moving communication."[21]

In Dewey's early analysis, democracy requires art because art is an enhancement of communication necessary for communion, community and, therefore, democracy. Eight years later, in *Art As Experience*, he develops the notion of art as *imaginative* experience, and so gives it a more fundamental role in the expansion and enhancement of human association.

He explores what he calls the "humane function" of art in his final chapter, "Art and Civilization." He explicitly contrasts his approach with those that presume "direct moral effect and intent to art." For Dewey, art operates "not directly, but by disclosure"; it offers a sense of unrealized possibilities, and so makes us aware of "constrictions that hem us in and of burdens that oppress."[22]

He quotes Shelley's statement that "imagination is the chief instrument of the good." It is the way in which individuals put themselves in others' places,[23] the way that human loyalties operate, the way that thought and desire are commanded. Art, Dewey says, "has been the means of keeping alive the sense of purposes that outrun evidence and of meanings that transcend indurated habit."[24]

Here we can see how, in Dewey's account, the arts function in ways much like science and communication—as ways to enhance social intelligence. They are not an intervening variable, but exemplars of creative, communicative human action. Art becomes one of the many ways that modern American life can be liberating and enlivening, while offering connection in community.

Dewey's vision of democracy, of communication, of art, is a simultaneous one—freedom in association, liberation in conjoint activity. Imaginative experience is the way that we both free ourselves from that which constricts and binds and connect ourselves with that which supports and sustains. As Dewey argues, the liberating and uniting potentials of art proceed from imaginative experience, which is the heart of its moral potency.[25]

Note that, in every instance, Dewey does not argue that art is in itself a power or force; it does not contain some substance that is transmitted from the mind of the artist to the waiting public. Instead, art is a form of imaginative kindling. It works against the local, the provincial, the mistrustful, toward a wider, more cosmopolitan and empathetic understanding. It needs to be acknowledged as a form of social relationship, not "treated as the pleasure of an idle moment or as a means of ostentatious display."[26]

DEWEY AND AMERICAN ARTS DISCOURSE

Using this sketch of Dewey's ideas about art, we can explore what happens to the arguments of previous critics if we deploy a Deweyan perspective of art as experience. Rather than represent myself as speaking for Dewey, I offer a Deweyan perspective, with evidence from his work, but without claiming to represent with certainty what he would have said. By doing this I hope to avoid the pitfalls of the intellectual parlor game of "if so and so were alive today," a game that collects a sampler of quotes designed to demonstrate that long-dead great thinkers support the position of the bricoleur.[27]

Instead I directly explore particular discursive claims, showing how they are transformed by a Deweyan perspective. This concern for consequences also makes my analysis pragmatist, rather than mainly rhetorical, in style and intent. With Dewey, I believe that the ways we think both constrict and enable experience, and therefore both constrict and enable our actions. The ways we have thought about the arts constrict the ways in which we understand and enact them. I offer Dewey's perspective as a better way to think about the arts in democracy, and to act toward them. Adopting Dewey's view of the arts can enable us to act in more just and respectful ways toward other people and our common life.

DEWEY, WHITMAN, THE YOUNG AMERICAN CRITICS

As Whitman described what a new divine Literature can supposedly achieve, he also argued that nineteenth-century social ills were connected to the inadequate art of the times—commercially successful culture. In Whitman we find an exemplary case for art that can redeem us. Ideal Art, created by a new race of orbic bards, is an otherworldly force, one that can move American society into its next, spiritual phase of development. Its new form may well spring from the mechanics and farmers and workmen of the West, but it has not yet arrived, its powers are not yet evidenced. Whitman sets up a belief in art's power that allows him to keep faith in an imagined new art form that would spring from an idealized new public, while deploring the current forms and predilections of the populace.

The Young American critics adopted Whitman's redemptive logic in a somewhat tempered form. The arts they called for were also American, also an alternative to commercial and aristocratic culture, but not necessarily mystical or spiritual. Yet the pattern of argument holds—a new form of art will create a new form of society. Art, in these versions, is an instrument for social change, brought into being by a particular group of creative people, and distributed to others so that they all may become enlivened and animated.

Here the similarities and differences with Dewey are most obvious. Writing at the same time, Dewey does *not* see art as something that can be distributed, as a commodity, for the transformation of people or groups. For Dewey, art is already a social relation, a process, a version of what people are up to. His vision does not require a new kind of art or a special group of people—just an arrangement through which the artfulness of the everyday can be more fully and freely expressed.

Dewey's vision does not, therefore, depend on a particular group of creative artists or orbic bards, or on a particular kind of art, democratic or divine, for its fruition. It does not anoint special forms of arts with special powers. It does not presume that bad art has led to bad people, and that good art will lead to good people. Instead, it presumes that people are already engaged in art-acts, and that society would be even better if such art-acts were more widely and more deeply shared and enjoyed.

This means that Dewey does not rely on the creation of a heretofore unknown cultural form to redeem the American dream. Instead, the dream of America is democracy, is community, is communication, is art—the American dream is an enacted relationship. It becomes our responsibility to maintain and enhance such activity in selective ways.

There are no simple causes or simple cures for what ails us, but there are ways to make things better, by doing what we already do. Dewey's vision is less dramatic and more inclusive—we each participate in, and have responsibility for, the larger project of democracy.

DEWEY AND THE NEW HUMANISTS

In stark contrast, the philosopher-king is central to the vision of the New Humanists. In their version of the world, a small group of people, because of their special abilities, are able to lead. Wisdom is not widely distributed because it is not easily available—wisdom comes from study and discipline. Dewey shares the New Humanist faith in wisdom through study and discipline, but unlike them, he believes that maximum participation is needed for social intelligence.

In New Humanist thought, only some people are capable of aesthetic work at the required high level. This means that an improved American life requires that truths of the past be protected and defended in the present by those few who can fully apprehend them. The modern world is full of Whitman's "gaud and fraud," and it is up to the "saving remnant" to recognize and protect the heritage of transcendent truth from the masses. While some New Humanists, like Stuart Sherman, attempted to construct a more egalitarian humanism, the elitism of the position is central to it—only some people have what it takes to understand, and to lead.

In dramatic contrast, Dewey believes, deeply, in the incorporation of all people into community, and so into democracy. His view is not, however, "leveling," and he is not in any way against excellence. This is a common, unfair misreading of Dewey. His belief is that excellence can and will be recognized and sought after, through common actions and activities, in community. Excellence is what inquiry fosters.

Because a Deweyan position is so often misread as either mechanistic or relativistic (or both), it is important to see how committed to "the good" Dewey is. For Dewey, Excellence and Truth and Beauty[28] do not reside in traditional objects of arts, to be contemplated and absorbed. But the ability to respond to the excellent, the true, and the beautiful is a central aspect of human life: it gives direction and meaning to our experience. Dewey is egalitarian without being leveling, and without eschewing the quest for excellence.

Unlike the New Humanists, Dewey does not presume that modernity involves the loss of much that is precious. The New Humanist vision, like most of American social criticism, presumes loss—of community, of felicity, of faith, of hope. Theirs is a rhetoric of decline, erosion, and corruption, one that becomes, as the century proceeds, a conviction that most nonintellectuals lead empty lives.

This means that, for them, the past becomes a repository of hope, where once there was community, abundance, faith, meaning. For New Humanists, the past was also purer, closer to the fundamental and transcendent truths that are now being eclipsed and therefore forgotten. The New Humanists rely on the past both for artifacts that contain and can bestow wisdom and for a vision of what must be defended against the corrosive flow of modernity.

This idealization of the past, and related desire to protect pockets of the past from a chaotic present and future, is antithetical to a Deweyan perspective. The past and present and future contain both good and bad, sweet and bitter, truth and falsity—the issue is the proportion and the goal is to enhance the good and decrease the bad. This is why Dewey is never a relativist—the social project is about making things better, not accepting whatever already is.

But for Dewey, the modern is not inherently corrosive, but is instead an ongoing transformation that requires concomitant changes in the ways we connect with each other. The key problem for Dewey is how we conduct our common life; art matters only in relation to the larger problem of democracy.

Dewey, too, is concerned with loss, but his concern is specific—the loss of the local, the face-to-face, the communal.[29] His solution is specific, too—policies and institutions that enhance the abilities of people to learn and question and understand in relation to one another, and in relation to the consequences of their own actions. That is why he focuses on education as one means to enhance those abilities; that is why he values scientific inquiry; that is why he values aesthetic experience. Dewey is ever tied to the concrete, the local, the particular, and puts his faith in the salutary influence of ongoing, examined experience.

There is no hallowed past, corrupt present, or mythic future in Dewey's thought. In history there is evidence of man's nature and of man's possibilities; in the present there are circumstances that occlude and enhance those possibilities; in a future we create together those possibilities can achieve a fuller fruition.

DEWEY AND THE MARXISTS

Dewey's moderate vision of social change frustrated his more radical readers. Yet Dewey was skeptical of corporate capitalism, and believed in the necessity of dramatic institutional and social change. His social and political activism was extraordinary. But his unwillingness to find villains, or to offer simple cures, made him incapable of allying with any particular doctrine or movement.

I have argued that Dewey's social criticism does not spiritualize and compartmentalize art, does not offer simple causes and simple cures for social ills, does not presume that some individuals have special insight and wisdom, and does not rely on a demonization of the modern. He views art as everyday experience, society as a mixture of good and evil, with individuals capable, through conjoint activity, of understanding and critiquing and improving that mixture. Modern life offers conditions favorable to such understanding, critique, and improvement—our common task is to take the opportunities modernity gives us.

But there is an additional aspect of a Deweyan perspective that differentiates him from most social critics, and it is most obvious when we compare his thought with that of his Marxist contemporaries. Dewey sees them, along with many others, on a quixotic and ultimately disabling "quest for certainty."[30] Dewey shared, far more than most people realize, the Marxist mistrust of capitalism, a Marxist faith in socialism, and a Marxist desire for social change. But Dewey's mistrust, faith, and desire relied on a very different vision of how human history proceeds. His mistrust is of *all* forms and forces that hobble the free play of intelligence. His faith is in the human ability to understand and create alternative social forms. And his desire is for ever-increasing experimentation with social possibilities.

Nothing ever ends, becomes final, or stays secure in a Deweyan perspective. His utopia resembles the best he finds in contemporary life—there is simply more of it, available for everyone. Unlike 1930s Marxists, he does not presume that there are laws of history, or immutable forces, or certain outcomes, nor does he believe that revolution can offer us a world in which social problems are solved. Not only is there no simple cause, no simple cure, no special sight, but there also is no certain outcome—not the certainty of revolution, nor the certainty that a revolution will bring us a better world. In this, too, he is Tocquevillian.

The understandable desire for certainty is what Dewey so thoroughly critiques; he offers in its stead endless transformation, humanly worked and reworked. The question is never *if* things will change, but *how* they will change—toward whose purposes, which possibilities, with what consequences. Change is unfolding, and is for the best when in response to the evidence it itself uncovers—change creates the understanding required for more and better change.

This is why a Deweyan perspective is antidoctrinaire. If there are no fundamental certainties or laws, there can be no simple statements that stand true for all times and places. Everything is up for revision, based on actual consequences. Life is a process of experimentation and evaluation, and change comes through experiencing its consequences, and deciding on alternatives. Change is always contingent on concrete experience, not doctrine or theory.

This is also why Dewey can strike some readers as vague, fuzzy, even contradictory, especially when he is contrasted with those who produce clean and quotable truths and elaborate, self-referential theories. His insistence on the connection between experience and evidence, between action and understanding, between the concrete details of life and the explanatory apparatus philosophers construct, means that his thought is by necessity tenuous, hesitant, responsive to changed conditions, and amenable to different angles of vision.

His thought is designed to be part of a conversation—with the expectation that we will act, talk, live out our parts in conversation with him. Dewey's writings can be seen as an extended attempt to participate in the conversations of his time, an attempt that was constantly subverted by his being exhorted to define his terms, take his stand, be consistent. Basically, most of his critics ask him to stop being a Deweyan and return to the assumptions and modes of thought he explicitly critiqued. I think that much of Dewey's work is a poignant attempt to clarify previous claims by working through new terrain, to address his critics (as he addresses aesthetic theories in *Art As Experience*) via detour.

Dewey's style exemplifies his philosophy not only for what it says, but for how it says it—in relation to what he has found to be true of himself and others. It is thought that proceeds from common sense: the sense-we-have-in-common. It is designed to interest and persuade the reader by pointing out things we already know but may not have thought through, and by suggesting consequences we might not have foreseen for how things are commonly viewed. Most importantly, it proceeds in a discursive, conversational mode, circling around and through examples that illuminate what happens when we adopt particular perspectives.

DEWEY AND THE ROLE OF THE INTELLECTUAL

Dewey's diffident mode of address, based in mundane examples and appeals to common experience, is congruent with his larger assumptions about the nature of social inquiry. Everyday people are all, in their way, artists and scientists, able to experience and explore, enjoy, and explain. Some people are particularly gifted in aspects of these enterprises, and some are also given the time and opportunity to more fully develop and express those gifts.

But the experimental attitude, the approach to knowledge that Dewey believes is necessary for democracy to flourish, must be more widely developed. It is an extension and refinement of the human desire and capacity for self-understanding, based in the evaluation of the consequences of everyday life. But opportunity for it is not distributed equitably.

Education can be arranged to more fully make use of, and develop, these capacities. Full reporting of people's findings and experiences can be circulated in modern life, via the media, to improve everyone's ability to evaluate and choose actions. Dewey's goals are always socially inclusive, assuming that democracy needs more of what it already allows—the development of people's innate capacities for social intelligence.

The role of intellectuals in this process is *not* as a special class of people whose aesthetic abilities make them better able to inspire, lead, or change the world. This is made clear in his chapter "The Crisis in Culture" in *Individualism Old and New,* where he expresses concern that "interest . . . in art and aesthetics . . . will readily turn into an escape mechanism unless it develops into an alert interest in the conditions which determine the esthetic environment of the vast multitudes."[31]

Dewey argues that a truly valuable modern culture must spring from the material realities of contemporary life. He chastises (gently) those critics who bemoan the barbarism of the present, and seek to escape it by fleeing to Europe. "Some flee to Paris or Florence; others take flight in their imagination to India, Athens, the middle ages or the American age of Emerson, Thoreau and Melville." (This last seems to be a response to Mumford's *The Golden Day*.) Dewey continues:

> Flight is solution by evasion. Return to a dualism consisting of a massive substratum of the material upon which are erected spiritually ornamented facades is flatly impossible, except upon the penalty of the spiritual disenfranchisement of those permanently condemned to toil mechanically at the machine.
>
> Escape from industrialism on the ground that it is unesthetic and brutal can win only a superficial and restricted success . . . the question is not one of idealizing present conditions in esthetic treatment, but of discovering and trying to realize the conditions under which vital esthetic production and esthetic appreciation may take place on a generous social scale.

His next sentence is, "And similarly for science. . . ."[32]

Dewey argues against the compartmentalization of both science and art, and says that intellectuals are likewise "dispersed and divided" by maintaining loyalty to science and the arts as abstractions. He argues instead for "a more intimate connection . . . to the scenes of social action," through "an active and alert recognition of the realities of an industrial age . . . planning to use them on behalf of a significantly human life."

This stance, while not elitist, is very much pro-aesthetics and pro-intellect. Its critique of intellectuals comes only when intellectuals separate themselves from other people. Such separation, a Deweyan perspective argues, guarantees that the social inquiry that results will not serve the needs of democracy.

In *Art As Experience*, Dewey develops this point in relation to criticism, in a gentle but ultimately devastating analysis of how aesthetic and literary criticism (and philosophy) proceeds. He begins, characteristically, by noting an aspect of human nature: "Desire for authority (and desire to be looked up to) animates the human breast." That desire means that much criticism is devoted not to explication, but to acquittal or condemnation, via appeal to authority. This explains the predominance of the "judicial critic" who "speaks as if he were the attorney for established principles having unquestionable sovereignty."[33]

He continues: "A judgment as an act of controlled inquiry demands a rich background and a disciplined insight. It is much easier to 'tell' people what they should believe than to discriminate and unify. And an audience that is itself habituated to being told, rather than schooled in thoughtful inquiry, likes to be told."[34]

Such an approach is disconnected from the shared experience that must inform inquiry—it is disconnected from the world we share. Both the critic and the people suffer, Dewey implies, because each has been cut off from the concrete world and from the "emergence of experiences that have a distinctively new character."[35] So Dewey concludes that the judicial critic succumbs to the temptation of authority and becomes a member of a self-enclosed, self-referential world. In short, he "erects the very things that are the dangers of his calling into a principle and norm."[36]

Dewey also describes these tendencies in the impressionistic critic who "goes off into irrelevancies and arbitrary dicta"; in formal critics who reduce art to particular categories; in psychoanalytic critics who use predefined factors to construct causal explanations; and in sociological critics who explain art solely by reference to historical and cultural and biographical information.[37]

These critics share a tendency to believe that their own theories and constructions are more valuable than the experience of the artist in producing the work, and of the viewer in experiencing the work. They therefore reduce the work of art to predetermined categories, categories that Dewey believes prevent both critic and reader from experiencing the imaginative possibilities that art offers.[38]

Dewey presumes a relationship among ideas, intellectuals, and the public that depends on mutual openness and responsiveness to common experience. By distrusting conceptual schemes, preconceived systems, explanation by reduction, and the theoretical apparatus in any version, Dewey presumes that all of us share the basic understandings needed to make good choices. The issue is not "who has access to the right information, insights, and theories," but "how can we enhance our abilities to make, as a group, good choices?"

So the question for the modern age is not, as Lippmann sees it, "who has enough of the best information?" but is instead, "how can we share the knowledge we gain from social inquiry?" This places the intellectual in a significantly different relationship to the public, and to the issue of expertise. The intellectual is "expert" only to the extent that he or she shares in the world he or she seeks to explain. She is valuable to the democratic process only to the extent that she is a member of a community that is engaged in some common enterprise, within and through which she considers and explores. His insights will be keenest, most useful, and most wise when they are most fully grounded in the concrete world of common experience. With every move away from that world—toward abstraction, toward theory, toward authority—the intellectual loses the possibilities of his or her calling—the possibility of sharing in the social conversation.

We can see the contrast between the Deweyan perspective and the *Partisan Review* position of the 1940s. The *Partisan Review* position combines aspects of the incongruent preceding perspectives in an innovative but ultimately arrogant way. For the *Partisan Review* intellectuals, criticism was art, a specialized practice of specialized people gifted with intelligence and sophistication. Such abilities involved dramatic social responsibilities, especially in response to the tide of mediated mediocrity that seemed to loom. The fear that the excellent and cultivated would be drowned out by the din of the brutal and vulgar animated those critics as they participated in the mass culture debate of the 1950s and 1960s. It is a fear that is based in their presumed difference from, and superiority to, the rest of the barbaric world. It is exactly the kind of dualistic, escapist, self-referential stance that Dewey writes against.

DEWEY AND MEDIA STUDIES

Does this mean that Dewey presages postmodern populism? Can we make Dewey into an early twentieth-century figure who finds in mass culture all kinds of liberating and subversive possibilities? No. Dewey is not arguing that popular culture is full of wise and clever possibilities that can be decoded by insightful critics, or apprehended in all their subversive possibilities by subaltern readers. He does not abandon judgments of differential quality, and he does not presume that all cultural expressions are of equal social benefit. He has strong beliefs about what is better and worse in a society—he simply does not presume that art can purify or that the media can corrupt.

By focusing on art-as-experience, rather than art-as-artifact, he can still ask about the quality of the experience. Dewey's concern will always be with the quality and equitable distribution of human experience, rather than with the quality of the artifact. So his concern is with what happens with art, with its experiential consequences. The consequences he describes are imaginative, and relate to broadening and deepening experience and to expanding the sympathies.

He writes to critique those theories that presume that art is something distinct and esoteric, outside of the realm of the everyday. He notes the origins of theories of art, grammar, and rhetoric in the Alexandrian period, and its loss of civic consciousness. "Instead of connecting arts with an expression of the life of the community, the beauty of nature and art was regarded as an echo and reminder of some supernal reality that had its being outside social life, and indeed outside the cosmos itself—the ultimate source of all subsequent theories that treat art as something *imported into experience from without*" (my italics).[39]

Dewey's purpose is my purpose too—to critique the consequences of all theories that treat art as something that comes in from the outside to transform us. In the mass culture debate, art is rhetorically positioned as a purifying force, while the media are positioned as a corrupting one. This supports a view of intellectuals as uncorrupted experts, protected from the crude world by their association with aesthetic exquisiteness. It allows intellectuals to write essays about levels of culture, the influence of mass culture on high culture, and the necessity for intellectuals to ignore the common life so that they can protect intellectual things.

The mass culture debate assumed that "the people" are being ruined by mediated and commercial art, and can be improved by traditional or modern art. Once art is imagined as an outside force, it can be invoked as a means to a desired end. The end that is desired, by this logic, is the saturation of the crude public in a refining bath of good art.

This fosters the concerns we still find in discussions of the arts, media, and commerce. There is concern about "dilution"—does good "real" art become lessened by being "mixed in" with the bad stuff? By appearing in the media? By being widely distributed? By being advertised and promoted? For many in the NEA debates, good art must remain pure and inviolate, ignoring, of course, that the art world has been a commercial world since its inception.

Many still believe that if lots more "good art" is added to the current bath of mediocrity, the level of culture will go up, people will become more rational and refined, and the world will be a better place. A Deweyan perspective cannot operate with such an instrumental

logic, because it cannot imagine culture as a force that has either redemptive or corrupting powers. Art is experience, experience is saturated with art. The issue is the *nature* of the experience, and experiences of all kinds can be imaginative, enriching, invigorating. The
issue, for Dewey, is the social efficacy of the ideas and beliefs that
come from an experience—the imagination is always tested and developed against experiences.

Dewey criticizes art that is shoddily made, dishonestly offered, or designed to pander, because he presumes that it offers a degraded experience, with less potential for imaginative growth. It is not poison, or corrupting, it is simply a *missed opportunity*—a possibility deflected or
denied. What Dewey wants is for the public to make the most of the opportunities that modernity offers, including the potentials of new devices of mass communication.

Art is a potent disseminator of the full scope of social inquiry.
Artists have always been, he says, the real purveyors of news, "for it
is not the outward happening in itself which is new, but the kindling
by it of emotion, perception and appreciation."[40] For Dewey, art is
both communication and experience at its most communicative and
experiential.

In an often-quoted phrase, Dewey says, "Of all things, communication is the most wonderful." He justifies this sweeping claim by
his belief that communication is the human process of creating and
sustaining a common world. Communication is democracy, in that
democracy is the co-creation of a social world in which to live, a creative process that engages us via experience. Our intellect, aesthetic
desires, and imagination are all aspects of our engagement in communication and in our community.

This means that the mass media, as information and as culture, can
be criticized for how well they help us in our social inquiry. What are
their consequences for our experience? Do they help us talk with each
other, sharing our understandings and insights? Do they circulate the
results of our inquiry? Do they help us achieve full and rich understanding of our common possibilities? Do they help us, as members of
a public, come to an understanding of ourselves, our allegiances, our
responsibilities, our potentials? The question is not "How can we
avoid, deflect, or mitigate the hypnotic power of the media?" but
"How can the media—and all other communication forms—help us
do whatever we can do to enhance democracy?"

These two questions are posed about forms of communication, but they can also be asked about intellectuals. From an instrumental perspective, the questions are different: how to either maintain or increase the presumably beneficial social power of art and of the intellectuals whose property art had become. Asked in this way, the answer involves an insistence that the public be exposed to good art/good thought—usually via educative institutions like museums and schools. Contemporary arts discussions have not yet moved us past these limited questions and answers. The NEA funding debates were about how to ensure that such "exposure" be retained and increased.

THE PUBLIC AND THE CRITICS

Our dominant arts discourse presumes that a stubborn public, as yet unable or unwilling to engage in good art and thought, needs to be uplifted. Belief in the social power of art comes from a belief that the public must be changed. The people need the salutary influence of some outside force like art to be able to do the difficult business of self-governance. Various institutions are proposed and supported in relation to their ability to transmit the necessary elixirs, so that they can do their magic work on citizens. Schools are designed to turn the clay of children into the model citizens of tomorrow. Parks are developed to give unruly immigrants the experience of clipped and orderly promenades. Theaters and museums are designed to expose citizens to the beneficial and healing powers of art. A system of cultural improvement is developed to transform an unsavory public into something more palatable.

Intellectuals draw from these currents a notion of their own importance in the process of public salvation. We come to see ourselves as specially constituted for the task. We have found congenial homes in institutions dedicated to public uplift. We cherish the art forms we like, and define them as most likely to improve others. We teach the courses that we have decided are most necessary for students' betterment. We write indictments of current conditions that demonstrate the hollowness of contemporary experience, and pierce the deceptive veils of contemporary culture. Intellectuals know more, and know better, than the public. The masses must be taught how to see and respond to things as we intellectuals do, and then democracy will be safe.

Dewey starts, and so ends up, in a very different place in relation to the public. His view of art, communication, and democracy ensures that he begins with the assumption that intellectuals are peculiarly drawn to thinking about certain problems in certain ways, and that these ways may well be useful if they spring from, are grounded in, and applied to, common experience. Dewey is adamant that soliloquy is not communication, that intellectuals matter only to the extent that we are participants in social practices and actions.

The public is muddled, confused, inchoate, to the extent that the means for social inquiry and conversation have not kept up with the changes in pace and scale in modern life. *The problem is structural, not intellectual.* The public is not crude, vulgar, or stupid, it simply has less access to the means and modes of social inquiry. Intellectuals have the privilege of time and energy to devote to creative thought and experience.

The Deweyan goal for education, mass communication, and intellectual activity is the same—to increase and enhance public engagement in its own problems. Dewey argues that schools need to be remade to help students develop an experimental attitude—the ability to decipher and evaluate conditions and consequences. The media should serve the democratic function of communication within and across communities, by offering experiences that will enlarge the possibilities of face-to-face discussion. Education, the media, and aesthetic experience can offer liberation from the deadening and limiting influences of habit, tradition, inertia, and provincialism.

For Dewey, intellectuals are fortunate because they have had greater opportunities to experience afresh, imagine the new, and develop an experimental attitude. The democratic goal is to increase the opportunity for *all* citizens to develop those same capacities, capacities that too often remain stunted. It is not up to intellectuals to transmit truths to the lacking public, but we can act to increase the chance for all members of the public to imagine, think, and decide in wise ways.

In American social thought, the key problem is democracy. I have shown how, explicitly or implicitly, American social thought seeks ways to increase the likelihood that the public will act prudently. For Dewey the answer lies in inclusion—including the public in the salutary processes of community, via communication. For Dewey, art is communication, and art offers a wider disclosure of possibilities, as well as of the constraints upon them.

"Art is the means of keeping alive the sense of purposes that outrun evidence and of meanings that transcend indurated habit,"[41] Dewey says as he explains what art offers democracy. "As long as art is the beauty parlor of civilization, neither art nor civilization is secure."[42]

To secure civilization, art needs to operate widely, fully, freely, inclusively. It need not be protected, dispensed, explained, or theorized by intellectuals. It does not contain wisdom and truth that must be inculcated into the masses. Instead, it is a means, as is all communication, by and through which the public can come to know itself.

NOTES

1. For a powerful overview of Dewey's life in relation to his social thought, see Alan Ryan, *John Dewey and the High Tide of American Liberalism* (New York: W. W. Norton, 1995). Robert B. Westbrook's masterful *John Dewey and American Democracy* (Ithaca, N.Y.: Cornell University Press, 1991), effectively locates Dewey's works in twentieth-century political, social, and cultural currents.

2. My analysis is oriented toward the consequences of Dewey's art thought for American social criticism, rather than for philosophy or traditional aesthetics. In *Pragmatist Aesthetics: Living Beauty, Rethinking Art* (New York: Blackwell, 1992), Richard Shusterman offers a subtle and wide-ranging account of Deweyan aesthetics, in the context of contemporary philosophy, with attention to rap music as well as Richard Rorty.

3. John Dewey, *Art As Experience* (New York: Perigee Books, 1980; originally published by Putnam, 1934).

4. Thomas M. Alexander, *John Dewey's Theory of Art, Experience and Nature: The Horizons of Feeling* (Albany: State University of New York Press, 1987), xix and passim. This book effectively integrates Dewey's aesthetic thought with the basic themes and concerns that characterize Dewey's approach to experience, and is a valuable overview. Philip W. Jackson's *John Dewey and the Lessons of Art* (New Haven, Conn.: Yale University Press, 1998) describes, in personable detail, how Dewey's thought can illuminate the nature and value of general human experience. Michael Eldridge's *Transforming Experience: John Dewey's Cultural Instrumentalism* (Nashville, Tenn.: Vanderbilt University Press, 1998) argues that Dewey offered more of a political technology for change than many of his critics allow. While this is why Eldridge uses the term *instrumentalism*, he does *not* read Dewey as claiming that art can change society. Rather, "thoughtful valuation" is the instrument of change, in the service of what he calls Dewey's "humanistic naturalism." With Eldridge, I see Dewey's "fudge factor" as intelligence, not art. Dewey's democracy-protecting intervening variable is the human capacity for weighing evidence and making rational decisions.

5. Dewey, *Art As Experience*, 4.

6. Dewey, *Art As Experience*, 5.

7. Dewey, *Art As Experience,* 10.

8. Dewey, *Art As Experience,* 11.

9. Dewey, *Art As Experience,* 274.

10. Dewey, *Art As Experience,* 19.

11. Dewey, *Art As Experience,* 185.

12. Dewey, *Art As Experience,* 332.

13. John Dewey, *The Public and Its Problems* (New York: Henry Holt, 1927).

14. Dewey, *Art As Experience,* 326.

15. John Dewey, *Individualism Old and New* (New York: Capricorn Books, 1962; originally published in 1929 and 1930).

16. James W. Carey has developed this aspect of Dewey's thought, tracing its implications for the study of communication. See *Communication As Culture: Essays on Media and Society* (Boston: Unwin Hyman, 1989).

17. Dewey, *The Public and Its Problems,* 155.

18. Dewey, *The Public and Its Problems,* 149.

19. See, in particular, Walter Lippmann's *Public Opinion* (New York: Macmillan, 1922). Robert Westbrook in *John Dewey and American Democracy* shows how much was at stake in the opposition, 294–300.

20. Dewey, *The Public and Its Problems,* 184.

21. Dewey, *The Public and Its Problems,* 184.

22. Dewey, *Art As Experience,* 346.

23. Here we can discern the influence of Dewey's friend and colleague (at the University of Chicago) George Herbert Mead, whose role in anchoring pragmatism in experience has been overshadowed by his reputation as a founding figure in symbolic interactionism.

24. Dewey, *Art As Experience,* 348.

25. Dewey, *Art As Experience,* 349.

26. Dewey, *Art As Experience,* 348.

27. For a memorable critique of this form of intellectual resuscitation, see John Rodden, *The Politics of Literary Reputation: The Making and Claiming of "St. George" Orwell* (New York: Oxford University Press, 1989) on the self-serving political uses of playing "If Orwell were alive today. . . ."

28. In my favorite Dewey footnote, he says, "The effect upon German thought of Capitalization has hardly received proper attention" (Dewey, *Art As Experience,* 252).

29. Obviously, Dewey's thinking is shaped by his time at the University of Chicago, especially in relation to Charles Horton Cooley.

30. Dewey's analysis in *The Quest for Certainty* (New York: Putnam 1960; originally published in 1929) can continue to apply to all positions that privilege theory over evidence, or presumptions that theories constitute evidence.

31. Dewey, *Individualism Old and New,* 130.

32. Dewey, *Individualism Old and New,* 137.

33. Dewey, *Art As Experience,* 299.

34. Dewey, *Art As Experience,* 300.

35. Dewey, *Art As Experience,* 304.

36. Dewey, *Art As Experience,* 304.

37. Dewey, *Art As Experience,* 314–18.

38. This is the reductionist fallacy; the other fallacy that concerns Dewey in this section is the confusion of categories. He believes that critics treat art as if it were "a reediting of values already current in other fields of experience." Critics wrongly presume that artistic material is actually moral, philosophic, religious, or historical, rendered "more palatable by emotional seasoning and imaginative dressing." This approach then criticizes the work of art in moral, philosophic, religious, or historical terms, rather than in relation to the aesthetic experience itself. (Dewey, *Art As Experience*, 317–19). Here Dewey's argument most directly reflects the beliefs of Albert Barnes, the eccentric art collector and philanthropist; see Howard Greenfeld, *The Devil and Dr. Barnes: Portrait of An American Art Collector* (New York: Viking, 1987). Barnes personally organized his extraordinary collection to enhance the direct, aesthetic experience he believed art must offer. Barnes insisted that aesthetic experience be direct, rather than mediated by prefabricated critical systems, including museums. This made for an interesting controversy when the Barnes Foundation decided, in the early 1990s, to take part of the collection out of Barnes's designed viewing context and put it on tour.

39. Dewey, *Art As Experience*, 328.

40. Dewey, *The Public and Its Problems*, 184.

41. Dewey, *Art As Experience*, 438.

42. Dewey, *Art As Experience*, 344.

Conclusion:
The Value of Expressive Logic

In today's culture wars, the instrumental power of art and criticism remains relatively unquestioned. Academics from a variety of political positions keep faith with a personal version: cultural criticism is social medicine.

We want our work to be culturally and socially powerful. Many of us long to be public intellectuals, whether from the right or from the left. We maintain continued faith in the power of language, the dominant form of academic art, to make a difference in the world. Which brings us back to Whitman and the problem of recalcitrant audiences. Whitman spent his life revising "Leaves of Grass" in the hope that it would kindle and transform the audience he sought to save. We professorial types are Whitman's heirs. The cultural forms we hope will help, if not save, the masses, are rarely appreciated by those we yearn to redeem. As academics, we have students we can (at least temporarily) engage, but as scholars and intellectuals we realize that what we have to offer is not appreciated by everyday people. How can this be?

We can blame, if not "the media," then "the marketplace" or "corporate culture." This explains why our students have such awful taste, why insipid television shows are on the air, why noxious music predominates, why violent movies make so much money. Our potential audience has been, and is being, poisoned. This is what must be preventing students from responding to what we know is good for them. It must be that the media—in themselves or as extensions of capitalism or commercialization or mass society—are ruining audiences for us, and for our art.

The instrumental view of culture—that it can serve as social medicine—offers satisfying explanations to the critic, artist, and scholar, and so it continues. The instrumental view allows academics to feel both potent and benevolent. We can do our work in the name of a vaguely defined democracy, feeling virtuously radical, progressive, or conservative as we wish. We are just calling for better culture to make people and society better. And we, like Whitman, do the stuff we love in the name of the people we support in the abstract but all too often deplore in the concrete.

POLICING MEDIA/ART/VERNACULAR BOUNDARIES

This is why it will never be easy to give up distinctions among "the media" "the arts," and "the everyday." The Manichaean distinction between bad media and good art lets academics, artists, critics, journalists, arts educators—let's just say "us," for now—cast ourselves as heroes in a bracing drama. With instrumental, redemptive, counterbalancing logic, we have something to blame for whatever we think is wrong with contemporary life, and with the contemporary public. Using this logic, we can imagine a force that will improve and ameliorate and make the world a place we like better. With this logic, we in universities or the arts are on the side of right, doing cultural work that is individually rewarding and socially valuable, creating truth, or beauty, or insight, or subversion, or critique, against pernicious commercial (and yes, alas, popular) crud.

We will never say this outright. We don't want to be perceived as simpleminded, or as snobs—by ourselves or by others. So we find ways to support what we believe to be truly democratic cultural forms, while ensuring they are never confused with their evil twin: commercial culture. We also dismiss the salutary power of such mundane noncommercial activities as knitting, leather tooling, and bass fishing. To keep our dramatic story line, and our heroic position in it, the arts must never ever be confused with the media or with hobbies.

Repositioning the arts as vernacular culture, a tactic used in contemporary defenses of arts funding, makes this heroic opposition more difficult to sustain. If the arts are what average people do, because they are fun and rewarding activities, then what do artists, critics, and academic folks have to offer?

BOUNDARY DISSOLVING AND ITS AFTERMATH

If the arts aren't simply the fine arts, but include any form of individual or group creative expression (even mass-mediated, commercial forms), then what? Can we go even further, and presume that all creative, aesthetic practice is art or (if the term needs to be changed) culture? Can we argue that it doesn't matter if culture/art is mediated or nonmediated? Can we with Dewey dispense with definitions of art as essentially higher than, or different from, other forms of creative, symbolic, imaginative practice? Can we fully and finally blur the distinctions, at least long enough to explore the consequences?

I am not alone in calling for the elimination of the conceptual boundaries that keep art separate, and so allow it to be imagined as socially potent and redemptive. John P. Sisk critiques "The Tyranny of the Aesthetic"[1]—the ways "our culture refused to give up on the image of the artist as an imperial and performing self for whom both the personal and aesthetic are political, and whose creations, however subversive they may appear by democratic bourgeois standards, will in the long run prove therapeutic." He suggests that we question the automatic association of aesthetic quality with any kind of personal or communal salvation, and even argues that democracy may not need more art and more museums, but "a way of protecting itself from the aesthetic impulse that it cannot help fostering."

Libertarian Charles Paul Freund questions the ways in which the arts are counterposed to commerce[2] and notes how arts defenders are defending their own tastes and status in the name of the masses. In another trenchant analysis of the logic of some NEA defenders,[3] he describes how current discussions have a complex social location in fears of barbarism, ambivalence about democracy, and in the status anxieties of educated art admirers.

If we agree that contemporary arts rhetoric is contradictory, misguided, and ineffective, then what can we offer in its place? If we agree that the mass culture debaters were rightly concerned about cultural quality, but faulty in their assumptions about intellectual ownership of the arts, how can we save the good questions, and jettison the arrogance?

I want us to find new ways to think about the arts, ways that both celebrate and respect *varieties* of aesthetic experience. To do this, I believe we must give up the instrumental view. We need to adopt a more

Deweyan expressive view, one that understands the arts as an ongoing symbolic process that is valuable in and of itself, and is widely and variously manifested.

Such a perspective is compatible with Ellen Dissanayake's biobehavioral view of the arts as the way we make sense of our everyday experience. She suggests that art is the basic, evolutionarily sensible, human activity: "when 'artifying,' one shapes or elaborates everyday, mundane reality, thereby transforming it into something special."[4] Dissanayake is arguing that art has a ritual function—making the ordinary extraordinary. Ceremony is the human way of making the world, making it orderly, and endowing it with meaning.

This ceremonial view of the arts resonates with a ritual view of communication, one which defines communication as, in Carey's words, "the process whereby reality is created, maintained, repaired and transformed."[5] This perspective has been used, by him and others, to illuminate the role of the news and of popular culture in American democracy. An expressive perspective on the arts would see the arts as a form of communication, understanding always that communication is something other than, and much more interesting than, the transmission of messages across space.

From the expressive perspective, the news, or various mass media like radio, television, film, or popular culture, and now the arts, don't simply transfer meaning from a sender to a receiver, or inject ideas, values, and beliefs into our fragile, vulnerable minds. Nor do they hail us into discourses that automatically contain, constrain, or even liberate us. Instead, these cultural forms are part of an ongoing, humanly constructed conversation about the reality we are shaping as we participate in it. This is the way we should think about the social role of the arts.

An expressive view of the arts, then, is a view that does not try to erase notions of high and low, authentic and commercial, arts and crafts, sacred and profane. It presumes, instead, that these distinctions are important because they are *important to the participants*. Lines of demarcation between good and bad culture are endlessly being constructed, sustained, repaired, and transformed. These distinctions matter, but they matter because they are part of an evaluative ritual—the ceremony of making and protecting worthiness. The arts are part of our vital ongoing conversation about what is valuable, human, exalted, sacred, pleasurable, challenging, and worthwhile, and what is not. And *that* is why the arts are so important and so valuable. That is why the arts are good for us. It is on these grounds that they should be supported.

An expressive perspective defines art without seams or divides—it can include both opera and gardening, in that it defines art, with Dewey, as lived experience, particularly valuable and pleasurable experience, but not any more—or less—sacred than many other human experiences. From an expressive view of the arts, it is good to have creative aesthetic experiences, and a good society supports such experiences as often as possible for as many people as possible. But there is no instrumental magic here. And perhaps (alas!) there is less reason for government funding, since massage, jogging, chess, in-line skating, and solitaire are also valuable human activities, but we don't expect government support for them.

THE CONSEQUENCES OF DE-SACRALIZATION

Before I explore the consequences of adopting an expressive perspective, let me anticipate the most common objections. I am not calling for the suspension of evaluation. I am not saying that we should define everything as equivalent, or that there's no such thing as exceptional ability, or that there is no way to distinguish between good and bad, truth or lies. I am not that impossible creature imagined by conservative critics, a postmodern relativist calling for the dissolution of all hierarchies of value. I am saying that, because we socially and symbolically construct our lives, we are constantly in a conversation about what is good, what is bad, what we want more of, what we want less of. When we challenge the automatic art/media/crafts distinctions, we can foreground how we evaluate. When instead—as in the instrumental view—we accept distinctions as natural, we lose touch with the very process we most need to pay attention to and respect.

Culture is a conversation about what matters most to us—privately, publicly, socially, economically, politically, and spiritually. It is the way that we keep reality—our interpretive world—going. Participatory culture—an inclusive, cosmopolitan, diverse conversation—is also the vital stuff of democratic life. And modern life is bursting with stories, contradictory, self-serving, persuasive, residual, emergent, and overwhelming. Therefore, especially in modern democratic life, we need to think and talk as wisely and well as we can.

We have not been thinking or talking wisely or well about the arts. This is because we have continued to imagine the arts as a magic substance that can do all kinds of wonderful things for us. That means that we argue for "more arts" when we should be arguing—directly— for what we believe and want, and for why we believe it and want it. Our instrumental logic leads us to spend time, money, and intellectual effort on an illusory intervening variable—the arts. The arts—not us— will save our kids. The arts—not us—will heal our sick, ennoble our elderly, encourage our poor. The arts—not us—will bind our communities, uplift our spirits, counteract our evils, make everything better.

We need to acknowledge that the arts can't do all that, because cultural forms don't work that way. There isn't magic "art" out there that can do these good things, and there aren't evil "media" out there doing us great harm. We have constructed a self-serving story based on a faulty premise—that cultural forms have the power to directly transform us in both good and bad ways. Art can't free, media can't enslave, and money doesn't corrupt. It is what we *do* with art, the media, and money that matters.

Here is the most difficult part of my argument. I am not saying that cultural forms are epiphenomena, less "real" or important than economics, institutions, social relations, or politics. Instead, I am saying that they are part of how we think and construct the world: they are symbolic forms that we endow with meaning, through an ongoing interpretive process. And interpretation always has real consequences— we make weapons, poverty, and injustice symbolically, too. We can be cruel, we can be kind, we can be harsh, sentimental, vicious, and/or compassionate in our private and our public actions. We do these things, always, in a web of significations we ourselves have spun.

From this perspective, cultural forms, including the high arts, folk arts, and the mass media, both spark and embody values, beliefs, and ideas. We can critique these forms for what they say to us, and for how well they seem to say it, and we can call for better, more thoughtful, wise, delightful, pleasing, even more subversive and disruptive forms. But we can do that based *not* on their membership in some a priori category—art or media or mass culture—but instead on what we think they are up to.

What we think cultural artifacts are up to is another interpretive moment in the ongoing conversation. We can think they are up to mischief, for example, and so we can argue that certain images cause violence or sexual attacks or anomie or uplift. But if we want to claim that we will need coherent arguments, as well as empirical evidence. It is because there is so little coherence in the arguments, and so little empirical evidence in the research, that I have come to doubt the good effects of the arts, and the bad effects of the media. This book is my attempt to offer a better way to think and talk about cultural effects.

Cultural forms, and the discourse that surrounds them, are among the ways we make and display our sense of the world. The arts, as a form of communication, are best understood as rituals rather than as transmitters of messages. They are activities we engage in; through our engagement we locate and express meaning. In our cultural conversations, that is in fact what we are doing, and such conversations both comment on, and enact, our social world.

In a free society, there may be few intentional limits to what we can talk about, but there are always interpretive limits—patterns, blind spots, constraints on how we can imagine and think. The liberal faith in the free and open marketplace of ideas is also a faith in the power of open discussion to allow greater wisdom than private thought, tradition, or formal decree. Free and open discussion is valuable not only through the winnowing of falsehood from truth, as in the classical liberal view, but also in the increasing capaciousness of constructs, and in the ability to take account of multiple perspectives and incommensurable differences, as in more contemporary liberalism. That is the democratic promise as I understand it, and as Dewey describes it. This promise relies on having a fundamental respect for, and appreciation of, the processes through which various peoples work out their own particular constructions of reality.

This asks a lot of us. Democratic life demands extraordinary levels of tolerance. It asks us not only to tolerate the habits and values of strangers, but also to share power with people we may despise and who may well despise us—or at least most of what we hold dear. The arts have become an intervening variable, in sophisticated social criticism as well as in everyday thought, because (as instruments of transformation) they appear to offer a way to make this most difficult aspect of democracy evaporate.

We would much rather share power with people whose tastes are like ours, because their cultural forms make sense: they confirm our own perspectives, and represent all that we think ourselves to be. If we believe that exposure to cultural forms are transformative, then, well—all we need is lots more of our culture, and those noxious others will become delightful neighbors, just like us!

Discussion, on the other hand, is not automatic transformation. It is, instead, an ongoing attempt to persuade, convince, and (ideally) to be persuaded, to be convinced. If we are to become wiser, we should be listening to people who don't see things as we do. Media-disparaging intellectuals should respect, or at least pay attention to, those who, unlike them, enjoy mass culture. And of course, I want people who think the arts are frills and foolishness to listen to me, who enjoys many examples of what they dismiss.

Like most arts supporters, I want people to realize how wonderful my favorite cultural forms are. As a professor, I am fortunately located—I can insist that my students achieve familiarity with what can be found in museums, libraries, theaters, concert halls, as well as radio, television, movies, magazines, newspapers. We who love high culture, or scholarship, or philosophy, or avant-garde art are far from marginalized; we certainly cannot claim we are being silenced. And we close down discussion when we imagine ourselves possessing an elixir that will make other people better by making them more like us.

I realize that I am enacting what I am warning against—I want you, the reader, to think like me. As in contemporary arts rhetoric, I am suggesting that you are being harmed by instrumental logic, and will be better off with expressive logic. The difference is, I hope, that I am seeking conversation about the terms in which we think—I'm asking you to reexamine how it is you think about arts, media, commerce, democracy, other people, modern society. I am offering a different way to think and talk about the things that we think ail us in contemporary life. My hope is *not* that you will be transformed by exposure to my message (would that it were so easy!), but that once you've recognized the dominant pattern and explored its consequences, you will choose to change the ways you think about art, media, and society.

Cultural criticism, at its most useful, is about the evaluation of consequences—what happens when we think this way, not that? On what evidence can we presume one thing to be true, and not another? Is that evidence reliable? Why? Why not? The social intelligence that Dewey counts on is formed in public conversation about the nature, costs, and benefits of particular styles of thought and forms of action.

We live, now, in a world that is saturated in stories. Narratives abound, and thanks to the range of recording devices, we can freeze, circulate, study, and critique those stories. Thanks to mass communication, we can circulate those stories across space as well as time, and we have access to an unprecedented number of ways of constructing the world.

All forms of storytelling offer ways to make sense of the world, and those who support the arts believe they offer better, more wholesome, more beneficial stories than those offered by the media or the marketplace. *It should be the business of cultural criticism to explain how and why this is so.* Cultural criticism that proceeds from predetermined categories—high art presumed, a priori, to be challenging and subversive or uplifting and sacred, while mediated art is formulaic and narcotizing—can't do that. All that can happen, using instrumental logic, is an endless reassertion of the presumed good effects of art, and bad effects of the media.

Only work that explores what various cultural forms mean and why, that explores what is being expressed to particular audiences by particular cultural forms, can presume to evaluate the benefits or dangers of particular kinds of culture. And then their conclusions would be up for discussion, because how are "we" to decide which beliefs are better or worse?

If, using the expressive view, we give up the notion of inherent differences in effects among commercial, popular, folk, and high art, we challenge ourselves to rethink how culture works, and also how we imagine audiences. How are we to explain the popularity of cultural forms that so many intellectuals and social critics find banal, vulgar, and dangerous? Do people really like what is harmful to them? Have we/they really been brainwashed? Are art and folk culture more real and virtuous than commercial culture? Why? If we acknowledge the constructedness of these categories, we see that we have also adopted an implicit account of "those people" who like the forms we don't like—they are either tasteless boors, or have been turned into tasteless boors, except for those few left untainted by commercialism.

This is a consequence I don't like, and yet it has been chronic (if implicit) in American social thought. Why should we presume that "we" are full of wisdom and resilience and "they" are foolish and vulnerable? If we examine, say, the quality of our personal lives, marriages, parenting, treatment of students, departmental politics, relationships with colleagues, care for aged relatives, or commitment to social service, we find little empirical evidence for our vast superiority. We who think of ourselves as having so very much to offer others do not necessarily lead lives that those others find exemplary or even enviable.

It is clear that many people find dedication to the arts, or to scholarship, to be eccentric, even amusing, often ridiculous. Absorption in such esoteric stuff strikes them as a bit pathetic, perhaps even absurd. And, of course, that's how I often see their dedication to, say, fishing and car racing. But notice that there is not necessarily a moral component here. I am not better, they are not worse, because we have such different tastes in pastimes. Once the moral influence of aesthetic activity disappears, these distinctions are indeed ones of mere taste, even as they construct social identity. But they need not necessarily construct social worth or wisdom—bad taste does not make bad citizens.

The people I know who like commercial culture and hang out in shopping malls are as actively judgmental, and disrespectful, as scholars, teachers, artists, and journalists. They are as cynical and as gullible, as full of doubt and as full of certainty. But they often have doubts and certainties very different from mine. A neighbor may love movies I think are tripe, while I like stuff that bores or repulses her. Should I presume she's been duped and I've been saved? What are the consequences for such a belief—not only for how I treat her, but for how I imagine all such "deprived" others should be treated?

As a professor, should I teach my students that they've been duped and I've been saved? This is the rhetorical position of much contemporary cultural criticism, and I don't like its consequences, either. But I believe I have an obligation to make my very best contribution to the cultural conversation. That means I help my students understand that their tastes (like mine) are already structured, and that there are many things they've not yet had the chance to think about or to enjoy. I believe I have an obligation, mandated by society, to show them how the stories they take for granted may not be the best stories for them to believe in or live by. And I must, humbly, remember that this is true for me, too.

We are all of us, always, participating in an ongoing cultural conversation about what is good, what is bad, what matters, and what doesn't. Such a conversation is structured in dominance. I have more access to mechanisms of public conversation than do many of my neighbors, or my students. I also think I'm better off with wider familiarity. So I can call for friends, neighbors, students, citizens to have broad horizons; I can explain why I think there is virtue in cosmopolitanism. But I must do this directly, rather than calling for More Art to make people More Wise and More Tolerant.

If each of us constructs, and is constructed by, stories, then we must find ways to choose stories to live by. Here is where the ability to evaluate consequences, to sift, to critique, to explore, to question— Dewey's social intelligence—is so crucial. This isn't something *art* does, this is something *we* do. Like Dewey, I believe that having more art is valuable. But that means I should call for, teach, and work on critical thinking, rather than counting on something called art to do that for me, too.[6]

This applies, also, to whatever I want done about crime, urban renewal, homelessness, and the plight of the elderly. It is absurd, and simplistic, to presume that art will make these things better. This "good for whatever ails us" logic is the most unpalatable element in contemporary arts boosterism. The way we have been talking about the arts offers us a self-serving and ineffective way to feel like we're making the world a better place, just by supporting the things we like.

Saving the world requires more grueling and mundane activities than cultural criticism and artistic creativity. Wise world-saving must respect the diversity of experiences and stories that are circulating, and find ways to listen to them, rather than anoint what "we" like as good, and denigrate what they like as bad. If there are things wrong with particular ways of seeing and being in the world, these need to be criticized, directly. Lies, viciousness, and evil can be located and deplored, and alternatives offered. Vernacular moral philosophy is our narrative sea; we are participating in it, as creators and commentators and critics, and readers and viewers and listeners.

Once we dispense with our instrumental logic, my hope is that we will be more likely to evaluate what is going on, clearly and directly. The current cultural, political climate is both timid and polarized. People are hesitant to explore their own conflicted beliefs because the conflict has been played out as a culture war, a conflict between Right and Left, and as a battle for the hearts and minds of The People. It's not nearly so diametric and simple, really. In current American life, we are part of an ongoing, sometimes stupid, often eloquent, unusually inclusive talk about what was, what is, and what should be. That talk is what democracy promises, and what American culture—high, low, popular, folk, nonprofit, and commercial—purveys. It is what modernity has made possible.

The arts are part of it. The mass media are part of it. The debate about the arts and the media are part of it. People pay attention to, and pay for, the parts they want more of, and ignore the parts that they don't like, or that they can't make sense of. That is as true of "them" as it is of "us." If there is wisdom to be gained, it must surely be in cosmopolitanism, in learning more about what *doesn't* yet make sense to us. This is also as true for us as it is for them.

If we can find ways to dispense with illusory causes and cures, we can focus instead on how we construct the world—the categories with which we think. Perhaps then we can imagine different categories, ones that are more generous or truthful or responsive or tolerant. We need to stop identifying demons and saviors, and get out of the business of trying to save whole groups of people via the elixir of art. We are better off recognizing that we would-be saviors of society are doing what all people do—trying to make sense of the world, and to bring others around to our ways of thinking.

If we want to change the world, we need to do it directly. The arts aren't good *for* us; they *are* us—expressions of us. We can't look to the arts to transform us, or to make the world a better place. To make things better, we need to dispense with instrumental logic and intervening variables, and find democratic ways to identify and engage in right action. It's up to us, not art.

NOTES

1. John P. Sisk, "The Tyranny of the Aesthetic," *The American Scholar* 63, no. 2 (Winter 1994), 119–23.

2. Charles Paul Freund, "Money Talking Art: Does Cash Corrupt or Communicate?" *Reason,* July 1997.

3. Charles Paul Freund, "Who Killed Culture? From Barbarism to Democracy, Elites Seek a Suspect in the Reported Death of Art," *Reason,* March 1998, 23–39.

4. See Ellen Dissanayake, *What Is Art For?* (Seattle: University of Washington Press, 1988); and *Homo Aestheticus: Where Art Comes From and Why* (New York: Free Press, 1992). This quote is from Dissanayake, "The Pleasures and Meanings of Making," *American Craft* 55, no. 2 (April–May 1995).

5. James W. Carey, *Communication as Culture: Essays on Media and Society* (New York: Unwin Hyman, 1989) remains an excellent introduction to his work; see also Eve Stryker Munson and Catherine Warren, eds., *James Carey: A Critical Reader* (Minneapolis: University of Minnesota Press, 1997).

6. For an example of how someone shaped by a Deweyan perspective connects art, education, and critical thinking, see Maxine Greene, *Releasing the Imagination: Essays on Education, the Arts and Social Change* (San Francisco: Jossey-Bass Publishers, 1995).

Bibliography

Aaron, Daniel. *Writers on the Left*. New York: Avon Books, 1965.

Adorno, Theodor, and Max Horkheimer. "The Culture Industry: Enlightenment as Mass Deception." In *Mass Communication and Society*, ed. J. Curran et al., 349–83. Berkeley, Calif.: Sage, 1977.

Alexander, Jane. "Our Investment in Culture: Art Perfects the Essence of Our Common Humanity." *Vital Speeches of the Day*, 15 January 1996, 210–13.

Alexander, Thomas M. *John Dewey's Theory of Art, Experience and Nature: The Horizons of Feeling*. Albany: State University of New York Press, 1987.

America and the Intellectuals, a Symposium. New York: Partisan Review Series 4, 1953.

Arendt, Hannah. "Society and Culture." In *Culture for the Millions? Mass Media in Modern Society*, ed. Norman Jacobs. New York: D. Van Nostrand, 1961.

Arian, Edward. *The Unfulfilled Promise: Public Subsidy of the Arts in America*. Philadelphia: Temple University Press, 1989.

Arvin, Newton. *Whitman*. New York: Macmillan, 1938.

Babbitt, Irving. *Criticism in America: Its Function and Status*. New York: Haskell House, 1969. Originally published in 1924.

———. "Genius and Taste." *The Nation*, 7 February 1918.

Baldwin, James. "Mass Culture and the Creative Artist." In *Culture for the Millions? Mass Media in Modern Society*, ed. Norman Jacobs. New York: D. Van Nostrand, 1961.

Barnes, Stephen H. *Muzak, the Hidden Messages in Music: A Social Psychology of Culture*. Lewiston, N.Y.: Edwin Mellow Press, 1988.

Barrett, William. "Our Country and Our Culture." *Partisan Review*, July–August 1952, 421–31.

Barzun, Jacques. "Our Country and Our Culture." *Partisan Review*, July–August 1952, 424–31.

Bendix, Regina. *In Search of Authenticity: The Formation of Folklore Studies*. Madison: University of Wisconsin Press, 1997.

Benjamin, Walter. "The Work of Art in the Age of Mechanical Reproduction." In *Illuminations*, ed. Hannah Arendt. New York: Schocken Books, 1969.

Berman, Marshall. *All That Is Solid Melts into Air.* London: Verso, 1983.

Blake, Casey Nelson. *Beloved Community: The Cultural Criticism of Randolph Bourne, Van Wyck Brooks, Waldo Frank & Lewis Mumford.* Chapel Hill: University of North Carolina Press, 1990.

Bourdieu, Pierre. *Distinction: A Social Critique of the Judgment of Taste.* Translated by Richard Nice. Cambridge: Harvard University Press, 1984.

Bourne, Randolph. "Trans-national America." In *The Radical Will: Randolph Bourne Selected Writings, 1911–1918,* ed. Olaf Hanson. New York: Urizen Books, 1977, 248-64.

Boyer, Ernest. "Lifelong Learning in the Arts." *Vital Speeches of the Day,* 15 October 1994, 15–18.

Brooks, Van Wyck. *Wine of Puritans: A Study of Present-Day America.* New York: B. W. Huebsch, 1924. Originally published in 1915.

———. "Young America." *Seven Arts* 1, December 1915, 144–51.

Browder, Earl. "The Writer and Politics." In *The Writer in a Changing World,* ed. Henry Hart. New York: Equinox Cooperative Press, 1937, 48–55.

Buchwalter, Andrew, ed., *Culture and Democracy: Social and Ethical Issues in Public Support of the Arts.* New York: New Press, 1992.

Burnham, James. "Our Country and Our Culture," *Partisan Review,* May–June 1952, 288–98.

"Campaign to Triple California State Funding to the Arts." thecity.sgsu.edu/CALAA, 1998 [accessed June 1998].

Carey, James W. *Communication as Culture: Essays on Media and Society.* Boston: Unwin Hyman, 1989.

Casey, Betty. "Is Your Child's School Flunking Art?" *Tulsa Kids* magazine, August 1998.

Cowen, Tyler. *In Praise of Commercial Culture.* Cambridge: Harvard University Press, 1998.

Crossman, Richard, ed. *The God That Failed.* New York: Harper & Brothers, 1949.

Culture and the Crisis. New York: University of Tulsa Special Collections, 1932.

Czitrom, Daniel. *Media and the American Mind: From Morse to McLuhan.* Chapel Hill: University of North Carolina Press, 1982.

Danto, Arthur. "Elitism and the NEA." *The Nation,* 17 November 1997, 6–7.

Davidson, Cathy N., ed., *Reading in America: Literature and Social History.* Baltimore, Md.: Johns Hopkins University Press, 1989.

Dell, Floyd. *Intellectual Vagabondage: An Apology for the Intelligentsia.* New York: George H. Doran, 1926.

Dewey, John. *Art As Experience.* New York: Perigee Books, 1980. Originally published by Putnam, 1934.

———. *Individualism Old and New.* New York: Capricorn Books, 1962. Originally published in 1929 and 1930.

———. *The Public and Its Problems.* New York: Henry Holt, 1927.

———. *The Quest for Certainty.* New York: Putnam, 1960. Originally published in 1929.

Dissanayake, Ellen. *Homo Aestheticus: Where Art Comes From and Why.* New York: Free Press, 1992.

———. "The Pleasures and Meanings of Making." *American Craft* 55, no. 2 (April–May 1995).

———. *What Is Art For?* Seattle: University of Washington Press, 1988.

Dunham, Mike. "Subsistence Art: Traditional Crafts Surface in Gambell, but Some Artists Long for a Freer Spirit." *Anchorage Daily News*, 21 September 1997, 16.

Eastman, Max. *Art and the Life of Action, with Other Essays.* New York: Knopf, 1934.

———. *Artists in Uniform: A Study of Literature and Bureaucratism.* New York: Knopf, 1934.

Eldridge, Michael. *Transforming Experience: John Dewey's Cultural Instrumentalism.* Nashville: Vanderbilt University Press, 1998.

Erkilla, Betsy. *Whitman, the Political Poet.* New York: Oxford University Press, 1989.

Ferment in the Field. Special issue of *Journal of Communication* 33, no. 3, 1983.

Fischer, Louis. Essay in *The God That Failed*, ed. Arthur Koestler. New York: Harper & Brothers, 1949.

Foerster, Norman, ed., *Humanism and America: Essays on the Outlook of Modern Civilization.* Port Washington, N.Y.: Kennikat Press, 1967. Originally published in 1930.

Frank, Waldo. *Our America.* New York: Boni & Liveright, 1919.

Frankel, Charles. "Ideals and Dangers of Mass Culture." In *Culture for the Millions? Mass Media in Modern Society*, ed. Norman Jacobs. New York: D. Van Nostrand, 1961.

Freund, Charles Paul. "Literature in Chains: Are Superstore Databases Turning Books into Pretzels." *Reason*, November 1997.

———. "Money Talking Art: Does Cash Corrupt or Communicate?" *Reason*, July 1997.

———. "Who Killed Culture? From Barbarism to Democracy, Elites Seek a Suspect in the Reported Death of Art." *Reason*, March 1998, 23–39.

Gans, Herbert. *Popular Culture and High Culture: An Analysis and Evaluation of Popular Taste.* New York: Basic Books, 1999. Originally published in 1974.

Getty Educational Institute for the Arts. "Educating for the Workplace through the Arts." National conference; excerpts in *Educational Leadership*, November 1997, 12–14.

Gilbert, James Burkhardt. *Writers and Partisans: A History of Literary Radicalism in America.* New York: John Wiley and Sons, 1960.

Gold, Mike. "Proletarian Realism." *New Masses* 7, September 1930.

Goldberger, Paul. "A Steely Humanist." *Harper's*, July 1989, 88–91.

Greene, Maxine. *Releasing the Imagination: Essays on Education, the Arts and Social Change.* San Francisco: Jossey-Bass Publishers, 1995.

Greenfeld, Howard. *The Devil and Dr. Barnes: Portrait of an American Art Collector.* New York: Viking, 1987.

Gussow, Mel. "Some Artistic Neighbors Try to Lower Their Fence." *New York Times*, 31 May 1997, section 1, 11.

Halperin, Jennifer. "Crafting for Dollars." *Governing* 10 (July 1997): 48.

Hawley, Anne. "The Fate of Art in Boston." *Boston Globe*, 11 May 1998, A13.

Hicks, Granville. *The Great Tradition: An Interpretation of American Literature since the Civil War.* New York: Macmillan, 1935.

Hindus, Milton. *Leaves of Grass: 100 Years After.* Palo Alto, Calif.: Stanford University Press, 1955.

Hirschman, Albert O. *The Passions and the Interests: Political Arguments for Capitalism before Its Triumph.* Princeton, N.J.: Princeton University Press, 1977.

Hluch, Kevin A. "A Revolutionary Concept: The Aesthetic Scale in the Art World," *Ceramics Monthly* 46, no. 1 (January 1998): 98.

Hoeveler, J. David Jr. *The New Humanism: A Critique of Modern America 1900–1940.* Charlottesville: University of Virginia Press, 1977.

Hook, Sidney. "Our Country and Our Culture." *Partisan Review*, September–October 1952, 569–75.

Horowitz, Daniel. *The Morality of Spending: Attitudes Toward the Consumer Society in America, 1875–1940.* Baltimore, Md.: Johns Hopkins University Press, 1985.

Horowitz, Helen Lefkowitz. *Culture and the City.* Lexington: University Press of Kentucky, 1976.

Howe, Irving. "Our Country and Our Culture." *Partisan Review*, September–October 1952, 575–81.

Hughes, H. Stuart. "Mass Culture and Social Criticism." In *Culture for the Millions? Mass Media in Modern Society*, ed. Norman Jacobs. New York: D. Van Nostrand, 1961.

Hughes, Thomas P., and Agatha C. Hughes, eds., *Lewis Mumford: Public Intellectual.* New York: Oxford University Press, 1990.

Hyde, Henry J. "The Culture War." *National Review* 42, no. 8 (30 April 1990): 25–27.

Hyman, Stanley Edgar. "Ideals, Dangers and Limitations of Mass Culture." In *Culture for the Millions? Mass Media in Modern Society*, ed. Norman Jacobs. New York: D. Van Nostrand, 1961.

Jackaway, Gwenyth. "Selling Mozart to the Masses: Crossover Marketing as Cultural Diplomacy," *Journal of Popular Music Studies* 11–12, 1999/2000, 125–50.

Jackson, Philip W. *John Dewey and the Lessons of Art.* New Haven, Conn.: Yale University Press, 1998.

Jacobs, Norman, ed. *Culture for the Millions? Mass Media in Modern Society.* New York: D. Van Nostrand, 1961.

Jarrell, Randall. "A Sad Heart at the Supermarket." In *Culture for the Millions? Mass Media in Modern Society*, ed. Norman Jacobs. New York: D. Van Nostrand, 1961.

Jensen, Joli. *The Nashville Sound: Authenticity and Commercialization in Country Music.* Nashville, Tenn.: Vanderbilt University Press, 1998.

———. *Redeeming Modernity: Contradictions in Media Criticism.* Berkeley, Calif.: Sage, 1990.

Jensen, Joli, and John J. Pauly. "Imagining the Audience: Losses and Gains in Cultural Studies." In *Cultural Studies in Question*, ed. Marjorie Ferguson and Peter Golding. London: Sage, 1997, 155–69.

Johnson, Dirk. "Does Art Change Things or People?" *New York Times*, 28 September 1996, section 1, 15.

Kammen, Michael. *The Lively Arts: Gilbert Seldes and the Transformation of Cultural Criticism in the US.* New York: Oxford University Press, 1996.

Koestler, Arthur. Essay in *The God That Failed*, ed. Arthur Koestler. New York: Harper & Brothers, 1949.

Kristol, Irving. "The Mass Media." In *Culture for the Millions? Mass Media in Modern Society*, ed. Norman Jacobs. New York: D. Van Nostrand, 1961.

Kronenberger, Louis. "Our Country and Our Culture." *Partisan Review*, July–August 1952, 439–46.

Lanza, Joseph. *Elevator Music: A Surreal History of Muzak, Easy-Listening and Other Moodsong*. New York: St. Martin's Press, 1994.

Larson, Gary O. "American Canvas: An Arts Legacy for Our Community." Report for the National Endowment for the Arts, 1997.

Lazarsfeld, Paul. "Mass Culture Today." *Culture for the Millions? Mass Media in Modern Society*, ed. Norman Jacobs. New York: D. Van Nostrand, 1961.

Lears, T. J. Jackson. *No Place of Grace: Antimodernism and the Transformation of American Culture*. New York: Pantheon, 1981.

Leonni, Leo. "Mass Culture and the Creative Artist." *Culture for the Millions? Mass Media in Modern Society*, ed. Norman Jacobs. New York: D. Van Nostrand, 1961.

Levine, Lawrence W. *Highbrow/Lowbrow: The Emergence of Cultural Hierarchy in America*. Cambridge: Harvard University Press, 1988.

Levy, Mark R., and Michael Gurevitch, eds., *Defining Media Studies: Reflections on the Future of the Field*. New York: Oxford University Press, 1994.

Lippmann, Walter. *Public Opinion*. New York: Macmillan, 1922.

Longine, Miriam. "NEA Goes Country." *Atlanta Journal and Constitution*, 26 April 1998, 1L.

Mailer, Norman. "Our Country and Our Culture." *Partisan Review*, May–June 1952, 298–301.

Marquis, Alice Goldfarb. *Art Lessons: Learning from the Rise and Fall of Public Arts Funding*. New York: Basic Books, 1995.

Marvin, Carolyn. *When Old Technologies Were New: Thinking About Electric Communication in the Late 19th Century*. New York: Oxford University Press, 1990.

Mather, Frank Jewett Jr. "The Plight of Our Arts." *Humanism and America: Essays on the Outlook of Modern Civilization*, ed. Norman Foerster. Port Washington, N.Y.: Kennikat Press, 1967, 116–26. Originally published in 1930.

McClay, Wilfred M. "Lewis Mumford: From the Belly of the Whale." *The American Scholar* 57, Winter 1988, 111–18.

Miller, Donald L. *Lewis Mumford: A Life*. New York: Weidenfeld & Nicolson, 1989.

Mills, C. Wright. "Our Country and Our Culture," *Partisan Review*, July–August 1952, 446–50.

———. *The Power Elite*. New York: Oxford University Press, 1956.

More, Paul Elmer. *Aristocracy and Justice*. New York: Phaeton, 1967. Originally published in 1915.

Mumford, Lewis. *Art and Technics*. New York: Columbia University Press, 1952.

———. *The Conduct of Life*. Harvest Books, 1960. Originally published in 1951.

———. *Faith for Living*. New York: Harcourt Brace, 1940.

———. *The Golden Day*. Westport, Conn.: Greenwood Press, 1983. Originally published by Beacon Press, 1926.

———. *Interpretations and Forecasts: 1922–1972, Studies in Literature, History, Biography, Technics and Contemporary Society*. New York: Harcourt Brace Jovanovich, 1979.

———. *The Myth of the Machine*. New York: Harcourt, Brace and World, 1967–1970.

———. *The Story of Utopias*. Gloucester, Mass.: Peter Smith, 1959. Originally published in 1922.

———. *Values for Survival*. New York: Harcourt Brace, 1946.

Munson, Eve Stryker, and Catherine Warren, eds. *James Carey: A Critical Reader*. Minneapolis: University of Minnesota Press, 1997.

Nachman, Gerald. "Break a Leg, Willy," *San Francisco Chronicle*, 30 November 1979.

National Arts Journalism Program. "The Future of Public Arts Funding." Forum held at Columbia University, published as NAJP Occasional Report No. 1, 1998.

North, Joseph, ed. *New Masses: An Anthology of the Rebel Thirties*. New York: International Publishers, 1969.

Obituary. "Lewis Mumford." *New York Times*, 28 January 1990, 21.

Peterson, Elizabeth. "The Changing Face of Tradition: A Report on the Folk and Traditional Arts in the United States." NEA Research Report No. 38, November 1998.

Phillips, William. "Our Country and Our Culture." *Partisan Review*, September–October 1952, 585–90.

Putnam, Robert. *Bowling Alone: The Collapse and Revival of American Community*. New York: Simon and Schuster, 2000.

Rabkin, Gerald. *Drama and Commitment: Politics in the American Theatre of the Thirties*. Bloomington: Indiana University Press, 1964.

Radway, Janice. "The Book-of-the-Month Club and the General Reader." In *Reading in America: Literature and Social History*, ed. Cathy N. Davidson. Baltimore, Md.: Johns Hopkins University Press, 1989.

Rahv, Philip. "Our Country and Our Culture," *Partisan Review*, May–June 1952, 304–10.

Rodden, John. *The Politics of Literary Reputation: The Making and Claiming of "St. George" Orwell*. New York: Oxford University Press, 1989.

Rosenbaum, Jonathan. "The Danger of Putting Our Cultural Destiny in the Hands of Business." *The Chronicle of Higher Education*, 17 April 1998, A64.

Rosenberg, Bernard, and David Manning White, eds. *Mass Culture: The Popular Arts in America*. Glencoe, Ill.: The Free Press, 1957.

Rosenberg, Bernard, and David Manning White. *Mass Culture Revisited*. New York: Van Nostrand Reinhold, 1971.

Rothstein, Edward. "Where Democracy and Its Money Have No Place." *New York Times*, 26 October 1997, section 2, 1.

Rubin, Joan Shelley. *The Making of Middlebrow Culture*. Chapel Hill: University of North Carolina Press, 1992.

Russ, Lawrence. "Art and the Mad Machine: The Spirit of Addiction vs. the Spirit of Life." *Omni*, July 1992, 6.

Ryan, Alan. *John Dewey and the High Tide of American Liberalism*. New York: W. W. Norton, 1995.

Salmagundi 49, Summer 1980.

Schlesinger, Arthur Jr. "Our Country and Our Culture." *Partisan Review,* September–October 1952, 590–93.

Schudson, Michael. *Advertising, the Uneasy Persuasion: Its Dubious Impact on American Society*. New York: Basic Books, 1984.

Schwartz, Delmore. "Our Country and Our Culture." *Partisan Review*, September–October 1952, 593–97.

Shils, Edward. "Mass Society and Its Culture." In *Culture for the Millions? Mass Media in Modern Society*, ed. Norman Jacobs. New York: D. Van Nostrand, 1961.

Shusterman, Richard. *Pragmatist Aesthetics: Living Beauty, Rethinking Art*. New York: Blackwell, 1992.

Siegel, Robert. "Arts Education vs. Artists." National Public Radio's *All Things Considered,* transcript #97091516-212, 15 September 1997.

Sisk, John P. "The Tyranny of the Aesthetic." *The American Scholar* 63, no. 2 (Winter 1994): 119–23.

Spender, Stephen. Essay in *The God That Failed*, ed. Arthur Koestler. New York: Harper & Brothers, 1949.

Spingarn, J. E. "The New Criticism." In *Criticism in America: Its Function and Status*, ed. Irving Babbitt. New York: Haskell House, 1969. Originally published in 1924.

Stovall, Floyd, ed. *Walt Whitman, Prose Works 1892*, vol. 2, *Collect and Other Prose*. New York: University Press, 1964, 361–426.

Tocqueville, Alexis de. *Democracy in America*, vols. 1 and 2. New York: Random House, Vintage Books, 1990.

Trilling, Lionel. "Our Country and Our Culture." *Partisan Review,* May–June 1952, 318–26.

Turner, Bryan S., ed. *Theories of Modernity and Postmodernity*. London: Sage, 1990.

Washington, Irwin. "Arts Education vs. Artists," National Public Radio's *All Things Considered,* transcript #97091516-212, 15 September 1997.

Weber, Bruce. "Building on the Arts: Cities Are Fostering the Arts as a Way to Save Downtown." *New York Times,* 18 November 1997, A1.

Weisberg, Jacob. "Bullwhips Yes; Barney No: The GOP's Kulturkampf Will Force Liberals to Rethink What Kinds of Art the Government Should and Should Not Fund. PBS Doesn't Make the Cut," *New York* magazine, 6 February 1995, 26–27.

Westbrook, Robert B. *John Dewey and American Democracy*. Ithaca, N.Y.: Cornell University Press, 1991.

———. "Lewis Mumford, John Dewey and the Pragmatic Acquiescence." In *Lewis Mumford: Public Intellectual*, ed. Thomas P. Hughes and Agatha C. Hughes, 301–22. New York: Oxford University Press, 1990.

Whitman, Walt. "Democratic Vistas." In *Walt Whitman, Prose Works 1892*, vol. 2, *Collect and Other Prose*, ed. Floyd Stovall, 361–426. New York: New York University Press, 1964.

Winer, Linda. "NEA Report Strikes at the Spirit of the Arts," *Newsday,* 17 October 1997, B2.

Wright, Richard. Essay in *The God That Failed*, ed. Arthur Koestler. New York: Harper & Brothers, 1949.

York, Alexandra. "Toward an American Renaissance in Art and Ideas." *The Humanist* 55, no. 1, January–February 1995, 29–32.

Zerubavel, Eviatar. *The Fine Line: Making Distinctions in Everyday Life*. Chicago: University of Chicago Press, 1993.

Zuckerman, Michael. "Faith, Hope, Not Much Charity: The Optimistic Epistemology of Lewis Mumford." In *Lewis Mumford: Public Intellectual*, ed. Thomas P. Hughes and Agatha C. Hughes, 361–76. New York: Oxford University Press, 1990.

Index

academic studies: commercial culture, and effects on, 136–37; mass culture, and effects on, 136–37

advertising, and arts as antidote for effects of, 160

A&E (Arts and Education) channel, 156

aesthetic experience: commerce, defined as, 173; democratic culture, role of, 201–2, 205–6; Dewey on role of, 169, 172–74, 180, 188, 190, 191; expressive view of arts, 198–99; mass media, role of, 201. *See also* authentic art

Alexander, Jane: arts, role of, 148, 154–55, 157; authentic experiences, 154; funding for arts, 160, 168n32; television, role of, 154

Alexander, Thomas M., on Dewey and aesthetic experiences, 191n4

American Canvas (Larson), 148–49, 150

American Movie Channel, 156

antidoctrinaire view, Dewey and, 182–83

architecture: democratization and, 21; Mumford on literature and, 58; Tocqueville on democratization and, 21

Arendt, Hannah, 118, 121

Aristocracy and Justice (More), 93

aristocratic culture: classical literature as reflection of, 24; Country House utopian vision, 60; democratic culture compared to, 13, 55; literature of, 23, 46; New Humanism view of, 93, 94; writing styles found in, 22. *See also* democratic culture

Art and Technics (Mumford), 64–65, 67–68

"Art and the Mad Machine" (Russ), 160

Art As Experience (Dewey), 172–76, 184–86

artists: authentic art, and role of, 130; Baldwin on role of, 125; classical traditions, role of, 92–93, 102; creativity of, 100–101; democratic culture and effects on, 20–21; elitist view of arts and, 149; intellectual class, and role of, 100; mass culture, and effects on, 115; modernism, and role of, 100; Mumford on role of, 70–71; political issues, and role of, 100; social criticism and relationship to, 90–92, 97, 98–101, 104; social issues, and role of, 85–89, 100, 105, 205; society, and role of, 81–84, 89; subversion view of arts, and role of, 98–101

About the Author

Joli Jensen's first book, *Redeeming Modernity: Contradictions in Media Criticism* (1990), analyzes how the media are blamed for the perceived ills of modern life. Her second book, *The Nashville Sound: Authenticity, Commercialization and Country Music* (1998), explores how and why musical genres change, in relation to concerns about culture and commerce. She has also written essays on media criticism, communication technologies, communication theory, the social history of the typewriter, and fans and fandom.

Dr. Jensen received her Ph.D. in 1985 from the Institute of Communications Research at the University of Illinois. She has taught at the University of Virginia and the University of Texas–Austin. She is a professor of communication at the University of Tulsa, where she teaches courses in media, culture, and society.